# C

# for Women
## (and Smart Men)

Reduce the risk, cost and grief
of auto ownership
and buying a new car

**by Alexander Law
and Susan Winlaw**

www.caradviceforwomen.com

**Publisher
Consumer Automotive Media Services
(CAMS)**

Cover and Interior Design and Production by
Consumer Automotive Media Services (CAMS)

**Printed and bound by Maracle Press Ltd., Oshawa, Ontario,
1-800-558-8604  www.maraclepress.com**

**Mixed Sources**
Product group from well-managed
forests and other controlled sources
www.fsc.org  Cert no. SW-COC-2080
© 1996 Forest Stewardship Council

**Published by**

**Consumer Automotive Media Services (CAMS)**
www.consumerautomotivemediaservices.com
Contact: Susan@consumerautomotivemediaservices.com

**Library and Archives Canada Cataloguing in Publication
1. Automobiles-Purchasing  2. Automobiles- Maintenance and Repair  3. Women Automobile Drivers**

**TL162.L38 2008          629.222'029          C2006-906454-7**

**ISBN 10:  0-9781931-0-5**

**ISBN 13:  978-0-9781931-0-2**

# A Book About Cars Women Really Need

We decided to write this book primarily to fill what we saw as an enormous and obvious gap in the automotive media marketplace -- information on owning or buying a car that women really needed. It was obvious the existing media had no interest in providing that. For example, just before we registered www.CarAdviceForWomen.com, www.CarNewsForWomen.com, and www.AutoSafetyIndex.com (among other names), the Wall Street Journal declared flatly that all of the good web addresses were already taken.

When we began to examine the existing advice about cars in general as it relates to women, we discovered that a distressing amount of it was simply wrong, or at least incomplete, and sometimes didn't address key items at all. Things about safety, quality, finance, the environment and many other issues that are presented as gospel in the media should just not be believed, while other issues important to women that should be pointed out are rarely, if ever, written about.

We mention this mostly because a lot of what we're going to tell you doesn't match what you might read elsewhere and we want you to be ready for that. We've used our extensive experience to cast a bright light on the hard facts, and we're confident that our advice is more complete and female-oriented than the other automotive advice in the media.

We've done our best to clear up what we like to call Old Husbands' Tales, some of which you might hear from your own husband and some of which will come from husbands who are auto writers or stock market analysts, many of whom tried to convince the world that Enron was a smart investment decision. We hope greatly that you benefit from our efforts, and we appreciate you buying our book.

Susan and Alex

**Alexander Law & Susan Winlaw**   3

## Buyers' Market Great For Car Shoppers
## And Maybe Bad For Other Car Owners

For people in the market for a new vehicle, the good news is that the general conditions of the automotive market are absolutely, positively in the customer's favor.

But a buyers' market also means that the profitability of the sellers is threatened, and that could have consequences for people who aren't even considering a new car.

Dealers looking at reduced profits from new car sales will try to replace them with increased profits from their service centers and by the sale of over-priced extended warranties when the sales agreement is being reached and whatever other devices they can come up with. This puts a lot more consumers at financial risk.

We try to cover all of these points in the book, but the advice often boils down to the need for you to be wary of everything you hear at a car dealer and to say no to anything that you don't like. Extended warranties are always available from various sources and you can get your car serviced at lots of other places. You still have the advantage.

For someone buying a new vehicle, it's the greatest buyers' market in history since sales are sinking and there aren't any really bad new vehicles any more.

The bottom line is that if there's a particular vehicle that you truly, madly, deeply want to have, you should be able to just go out and get it without having to worry about it biting you in the backside. The fact that it may not be the safest car for you or the best buy in the segment or the smartest business decision are other matters. If you really want a specific car, it will probably run fine and not go bad while you own it, if you behave sensibly and don't abuse it -- and even if you do it will likely keep going.

Three realities control the new car market today:

1) New vehicles have never been as good (i.e. reliable, safe, responsive, well-equipped, fuel-efficient and so on) as they are now, nor deliver as great a value. If you look back at new vehicles from even five years ago, it's easy to see this is true.

2) The car companies are all chasing a bigger share of the market, using a stream of offerings that didn't exist before and familiar models that have been extensively revised to compete with the improving competition. Consider that, in 2000, there were about 350 models on the market, and by the end of the decade there should be about 450.

3) The new vehicle market won't expand to accommodate all of those car companies' sales goals. Right now, it's going through a downturn that tightens the screws on the car companies more than ever.

On top of that, the price of gasoline and the endless talk about plug-in hybrids like the Chevrolet Volt and other technologies has people standing back to think about what might be coming and how they should respond.

So that's one-two-three a buyers' market, at least for the next few years.

The single most important thing to remember if you're buying a new car is that you have the upper hand. All it takes to exercise your advantage is a willingness to spend a little more time scouring the market for a deal that pleases you and being willing to just walk away if it's not what you want. Just say no, in other words, until the car dealer says yes to the deal that please you.

All kinds of sellers trying hard to sell you something from a huge selection of the best cars in history, and all of them highly motivated. A textbook definition of a buyers' market.

The pressure is even starting to show in the premiums that car companies like Toyota have placed on their hybrid vehicles, which could make them smart decisions at long last.

# Some Of The Most Important Things You Should Know About Cars

-You are likely too close to the steering wheel. Page 8

-Feel free to buy the car you really want. Page 4

-The smaller the car, the bigger the risk. Page 18

-Never let the tank get below three-quarters. Page 14

-Should pregnant women be in cars? Page 24

-Inflating the tires really matters a great deal. Page 111

-Loose objects in the car are a big safety risk. Page 10

-Pay no attention to those quality studies. Page 148

-Try not to buy more car than you need. Page 157

-Most hybrids won't help you save money. Page 108

-Leasing can be smartest way to buy a car. Page 158

-Maximum safety requires crash notification. Page 38

-Car alarm can keep you safer in the house. Page 12

-Hiring someone is the best way to buy a car. Page 138

-You don't need back-up aids to protect kids. Page 30

-What a serious emergency kit contains. Page 46

## In Which We Explore The Verity
## Of Some Old Husbands' Tales

-Change your oil as often as you can. Page 226

-Yeah, we have to pay the transport charge. Page 144

-It's the "Best Car" so we should get it. Page 154

-Sure it's safe, it has a 5-star crash rating. Page 18

-All insurance companies charge the same. Page 197

-We need some more expensive tires. Page 288

-All cars come with roadside assistance. Page 95

-Forget the seatbelts, we have airbags. Page 9

-I know where we are, we don't need GPS. Page 238

-It's got that flux-capacitor, which is cool. Page 179

-They wouldn't sell it if it weren't safe. Page 28

-With all that horsepower, it must be quick. Page 170

-Get the upscale model for better handling. Page 242

-Carfax reports tell you all about used cars. Page 209

-Residual rates are like a guaranteed thing. Page 200

-Yeah, we can only use premium gas. Page 181

# Sitting Too Close To The Wheel Is A Real Danger That You Should Address Now

There's considerable risk in sitting too close to the steering wheel of any vehicle, but that's what millions of women do every day on this continent.

In general, if every part of your head and torso isn't about a foot away from the steering wheel you're putting yourself in harm's way.

You do not want to have an airbag hit you if you are any closer to the wheel than 10-12 inches, and the more space the better. Injuries (bruises, black eyes, broken bones) will almost certainly occur, and there's a chance you'll be killed.

The situation's even worse if you're short in the torso and your head's so low that it will be hit full-force by the airbag.

The immediate solution is to move away as far as you can while still being able to reach the pedals. You should do this even if it means tilting the seat back to an angle that makes you uncomfortable.

Then you need to go to an automotive supply store or look online for pedal extenders. They attach to the pedals in your car and give you two or more inches to move away from the steering wheel. As well as keeping you safer, they should also make it more comfortable in general to drive your car. With installation, the pedal extenders should cost about $150 to $200.

When the time comes to shop for a new vehicle, consider a model that has adjustable pedals and a steering wheel that telescopes as well as tilts. The other key part of the triangulation is of course the seat, but they all slide back and forth and recline now.

This may not sound important to you, but sitting too close to the steering wheel is probably the biggest safety hazard you face on a regular basis.

# Princess Diana's Death Brings The Most Important Car Safety Issue Into Focus

"Princess Diana's last public service announcement" is the way an unhappy Mercedes executive once described her death in a car crash. This gentleman's thinking was that Diana's demise in a bad but not necessarily fatal crash in one of the world's safest cars (a Mercedes S-Class) was almost completely due to the fact that she was not taking advantage of the single most important safety device ever invented -- the seatbelt.

Almost certainly, if Diana had been wearing a seatbelt that fateful night in Paris she would have lived, possibly without any serious injuries. The only person in the car who did survive that crash was the only one wearing a seatbelt, and he was in the front passenger seat which is almost always a more dangerous spot than the back seat --- unless you're not wearing a seatbelt.

You've heard this about seatbelts before, but it bears repeating because it's easy to think that the apparently endless array of airbags that come in new vehicles now will protect you in a crash and you don't maybe need the seatbelt any more. In truth, those new airbags are all worth having and should slightly increase your chances of surviving a crash. But none of them will restrain you in a crash the way seatbelts will, and in many crashes it's critically important that you are not flying around inside the vehicle.

The same thing holds true for other people and pets in the vehicle with you, by the way. Unbelted passengers are a great risk to themselves, but they can also do great harm to other people if they're sliding, flopping or even flying around. True at the start, and just as true now -- seatbelts save lives.

If Princess Diana had been wearing a seatbelt that night, she would almost certainly have survived.

## Objects In Car May Be Harder
## And Deadlier Than They Look

For a quick, real-world appreciation of this section, get someone to stand close to you and throw a dime in your face, then a small battery, a pen and maybe a cell phone.

If that doesn't do it, get them to toss an umbrella at the back of your head as if it was coming off the "parcel tray" in the rear window of a sedan, then a pair of ice skates as if coming from the second row of an SUV, or a ski pole launched from the cargo space in the rear of a minivan. Let's not even think about how you'd feel if it was your beloved pet that crashed into your skull.

But we bet you'll have a grasp of the dangers of UFOs (Unrestrained Flying Objects) long before the sports equipment starts to fly. In this you will be part of a significant minority across the continent, since this is a genuine danger that goes almost completely without comment.

How big a deal is this? Well, if we adjust a British study for our population, it means more than 400,000 people a year are injured by some loose object bouncing around after some kind of emergency event.

We're not really sure why the dangers of objects flying around your vehicle aren't better appreciated by most people, but lots of the folks who've been in a hard braking incident, a crash or (particularly) a rollover can explain it to you. If your vehicle is going as slowly as 30 mph when it crashes into something solid, like another vehicle, the force of the collision is going to cause the rear end of your vehicle (tires and all) to lift into the air. So do not think for a minute that it won't take anything loose inside your vehicle and propel it towards the front. Sharp instruments left in the trunk have been known to go through seatbacks, while laptops and cell phones have knocked drivers out, and all kinds of things have blinded people. And it's worse in a rollover, since the tossing around is repeated.

The rule to remember is not to leave anything loose in the car that you wouldn't want to hit you in the head while it's moving at, say, 40 mph.

So put all those loose items away in the glovebox or the storage bin or wherever. Instead of leaving things loose on the rear seat, put them on the floor as far under the front seat as you can.

Best of all, keep everything loose in the trunk. If you have a crossover, SUV, minivan or hatchback, use the netting that may have come with the vehicle or get some and install it in the cargo compartment. Even better is a cargo box that can be permanently attached.

This may not sound like a serious risk, but you won't think that if you try that dime, battery, pen and cell phone test.

## Pre-Phone For Help If You're Worried

If you're nervous about where you have to park, it might be a good idea to phone someone you trust before you get out of the car or leave where you are and head for the car.

Tell them exactly where you are before you leave the safe place you're in and have them stay on the line until you're safely where you're going.

Using a loud voice makes it clear that you're actually on the phone with another person and helps give the impression that you're self-confident, which is supposed to dissuade attackers.

Make a point of telling your friend again where you are and where you're going if you see someone who looks suspicious or worries you in any way.

If worse comes to worst, your phone friend will know immediately and can call the police and direct them to your precise location.

# Car Alarm Can Also Provide You With Extra Safety Measure In Your House

It may not be the perfect personal security system, but the car alarm that comes on many models sold in the last couple of years might be useful in an emergency. It could frighten off an unwelcome visitor, thief or intruder, and if you organize it correctly it could act as a remote warning system in your neighborhood, for you and other women.

Phoning the police is of course the first thing you should do if you're worried about someone lurking around your home or, worse, trying to break in. But it might not be a bad idea to set off the horn-blaring, headlight-flashing alarm system on your car after that, or after you've checked to make sure the doors are locked. It might put the villain off staying where he is or doing what he's doing, and that's the prime objective in a situation involving your personal safety.

Most of those keyfob-based alarm systems will actually work through the walls of your house and over some distance, as long as they're pointed in the general direction of the car. The smart thing to do is test the car alarm system from your apartment or house to see what happens before you actually need it. Most systems should also turn the alarm off with a second push of that alarm button, but the test run will show you that as well.

It might be worthwhile to work out a sequence of alarm sounds and tell your trusted neighbors what it means, so they'll know what's going on if they hear a series of short blasts of an alarm coming from your vehicle.

Your area could even accept that as the general code for an issue involving personal safety, sickness or any emergency. If someone's at risk, they could sound the agreed-upon signal and her neighbors will know to see if she needs help.

This system would also work if there was already someone

in your house whose behavior was starting to scare you, since it could be a more subtle and perhaps quicker method of getting help than using the phone.

Remember that car alarms will also work even if the power goes out to your house, so it could be a backup to a built-in alarm system.

If your car doesn't already have an alarm system, you can probably have one installed at a decent auto parts store, which can be found in abundance on the web.

## Be Careful You Don't Get Stuck With A Post-Crash $2,000+ Tow Charge

To save towing costs that sometimes defy belief, some insurance companies are starting to decline charges from tow-truck firms they haven't pre-approved.

So if your car's in a crash that leaves it un-drivable and you use a truck from a non-approved towing company, you could be left to pay $2,000 or more.

The smart move is to check with your car insurer and see if they have a policy on this or other crash-related issues. If so, write down the particulars and put that information with the insurance papers you're required to have with you at all times.

Then, if you are in a crash and you can't drive your car away, you will know what firm to call and be able to avoid paying the huge towing fee.

The insurance companies are doing this because some tow firms see crashes as an opportunity to make money from insurance companies, which of course means making money from you through higher premiums.

In general, the tow trucks you probably shouldn't use are the ones who listen to the police radio and race to the scene of any car crashes, which means they'll be the ones offering to tow you car away.

# Filling Up The Fuel Tank Is A Critical
# Safety Aid In Many Situations

One of the best ways to increase your overall safety level involves a simple change in behavior rather than a new product or learning a new driving technique, and that's trying to keep the fuel level in your car full.

Yes, we mean full as in keeping the needle as close to the F on the gas gauge as possible, and we mean all the time. Of course that's not actually possible unless you fill the car and never drive it, but you understand the point.

The primary value of a full tank is that you will be better able to keep yourself and your family alive and well if you get stuck somewhere in an emergency, since the car's fuel provides you with heat, light, information, and communication (recharging the cell phone). Sure that's not likely, but neither are many of the other things you're careful to guard against and you still do them.

If the kind of nightmare that struck Jim and Kati Kim in Oregon in 2006 doesn't worry you (he died when he left their stuck car to go for help), then there are other dangers that a full tank can keep you from.

There's no chance you won't run out of fuel somewhere that scares you, or even be forced to stop for fuel there.

If an emergency comes up and you have to get someplace as quickly as possible, you probably won't have to stop for gas on the way if your car's tank is full.

It doesn't even have to be the kind of thing that wouldn't be an emergency if you were there on time. If you're picking up your daughter after a dance class when the building's open it's not an emergency. But leaving her standing alone in the dark for 15 minutes because you had to stop for gas (or even ran out) is something else.

Feel free to insert your own nightmare of that kind here.

Let's not forget that getting gas under circumstances that you create is always better than getting gas under circumstances that are forced on you, since it probably means a station and a time where you feel secure.

No matter how you slice it, the more fuel you have in your car the safer you and your family are.

## Flat Tires Don't Mean You're Immobile

The key thing to remember about a flat tire is that it does not necessarily mean your vehicle cannot be driven any farther. You can drive a vehicle with a flat tire (or even four flat tires), but there will be mechanical and financial consequences. The car will be slow and harder to steer and you stand a very good chance of causing significant and expensive damage to the tire, the wheel it's wrapped around, and the suspension and brake bits that are connected to it. Generally, the risk of doing damage and the costs associated with it go up with the speed you drive on a flat. In the wrong circumstances, driving on a flat could result in a very expensive repair bill.

But if you're in a situation where you genuinely believe your safety to be at risk, you can absolutely drive a car with a flat tire. It will make a lot of noise and create an awful smell, but it will take you to another location. It's your decision..

## Crashes More Likely With Sleep Apnea

Sleep apnea sufferers are three to five times more likely to be in a serious car crash involving personal injury, a recent study has found. With sleep disrupted by a breathing disorder, people with sleep apnea are more likely to be drowsy during the day and that can lead to loses of consciousness that create crashes. Officials suggest that people who know they have sleep apnea take extra precautions, and that people who might have it should find out for sure. There are treatments that can help with this problem.

## The Sad Reality: You Can Be Safer But Not Totally Free From Harm

When the concept of automotive safety began in earnest about 45 years ago, it was widely rejected as unnecessary by most consumers and even dangerous by some. If people know they'll die if they do something stupid, the theory went, they'll be more careful. This led to an idea that every steering wheel should have a sharp blade sticking out of it, to remind drivers of the risks involved.

When the best safety device of all time -- seatbelts -- arrived on the scene, the "common sense" rampant at the time suggested it was better to be thrown clear of the vehicle. There were also widespread concerns about the way the seatbelts wrinkled your clothes.

Now, of course, safety is usually the number one feature named by female respondents to a survey on what you might like in your next new vehicle, and goodness knows the car companies have done a remarkable job of giving you new levels of shelter from risk. Every year, lots of people walk away from crashes that would have killed them 30, 20, 10, even five years ago.

A few years back, safety levels did hit a bit of a flat spot when the meaningful passive safety devices (seatbelts and front airbags) were going into every car. So there was a switch to creating more active safety technologies to reduce injury, such as active head restraints and so on. We're seeing a lot of those active features now, with cars that act to avoid skids and apply the brakes and nudge you back into place if you drift out of your lane and all kinds of things. They're useful at reducing injuries and damage from fender-benders, but not really game-changing in terms of saving lives.

These features will continue to flow from engineering centers around the world and eventually they will help us achieve the safety technologies dream -- the system that programs cars to talk to each other and not let themselves collide. That system will likely debut in a few years and crashes will start to drop as a result, but the benefit won't be maximized until every car in the world is wired into the network that keeps them from making contact. That would be 2030 at the earliest, though many of the benefits will be seen before then.

You probably noticed that the key to getting road deaths to drop even lower than they are now is the removal of the driver's influence at critical moments. Stability control began that process to great affect and all the other systems will make it complete in due course.

Arguing about the morality of removing the driver from the driving experience is the normal course of the discussion at this point, but it's more useful to take a different path.

So there's no technology or technologies available now or in the medium-term that will ensure absolute protection for you and your family, and there's very little you can do to improve things for the foreseeable future.

All you can do is remember the harsh physics of motor vehicle crashes and the endless variety of methods human beings come up with to put themselves and others at risk. That should at least give you pause. It may not be as effective as a sharp blade sticking out of the steering wheel, but it makes the same general point.

## Keep Car And House Keys Apart

Never turn over your house key when you give anyone the key to your car, whether it's a valet parking person or anyone else. That includes the service department at your dealership, which likely has a facility on-site for duplicating keys. Be sure to make this policy clear to anyone else in your house, but particularly the men, who don't always think broadly enough on issues like this.

# The Big Lie About 5-Star Crash Ratings Can Put Your Life At Risk

Whatever a vehicle's frontal "crash rating" from the government may be -- 1, 2, 3, 4 or 5 stars -- it only measures how that vehicle behaved as compared to other vehicles in its weight class during a specific set of collision circumstances.

Specifically, those ratings only count if your vehicle hits something that weighs 250 lbs more to 250 lbs less than your vehicle head on at 35 mph.

So it's not true that a compact sedan with a five-star score will protect you as well in a collision as even a slightly larger mid-size sedan with five stars will. In fact, a mid-size sedan with 4, 3, 2 or even 1 star might protect you better, and the truth of that grows with the size of the other vehicle. For verbatim evidence of this, see the accompanying details from car crash experts around the world on Page 20.

The best analogy on this point involves the contact sports you see at the Olympics. Boxing, wrestling and judo athletes are all strictly divided into weight categories so that the larger opponent doesn't get the natural advantage that greater mass delivers in such situations. That is the regulated version of "pick on someone your own size".

Even inside each weight category there is considerable difference in potential injury between the various star ratings. Perhaps the best way to look at it is that, for every star the vehicle scores under five, her chances of being injured more or less double.

The National Highway Traffic Safety Administration, which usually goes by the name NHTSA, explains that "Frontal star ratings indicate the chance of a serious head and chest injury to the driver and right front seat passenger. A serious injury is one requiring immediate hospitalization and may be life threatening."

Remember that these ratings only apply when your vehicle strikes a vehicle of roughly the same size.

So, the chance of you sustaining a serious injury in a vehicle with

-a 5-star rating is 10 percent or less
-a 4-star rating is 11-20 percent
-a 3-star rating is 21-35 percent
-a 2-star rating is 36-45 percent
-a 1-star rating is 46 or greater percent

It's also worth noting that all of the crash ratings available pertain to a very specific set of carefully-controlled collision circumstances governing vehicle mass and speed, among other factors.

This is done so the results from one vehicle test can be compared with the results from another vehicle test, which is a good thing.

The downside of this comparison is that those two vehicles could very well behave differently if the crash circumstances were even slightly varied.

As a result, the star-based ratings are of no use to you whatsoever in judging how a particular vehicle will protect you in a crash with a heavier vehicle, and are of only limited value in telling you how it would protect you in a crash with a vehicle of a similar size that doesn't mirror the government tests.

Every crash is different, after all.

Those ads and TV commercials that say such-and-such a vehicle has the "highest government crash rating" aren't exactly lying since five stars is the highest rating that NHTSA gives, but they're not exactly telling the whole truth either.

Saying that is enough of a distortion that it could trick you into doing something that risks your life and the life of your friends and family.

# Experts Make Clear The Importance Of Vehicle Weight When It Comes To Safety

### National Highway Traffic Safety Administration

"A heavier vehicle will generally better protect you in a crash. This is particularly the case in two-vehicle crashes. NHTSA research historically has shown that occupants in passenger cars are at a greater risk of being fatally injured when struck in the front or the side by a heavier and higher-riding light truck such as a pickup or SUV."

### New Car Assessment Program (Europe)

"In frontal impacts ... the occupants of the heavier car or the one with higher structures tend to fare better than those travelling in lighter, lower cars. As these effects are currently impossible to overcome, Euro NCAP only makes comparisons within size categories. The rating of a car within its size category is a function of the quality of its safety design."

### Insurance Institute Of Highway Safety

"The first crashworthiness attributes to consider are vehicle size and weight. Small, light vehicles generally offer less protection than larger, heavier ones. There's less structure to absorb crash energy, so deaths and injuries are more likely to occur in both single- and multiple-vehicle crashes. So if safety is one of your major considerations PASS UP VERY SMALL, LIGHT VEHICLES."

### Australasian New Car Assessment Program

"Results can be used to compare the protection offered to occupants in the event of a severe frontal offset or side impact crash for vehicles of similar size and weight. Care must be taken when comparing results for different vehicles as only those vehicles of similar mass can be correctly compared. As a heavier vehicle will generally provide better protection in a collision with a smaller and lighter car, any result comparison should be restricted to cars of a similar class."

# Small Asian Cars Score The Worst
# For Personal Injury In A Car Crash

While there's certainly some value in knowing exactly which cars have the worst records for personal injuries between 2004-2006, the bigger lesson is that nine of them were small four-door sedans and the other was a mid-size four-door sedan.

More proof, in other words, that the occupants of small cars are more likely to get hurt in a crash than the occupants of any other size of vehicle.

The number for each car represents the relative value in this category, with 100 being the average for all cars sold in the U.S., and with many other vehicles scoring under 50, which is much better.

The scores for the following cars are in the Substantially Worse Than Average Category.

Eight of the worst models in the personal injury results were Japanese and two were Korean.

The results were compiled by the Highway Loss Data Institute and are available from www.iihs.org.

| | |
|---|---|
| Mitsubishi Lancer | 220 |
| Suzuki Reno | 220 |
| Suzuki Aerio | 217 |
| Suzuki Forenza | 211 |
| Nissan Sentra | 200 |
| Mitsubishi Galant | 196 |
| Kia Spectra | 189 |
| Nissan Sentra SE-R | 184 |
| Scion tC | 179 |
| Hyundai Tiburon | 178 |

# NHTSA Crash Rates Vehicle Categories By Weight

The National Highway Traffic Safety Administration (NHTSA) categorizes vehicles by vehicle class and "curb" weight. Curb weight represents the weight of a vehicle with standard equipment including the maximum capacity of fuel, oil, coolant, and air conditioning, if so equipped. Passenger cars are further subdivided.

When the time comes to judge your vehicle's overall safety rating, remember that its crash rating (the famous five-star rating) only applies to other vehicles in the same class. So a five-star light passenger car isn't as safe as a five-star compact car and so on. Here are some examples.

Passenger cars – mini (PC/Mi) (1,500-1,999 lbs. curb weight): Mercedes Smart.

Passenger cars – light (PC/L) (2,000-2,499 lbs. curb weight): Chevrolet Aveo 5, Hyundai Accent, Mazda Miata, Toyota Yaris

Passenger cars – compact (PC/C) (2,500-2,999 lbs. curb weight): Chevrolet Cobalt, Ford Focus, Honda Civic, Hyundai Elantra, Mazda 3, Nissan Rogue, Toyota Corolla

Passenger cars – medium (PC/Me) (3,000-3,499 lbs. curb weight): Chevrolet Malibu, Ford Fusion, Honda Accord, Hyundai Sonata, Subaru Impreza, Toyota Camry

Passenger cars – heavy (PC/H) (3,500 lbs. and over curb weight.): Chevrolet Impala, Ford Five Hundred, Hyundai Azera, Nissan Maxima

Sport utility vehicles (SUV): Chevrolet Equinox, Honda CR-V and Pilot, Hyundai Santa Fe, Toyota RAV-4

Pickup trucks (PU)Chevrolet Silverado, Ford F-Series, Honda Ridgeline, Toyota Tundra

Vans (VAN): Dodge Caravan, Honda Odyssey, Hyundai Entourage, Toyota Sienna

# Stability-Control Is The Best New Safety Feature For Cars Since Airbags

Not only does stability control go a long way toward preventing the skids that create crashes and rollovers, it also requires no extra effort, training or even thought on behalf of the driver.

Technology doesn't get much more user-friendly than that, and it's often included in the sticker cost of most vehicles, so stability control probably won't cost you any extra money.

Anyone buying a new vehicle should make stability control a priority, but its importance increases the taller the vehicle. Vehicle height has a lot to do with where its center-of-gravity is, and the higher a vehicle's center-of-gravity the greater the chance it will roll over, which you absolutely do not want to happen.

All the driver has to do is behave sensibly for the existing road conditions (go slower on snow or ice or standing water, for example) and the stability-control system will perform actions to avoid a skid that even the best driver can't take. In certain situations involving a loss of control, applying all the brakes is the last thing you want to do, while applying one specific brake can stop the skid. The driver can't do that, but the stability control system can.

While it's not universally available yet, stability control is pretty common on the vehicles that most need the help to prevent rollovers -- top-heavy models such as SUVs, crossovers, and large vans.

A comprehensive list can be found at www.safercar.gov but the choice will increase constantly as the car companies work to take advantage of its growing appeal to consumers.

The technology's marketed under different names by different car companies, but everyone will know what you mean if you ask about stability control.

**Alexander Law & Susan Winlaw** 23

# Pregnant Women Should Reconsider
# The Safety Issues Of Being In A Car

Society's response to the risks facing pregnant women in cars is still open to consideration, and there may be steps we can take to make things safer for women and their unborn children in the future, through better vehicle design and technology and refined safety regulations.

Certainly we should all promote research into the issue and demand whatever changes are required, since the health issues related to pregnant women in cars may be greater than we know.

But above all that, in the world we live in today, it seems quite clear what a pregnant woman should do to keep the risk to her life and the life of the unborn child as low as possible:

-stay out of cars (or trains and buses) as much as you can

-if you must drive get in the largest vehicle possible

-get someone else to drive so you don't have to get behind the wheel

-if you have to drive, sit as far back from the steering wheel as you can

-wear the seatbelt at all times no matter which seat you're in (see the accompanying item for guidelines on that)

-no matter who's driving (but especially if it's you), go as slowly as possible and maintain a rigorous defensive driving attitude at all times so as to avoid any hard braking or other action that will cause your body to move around

These tips may not always be feasible or even agreeable, but they are the logical methods of dealing with the risks that present themselves to a pregnant woman and her fetus while her body's in motion at certain speeds. After all, research shows that the biggest risks to the unborn child in a car crash are the mother's death, separation of the placenta, a ruptured uterus, and fracture of the baby's skull.

For those things to happen, there has to be an impact between the car and something else, such as another vehicle, a wall, a guardrail or whatever. The greater the force of impact (which is directly dependent on speed) the greater the risk to the mother and the unborn child.

The mother doesn't even have to be injured in a car crash for the baby to be put at risk. A 2005 study found that pregnant women with no recorded injuries from car crashes were found to have significantly greater risk of pre-term labor and placental abruption, and that their babies faced greater risk from pre-term delivery and low birth weight than pregnant women not involved in crashes.

Being behind the wheel is dangerous because you were probably already sitting too close when you weren't pregnant (see story on Page 8) and the pregnancy just puts you closer to the point of impact.

Picking the largest and heaviest vehicle you can find makes sense for everyone, since the vehicle mass can help deflect the force of the crash from getting to you and perhaps reduce the amount your body and its organs are put under stress.

There's even a risk if the car has to decelerate rapidly, since the placenta is not restrained the way the mother is and that can result in separation, which can harm or even kill the unborn child. And, no, leaving the mother unrestrained (i.e. without a seatbelt) is not the answer to that problem. Not being in a fast-moving car is the answer.

Talking about the forces at play between the body and the internal organs brings us directly to the issue of placental separation, which brings enormous risk to the unborn child. Indeed, a separated placenta is the most documented injury to an unborn child in a car crash, but other problems include fetal distress, early delivery, breathing and nervous disorders, direct fetal injury, and arm and leg injuries.

"Placenta abruptio" involves the premature separation of

the inner wall of the uterus from the placenta before the baby is born, which means the unborn child loses its direct connection to the nutrients and oxygen that it needs. As you can imagine, this can lead to all kinds of bad things for the mother and the unborn child, including maybe death.

What's missing from the research into the risks for pregnant women is hard data on when these different problems occur, or why. This is unfortunate, since it would be nice to know what vehicle speed must be reached before placental separation moves from being the cause of injury to the cause of death for an unborn child.

This is not a minor problem, since about 130,000 pregnant drivers a year are involved in car crashes that are reported to the police across North America, and there are undoubtedly many more that aren't reported to the authorities in Canada or the U.S. Some researchers believe that car crashes account for as many as 750 fetal deaths a year across the continent, which is about the same number of deaths a year in car crashes for all children up to four years of age.

On top of that, of course, are the unknown health problems for the child and/or the mother that may be created by the crash but may not be recognized as such. The idea that a pregnant woman's hard-braking maneuver to avoid crashing into another vehicle on the highway might have caused some degree of placental separation that later causes some kind of health problem for the child in 5, 10, 15 or even 50 years doesn't even seem to be on society's radar.

In light of all that, the prospect of letting someone else drive, taking the slow route, being extra cautious or even staying home may not strike a pregnant woman as being so ridiculous. She could use the time at home to fire off letters and e-mails to the government and the car companies demanding more research into the safety of pregnant women and their unborn children in cars.

## Technology And Technique Can Be Used
## To Reduce Dangers Of Driving In Fog

There aren't many driving experiences that can bring on fear as quickly as disappearing into a dense fog at 65 mph, and even fewer driving experiences that deserve that feeling as much.

As those amazing multi-car pileups prove with sickening regularity, there is apparently no way to avoid danger inside a stretch of fog-bound road. You can be driving along with no vehicles in front of you for miles and roll into the fog thinking you're okay only to smash into the back of a crash that happened 10 minutes before you showed up. Or you can follow some easy-does-it tractor-trailer into a fog knowing that his bulk will protect you from plowing into the back of an existing crash and someone who's not so careful will drive into the back of your car.

The only absolute answer to avoiding danger in a fog is not to drive in it. Failing that, you could wait for some trucks (maybe under police direction, as California is now doing) to form a safety convoy. They stop at the edge of a fogbank and wait for a line of traffic to form behind them so everyone can traverse the low-visibility zone in a controlled, orderly manner. If they're in contact with other truckers or the police by CB radio who can advise on how thick the fogbank is and what's in front of them, the whole thing can be fairly easy.

If that kind of assistance or an alternate route's not available, there is technology that can help you -- active cruise control. The purpose of active cruise is to keep your car going at a steady speed when traffic allows, and slowing it down when traffic is heavy and then bringing it back to your steady speed when possible. These systems work in the fog, snow and rain, so they can help you avoid crashing into the back of another vehicle in poor visibility conditions.

# The Third Row In A Compact SUV
# More Dangerous Than You May Think

People in the third row of various compact or mid-size vehicles are absolutely in more danger than people in the front or middle rows, and don't let anyone tell you they aren't. This started out as a minor issue in a few vehicles, but with the growing popularity of crossovers (a mix of a minivan and an SUV) more people will be put at risk.

Simply put, passengers in the third row are close to three potential points of impact -- rear, side and roof, but most critically the rear. The last place in the world you want your kids to be if a larger vehicle crashes into the back of your smaller SUV is in a seat close to the rear of the vehicle.

We're talking here about those compact SUVs and crossovers that have crammed a third row of seats into what should be the cargo area. The general rule here would be that the less cargo space there is behind the third seat, the less safe that third row is. Bear in mind that the auto companies also call the space behind the second row a "crumple zone" since it provides room for your car to crumple and absorb the enormous force from another vehicle hitting it from behind. If it's doing that, it can't also be a safe place to put kids or pets or anything inanimate that you cherish.

On top of that extremely dangerous attribute, many of the head restraints in the third-row seats of such vehicles don't adjust, which provides more opportunity for injury.

In virtually any circumstance, the safest place in any vehicle of any size during a crash is as far from its exterior as you can be, which effectively means the middle seat in the second row. But the smaller the vehicle, the more important that rule is.

Yes, the auto companies are doing wonderful things with body structure and airbags and seatbelts and all that, but as engineers are fond of pointing out about safety features: "The rules of physics still apply." That means they can't make vehicles that don't squash or "deform" in all crashes, and even if they could they can't stop the occupants from being tossed around in bad collisions.

Cars rarely carry more than four people, so the biggest danger would be for families who allow one of the kids into the third row to help reduce the shared-space friction.

Before you choose a vehicle with a third row, be sure to go back and sit there during the test drive to experience for yourself how cramped it feels and how close you are to other vehicles when they stop.

There isn't much clamor in the public arena about this danger, but that's because this specific size/seating configuration has only recently become popular. Previous vehicles usually didn't have a third row of seats unless they were big enough to hold them safely and comfortably. But unending consumer pressure for more features and ongoing auto company desire to meet that pressure has resulted in these vehicles.

If you must have a vehicle with a third row of seats that is close to the rear door and sits higher than the others, keep people out of it unless there is absolutely no choice, and even then you should consider taking a bigger vehicle or a second vehicle or making two trips.

## Renting Someone Else's Car

Renting someone else's car, or renting your car to someone else, is the idea behind www.RentMyCar.com.

The New York-based firm just got started but it already has dreams of being a global broker of car rentals. It promises to create a situation where you can trust the renter and the renter can buy some short-term insurance.

Don't know if this will work, but we thought you should know it was out there. The rest is up to you.

# Adults Can Reduce A Deadly Issue For Kids By Being More Active In Safety Measures

The bright spot of the ongoing tragedy involving cars backing over children in driveways and parking lots is that solutions are readily available for every type of vehicle owner right now. More technology in cars isn't necessary to keep them safer. All it takes is more effort from the adults.

The best solution to the problem that kills at least two children a week and sends thousands more to the emergency room is simple, free and virtually fool-proof. Get out of the car before you put it in gear and look to make sure that no one's behind your vehicle, and do not move the vehicle unless you see everyone standing well clear.

A good complement to this method is having another grownup or a responsible child (whom you can see at all times) walk by the rear of your vehicle as you're backing it up to make sure no person or animal wanders into the danger path.

If you have a minivan, SUV or any other vehicle with a rear hatch, you can also open that up when you're at the back checking to see if any children or animals are in your vehicle's blind spot. This will give you a lot more vision to the rear, but there will still be a space that you cannot see, so having someone walk back there is important.

If you want to throw some technology at the problem, there are systems available that include rear-facing cameras that project the zone behind your vehicle onto a monitor you attach to the instrument panel. These may cost less than you think and will provide an extra level of safety even after you check the driveway yourself.

Increasingly, such systems are becoming part of the long list of equipment being offered on new vehicles, and that availability should continue to grow.

There is a lot of chatter about SUVs and minivans and other high-backed vehicles increasing the danger because of their reduced line of sight at the rear, but that's mostly a smokescreen. No vehicle in the world lets you see someone or something small immediately behind the vehicle, and at least minivans and SUVs have rear gates that can be lifted to provide a better view from behind the wheel.

In general, all of the discussion about driver height (the shorter you are the longer the blind spot) and vehicle sight-lines are a method of shifting responsibility from the driver (who is often the parent of the child hurt or killed) to the vehicle itself.

Everyone can appreciate that a parent who has just run over her own child is deserving of as much sympathy and understanding as possible. But if this tragedy is to be stopped immediately, it's necessary to make the point that the driver is ultimately responsible for this kind of accident and that simple, no-cost and really effective methods of avoiding it are available to virtually anyone.

Other prevention tips that might decrease the chances of a backover include:

-teaching children not to play in, under or around any vehicles -- ever

-avoid making the driveway a play space, especially when cars are present

-if kids are playing in an empty driveway, leave something in the driveway (a kid's toy, for example) near the entrance from the street to warn people who might drive in

-never leave vehicles running when you're not in the car, to prevent kids from putting the car in gear, though a brake interlock system can make that much harder (see Page 68)

-talk to parents in your area about backover incidents and ask them to teach their children not to play in or around any vehicle or driveway.

## Saturn Outlook Is The Safest Vehicle
## You Can Have In Most Situations

The biggest, most agile and newest OnStar-equipped vehicle you can afford is the short answer to the popular questions: "What is the safest vehicle I can drive?". For most people at the moment that would be the Saturn Outlook, which is something of a blend of a minivan and an SUV, which helps explain why the auto industry calls it a "crossover utility vehicle."

It's impossible to be any more specific about the safest vehicle for you unless we know as much as you do about your driving habits, including how many people ride along with you (and what their ages are), your precise physical dimensions and mental acuity at the time of the crash, where you live, what kinds of roads you use and, most importantly, the precise circumstances of the life-threatening situation you will be involved in.

All this is necessary to picking out the safest vehicle for you because each and every crash or other life-threatening situation is different, thanks to a stream of variables so long it can't be outlined here or anywhere else. Suffice to say that every crash that's ever happened is different from every other crash in some way, so their outcomes are always slightly different. A hazard that you might avoid at 9 a.m. when you're awake and rested might kill you at midnight the same day because you're too tired to respond correctly.

This all means that you have to consider the reality of your driving habits and the totality of the risks you might face when you buy a vehicle, and adjust your requirements accordingly.

But a Saturn Outlook with OnStar is perhaps the best vehicle because it has skills and attributes that go a long way toward delivering the safest all-round vehicle for anyone.

Agility could help a vehicle avoid some of those life-threatening situations, and not crashing is the best solution by far. Features that promote agility include an engine powerful enough to get you out of harm's way quickly, anti-lock brakes, nimble handling, good tires, and stability control.

The larger a vehicle is, the greater protection it provides its occupants during a crash that couldn't be avoided, and this applies to the amount of space it provides around the people it carries as well as its weight. You want to be as far away from another vehicle, or a wall, or a pole or whatever's likely to do you harm as is possible, and you want as much weight as possible to keep the forces of the crash from reaching you.

On this point, it must be mentioned yet again that not all five-star vehicles are created equal. Each vehicle is measured against other vehicles in the same weight class, so if a five-star subcompact crashes into a five-star truck, the people in the subcompact are much more likely to suffer injuries than the people in the truck. In a crash, bigger is almost always better.

Whatever you drive, you should also be as far away from the steering wheel as you can possibly get to reduce your chance of injury in a front-end crash, and have the head restraint positioned correctly to avoid neck injuries in a rear-end crash. For the former look for a vehicle with a tilt/telescope steering wheel and adjustable foot pedals. For the later, the best choice is a vehicle with active head restraints.

Having OnStar in a vehicle ensures that first aid gets to you as quickly as possible, and that is a lot more of an issue than you probably appreciate. Many people who work in emergency services (including many trauma doctors) would love to see crash notification systems in every vehicle since it would save lives. A crash-notification system calls for help even if you can't, and sends it to your precise location. There are some aftermarket crash-notification systems available, but they aren't as good as one that's built into your vehicle because their signal strength is weaker and they won't work where cell-phones don't work.

GM's OnStar system is by far the most sophisticated crash-notification network in the world, and works where no others will because of the strength of its communications signal.

And if you think a cell phone's as good as OnStar you couldn't be more wrong; see Page 99 for more details on that.

Thanks to the ongoing focus on safety, it's fairly safe to say that newer vehicles are better equipped to protect you than older cars, since the modern models have the benefit of more refined crash protection design and extra safety features.

As for those extra safety features, the list grows longer with every model year. Many of them (like brake assist) might help you avoid a crash, and as mentioned that is the best scenario. Others, like airbags above the side windows, might reduce the injuries you sustain in a crash. How many of them you can afford is up to you.

If you ever do get into a hazardous situation, you'll probably wish you spent that $1,000 on anti-lock brakes and stability control rather than an upgraded stereo system.

In ordering extra safety equipment, you really should consider your regular driving circumstances and try to equip the vehicle accordingly.

For example, if you drive in areas where winter conditions are bad, you want to be sure you get snow tires and stability control to help reduce the chance of losing control on ice, and look for crash-notification as well.

If you live somewhere where fog is a regular issue, consider active cruise control, since it will keep you from driving into the back of a stopped vehicle that you can't see in front of you.

If you live anywhere where it gets cold, you might also want to think about a really sophisticated emergency kit to suit your needs. See Page 46 for more on that.

Having the safest vehicle for you is a lot more complicated than it looks at first blush, but the biggest, most agile and newest OnStar-equipped vehicle you can afford is always a good place to start, and the Saturn Outlook is probably an excellent choice for many people.

On top of everything else, it's easier to buy because Saturn practices a no-dicker sales policy and usually treats its customers as people rather than marks. That makes it easier to buy, which improves its safety value.

In terms of price, for the time being Outlook is at the bottom of GM's crossover fleet range, which includes the Buick Enclave and the GMC Acadia. When the Chevrolet Traverse model arrives as a 2009 model, it should be slightly less expensive and offer about the same safety benefits.

## Toxic Chemicals In Cars And Child Seats

For anyone deeply committed to the environment as it relates to the use of chemicals, their creation and their disposal, there's probably no better source of information than www. HealthyCar.org.

This site attempts to give consumers the full story on exactly what chemicals can be found in new cars and new child car seats.

There are many people who say that the chemical emanations from various cars makes them ill, so this site will be particularly useful to people with known reactions to certain substances.

Since people who write to praise the site say they found that their new car made them sick almost right away, it at least underscores the necessity for a longer-than-average test drive.

# Vehicles Can Still Roll Away From
# Driver If She's Not Careful

Even though few people know what they are or what they do, brake-shift interlocks have done a great job making cars safer over the last few years, cutting down markedly on problems of vehicles rolling away on their own.

Brake-shift interlock won't let a vehicle's automatic transmission go into a driving gear (D, R, L) without the driver first putting her foot on the brake pedal. It's a hugely helpful device but is unfortunately still not on all cars on the road.

The device was created in the 1980s when several crashes were blamed on "unintended acceleration," a condition that imagined that the engine and braking systems in a car could fail simultaneously and cause a vehicle to move forward without the driver being able to control it. This has since proved to be as unlikely as it sounds, or even simply impossible.

Brake-interlock was intended to overcome mistakes by drivers who actually had their foot on the gas pedal and not the brake, as they thought. Brake-interlock put an end to that delusion, but was never intended to solve the problem of rollaway vehicles.

There are still many cars that will move forward on their own if the engine is running and a child playing in the car, for example, knocks the gearshift into Drive. Not so long ago, in fact, a woman and three children drowned in a neighborhood pond with lots of people around to help when such a rollaway happened.

The answer is obvious and has value beyond putting an end to this problem -- do not leave a vehicle running when you get out from behind the wheel, most particularly if there are children in the car. If you must do that, put the emergency brake on and tell any kids to stay away from the steering wheel, but even then....

# The Danger From Airbags
# Can Be Greater Than You Imagine

To a degree that would probably surprise you, a deploying airbag makes contact with the person in front of it with surprising force. You would probably also be surprised to learn that many people have no memory of the airbag deploying and deflating, but that's another story.

So you can be hurt by a deploying airbag, but there are things you can do to lessen the risk. Most importantly, make sure your seatbelt is fitted tightly around you, and sit as far back as possible from the steering wheel.

Just as importantly, do not have anything in your mouth when the airbag deploys. That includes cigarettes, cigars and pipes, but also pens or anything else that you do not want forcefully inserted into your throat. You may be busy when a crash is imminent, but spitting out that pen or candy cane or whatever could be very important.

There is a perception that glasses can cause damage and that's slightly possible, but in-depth studies or real accidents show that glasses might actually protect the eyeball from being scratched by the fabric of the airbag.

The big airbag risk involves broken arms, which usually happens if the driver has her hands crossed on the wheel to steer the car away from the crash. But it can also happen if you're just holding onto the wheel. The smart move is to let go of the steering wheel when you know the crash is inevitable and put them at your side, away from the wheel. There's also a suggestion that you pull your feet back at the last possible second as well, since "vehicle intrusion" in a crash almost always involves the foot well where the pedals and feet are. But keeping your foot on the brake to reduce as much speed as possible can also be critical, so involve your own instincts if such a situation arises.

**Alexander Law & Susan Winlaw**

# Crash Notification System Is Simply Ignored By Most Car Companies

Normally the auto industry stays pretty bunched up when it comes to offering important safety features to consumers, but the experience of some women in the last few years show there's a serious safety disparity in the market right now.

They were ordinary women whose lives were put at risk because they slipped into one of those cracks in the public safety net that exist in most civilized places around North America.

Consider a Seattle woman named Laura Hatch, then 17, who nearly died after being trapped in her Toyota Camry for eight days in October, 2004.

You're probably thinking she was stuck out in the wilds of Washington State, but the Toyota was stuck in some trees just off a busy road less than a mile from the city hall of Redmond, which is of course home to Microsoft. So it was not some backwater with no services or smart, caring people around to help her.

Hatch's Camry skidded off the road and slid about 65 yards down an embankment before crashing into some trees. Search parties went along the road but did not look down the hill for a week, at which time the girl was found badly injured and severely dehydrated. Local authorities said it was a miracle that she survived that long without food or water, or from a lack of treatment for her injuries. Her youth probably had a lot to do with that.

It must have been horrible for her, but it's easy to imagine it worse. What if she'd had children with her, or an ailing grandmother?

The safety technology that could have helped Laura Hatch and lots of other people who are trapped in their cars after a crash but is NOT used by Toyota, Ford, Chrysler, Nissan,

BMW, Volvo, Hyundai, Kia, Subaru, Mitsubishi, Volkswagen and others is called crash notification.

This system can send emergency assistance (ambulance, fire, police) to your exact location if you ask for it, or if your vehicle crashes and you aren't able to call for help yourself. If crash notification is imbedded into your car correctly, it operates virtually all over North America, which includes lots of places where no cell phone would ever work. And unlike cell phones, this system works if you can't reach it because you're trapped or the phone's been tossed into the back seat by the crash, or even if you're not conscious.

Crash notification is high on the wish list of many of the continent's emergency service providers and hospital ERs, since they all know how critical it can be to reduce the time between an injury and its treatment. As a result, they have formed an alliance dedicated to promoting crash notification, making the case that it reduce the cost of emergency services as well as save lives.

At the moment, the primary provider of this service is General Motors, as part of its OnStar service. The company has offered OnStar for about a decade now and is constantly expanding its features (including route guidance, data on local attractions) and the vehicles it's offered in, but crash notification is its heart.

There are a few variations on the OnStar system from a couple of other car companies, but nothing comes close to the thoroughness of GM's system.

GM's crash notification uses an abnormally strong cell signal and a built-in GPS locating device to provide emergency assistance for its OnStar subscribers. Because the GM vehicle with activated OnStar is essentially a dial tone on its own, it's able to use a signal that's much stronger than anything in a regular cell phone. So it will connect with the OnStar service center from virtually anywhere in North America that there's a road, or perhaps more importantly even where there isn't

When the driver presses the OnStar button in the car, she is immediately connected to an advisor 24 hours a day, with service in English, French or Spanish. If the driver needs help, the advisor will call the emergency service closest to where the vehicle is and send it to the precise location as provided by the car's GPS system.

If the vehicle's airbags deploy, its crash notification system alerts OnStar by itself. An advisor then calls the driver and asks if she needs help. If no one in the car responds, the advisor immediately contacts local authorities and sends them to the exact location of the crash.

Consider the experience of Michelle Creager of Fort Wayne, Indiana, whose Pontiac Montana minivan hit a slick spot on a two-lane highway and plunged down an embankment before slamming into a tree and landing in a ditch filled with water.

Creager says her cell phone was thrown from the car during the crash and she was drifting in and out of consciousness. "Out of nowhere, there was a voice and she said help was on the way," says Creager. "The advisor heard my son's cry for help and she knew exactly where we were and what kind of help to send."

You don't even have to be alone for crash notification to help. In 2004 a rental car with OnStar collided with another vehicle somewhere in Yosemite National Park and the car's GPS locater placed the car precisely in the 1,189 square-mile region so the park's emergency team got there in time.

On many of the most recent GM models, the crash notification system has been upgraded to alert OnStar even if the airbags don't deploy. The new system records the severity of the crash, the direction of impact force, velocity change, if an airbag was deployed and which one (i.e. frontal), and rollover if present, information that the advisor can pass along to the nearest emergency service.

About 20,000 OnStar subscribers a month call looking for emergency help, and that doesn't include the 20,000 doors that are unlocked remotely, the stolen car tracking, or thousands of calls for roadside assistance to fix a flat or bring fuel or whatever.

Given all the advantages of crash notification and the ongoing consumer interest in safety and security, it's surprising that more companies are not providing their customers with such a service and that more consumers are not making sure it's part of their overall vehicle safety package.

For people serious about safety, it's a difficult service to ignore.

## Medical Info For Emergency Workers

To make sure that people in particular risk receive the best and quickest medical care in the event of a car crash, the authorities of Will County, Illinois, and other municipalities are using the Yellow Dot program.

People who normally ride in a specific car prepare a record of pertinent medical information (with a picture of their face for easy ID), leave it in the glovebox and put a yellow dot on the rear window.

That way, if police or emergency workers find them unconscious and see the yellow dot, they know to check the glovebox for whatever medical information (drugs and doses, existing conditions, etc) they might need to know.

The theory is that this can improve the type of emergency care they get if they're not able to impart this information themselves.

The county is using a similar program for the home called File For Life.

Search "Yellow Dot emergency" on the web and you should discover the latest information on where the service is and how it works.

# Tiny European Car May Not Be
# A Smart Safety Decision

Under no circumstances would we want someone we love to use the Smart ForTwo that's just come on to the market.

The new model did get a better frontal crash test rating than the last model -- four out of five stars, compared with three out of five for the model that was previously sold in Europe and Canada.

But it's extremely important to remember that those ratings are good only in comparison with mini-cars that are a lot smaller (about 700 lbs) than the smallest cars on North American roads. This means that the Smart wouldn't even be as safe as some other cars as tiny as it is (if they were sold here), let alone bigger models. (See Page 19 for story on what the ratings mean in terms of injuries.)

The fact that the new ForTwo's scores better than the previous model owes much to the fact that it's bigger than the previous model, which ought to tell you something. The four-star frontal crash rating means the Mercedes-built two-seater will be the only vehicle in NHTSA's "passenger cars mini" segment (1,500-1,999 lbs) and it still doesn't get five stars.

Smart ForTwo weighs about 1,650 lbs (750 kg), which makes it about 700 lbs (317 kg) smaller than the next smallest vehicles on the road, which would be the Chevrolet Aveo, Kia Rio and subcompacts like that.

Virtually everything else on the car side that's already on the road or is sold today is about twice as heavy, and much of the stuff from the truck side (pickups, minivans, SUVs, crossovers) weighs three or four times as much as a ForTwo.

Bear in mind too that those scores only represent a vehicle's performance in a specific kind of event, which represents only a narrow portion of the crashes that happen every day and which the car companies design vehicles to prepare for.

Who knows how the Smart ForTwo will fare in the chaotic traffic in North America that involves many kinds of crashes? You don't have to spend very much time in one to appreciate how exposed you feel, since there is virtually nothing beyond the metal frame you sit inside.

Smart's middling safety record in Europe was also earned in an automotive community that features many other tiny cars for it to hit, and very few SUVs, minivans and pickup trucks for it to be hit by. Here in North America, Smart will always be the smallest car in any crash, and that's not a good position for you to be in.

Consider this warning from the Insurance Institute for Highway Safety: "The first crashworthiness attributes to consider are vehicle size and weight. Small, light vehicles generally offer less protection than larger, heavier ones. There's less structure to absorb crash energy, so deaths and injuries are more likely to occur in both single- and multiple-vehicle crashes. So if safety is one of your major considerations PASS UP VERY SMALL, LIGHT VEHICLES."

The capital letters were put in by the IIHS, by the way.

## Drunk Drivers Get Web Exposure

In the latest attempt to shame alcohol-impaired drivers off the road, authorities in the Phoenix area have launched a web site (with supporting roadside billboards) that show photos of the people involved.

If you go to StopDUIAZ.com you'll see photos of the people convicted of driving under the influence in Maricopa County.

No word on what effect it's had on the incidence of drunk driving in the Phoenix area, but it's surely raised the profile of the man who holds the elected post of county attorney.

About 30 people a year die every year in Arizona car crashes that involve drunk driving.

# Driver Death Rates In Various Car Models Put Occupant Safety In Perspective

When it comes to casting light on real-world safety in different kinds of vehicles, little compares with the Insurance Institute for Highway Safety's report on driver deaths.

The smart consumer will review the study at www.iihs.org and pay close attention to its general advice -- that greater vehicle weight means greater protection in a crash, and that newer vehicles usually come with technologies that are significantly improving people's chances of sustaining fewer injuries in a crash (all those extra airbags) or avoiding a crash altogether (electronic stability control).

But the very smart consumer will NOT use the IIHS findings too specifically. By that we mean they will take notice of which types vehicles rank better (i.e. get lower scores), but if one vehicle in a category gets a lower score than another it does not necessarily follow that the vehicle with the lower score is always going to be safer.

In the first place, the most recent IIHS study involves vehicles from the 2001-to-2004 model years. Most of those vehicles will have been upgraded or completely revised since they were new, so their successors will almost certainly come with improved safety levels.

Furthermore, the IIHS study cannot take into account all of the individual factors of the types of people who buy certain kinds of vehicles, or the likely use of the vehicles. For example, sporty cars often have worse driver death rates than other cars of the same general weight, and we know that's because their drivers are probably driving them more aggressively, which puts them in greater danger. Similarly, larger wagons have higher death rates on the IIHS study than small wagons, which makes sense when you learn that old people drove a lot of the large wagons and they tend to get in more accidents as the general publc and their bodies aren't as resilient to injury.

This means that if you forced all young men to drive, say, large family sedans instead of small sporty cars, you would see the death rate for large family sedans go up. So the safety of the car depends greatly on the behavior of the driver.

However, the IIHS study reinforces the most important safety truths -- bigger and newer is better, but the driver is the biggest safety feature of them all.

## Alcohol Detector For All Cars Is Coming

In an effort to stop the alcohol-impaired driving that claims thousands of lives a year, an effort has been launched to create an in-vehicle alcohol technology for all cars.

If things go as planned, the technology could be part of new vehicles by the middle of the next decade.

The Automotive Coalition for Traffic Safety (ACTS) and the National Highway Traffic Safety Administration (NHTSA) have entered into a "cooperative research agreement to explore the feasibility, the potential benefits of, and the public policy challenges associated with a more widespread use of in-vehicle technology to prevent alcohol-impaired driving."

This semi-legalese is thought to be necessary because the organizations involved don't want to guess how the technology might work, or be applied. But there is now a concerted effort to try to make something happen, since all the public service announcements and legal punishment in the world doesn't seem to have any affect on the entire population.

To stay in touch with this, check out www.dadss.org.

## Car/RV Insurance For Your Pets

At least one insurance company -- Progressive -- is now offering coverage (up to $500 for no charge) if your pet is injured or killed in a crash. Expect other firms to follow suit.

# A Serious Personal Emergency Kit
## For Life As You Really Drive It

Except for always keeping your car's gas tank as full as possible at all times, it's impossible to prepare perfectly for an emergency situation unless you can precisely forecast the details and duration of that emergency.

That's not possible, however, so the best you can do is prepare for the types of emergencies that might befall you, given the place you live, the weather you're likely to encounter, and the people you regularly have in the car with you. For example, if you live in the Florida panhandle and almost always drive alone, you'll need different things than if you live in Colorado anywhere west of Denver and take your family with you all the time.

But first a word for those folks who think they might never need an emergency kit because they live in a big city: Never forget the woman whose Toyota Camry slid down an embankment in a well-developed area a couple of miles from the Microsoft complex near Seattle and spent a week trapped there.

But you can prepare to survive the kind of situation that might put you and yours in danger or away from the things you need to be comfortable. So you should consider the range of emergencies that are most likely to hit you and put together a kit that would suit those circumstances. Once you imagine and create that package, you then need to carry it in your vehicle at all times.

Imagine what you will need to cope with spending several hours or maybe even a couple of days in your vehicle, with no access to the things you have at home. This can happen in a winter storm or in a really bad traffic jam on a rural highway with no services nearby, or if you slide off a road into a shallow ditch and get covered with snow, or for whatever situation seems reasonable to you in your own life. What would you need to keep your family safe and comfortable for some time without outside aid or supplies?

For example, you'll want to have some pressure bandages on hand in case someone is badly cut in a crash, but you might also want to have a supply of feminine sanitary products in case you're stuck in your car for long periods. No pun intended.

Before we discuss suggestions for items you might want to carry in your vehicle, the most important thing you need to do is make sure your vehicle is always at least three-quarters full of fuel, but more is always better. The vehicle's engine is your primary source of heat, light, power and information (the radio) in an emergency, and the longer you can keep it from running out of gas the better it could be for your family.

The obvious place to go after that on any emergency list is a supply of any medicines a family member might need, and enough water and food to keep everyone hydrated and not hungry for a couple of days. There are special high-energy foods created for just such an occasion, but cans of soups and stews are also good, and a can opener of course. Indeed, this is where one of those multi-purpose tools from Gerber, Leatherhead or the Swiss Army would finally come in handy.

There are inexpensive (about $10-$15) little devices called "beverage immersion heaters" that use power from the car's auxiliary plug to heat water for coffee or tea or cans of soup or whatever you like. If you think this is all too much, imagine how your children will behave if they have to go without food for a day and how well you'll be able to cope without caffeine.

Candles are also good for creating heat in an enclosed space, and could also help to warm up some of those canned goods, which means matches would also be smart.

You should also think about how you're going to dispose of that food when it's done its job by including a bedpan, potty or pail in your emergency kit, and toilet paper.

If you live where it gets cold, you would want to include blankets and coats, and candles as a heat source, along with boots and hats or other winter gear in case you have to walk any distance for help. If you live in or regularly visit a hurricane zone, then rain slickers or umbrellas make sense. Whatever it is, do you want to walk through bad weather for help in your favorite heels?

If you do leave the car, a flashlight or lantern of some type would be useful, which of course means extra batteries unless you get one of those lights that you shake to recharge.

Put a utility knife and hammer in the glove box to cut through the fabric in the door or seat or to break the windows or wherever you need to do to help you get out, or to use as a weapon if necessary.

Other ideas include gloves, a whistle, a crank-operated radio/lantern or one of the many new devices designed to supply light, radio service, cell phone rechargers and other important things that are sold on the net or in serious auto supply stores.

Yeah, sure, it all sounds like a scene from Jericho or one of those 1950s films about an ordinary family having to flee an invasion from outer space, but that's the nature of emergencies. At least with a little foresight and work you can be ready to be stuck in your car for a day or two.

Such an emergency kit might be pretty silly if you never leave the downtown area of a major city, but it generally becomes more sensible the farther you live from a heavily-populated area. You have to make that call for your own life. And always remember that woman who was trapped in her Camry for a week. Think what that would be like with two children.

# Women Drivers Most At Risk
# When They Get Older

It seems that older women are more likely than older men to pay attention when someone asks them about the changing nature of their driving skills, which is great since there are more hazards for elderly drivers, but particularly women.

All kinds of studies and statistics make it clear that there is also likely to be more risk for other people on the road from aging drivers, so for the sake of someone in your family or maybe even yourself, the reality of an aging driver must be faced.

Such an undertaking is fraught with emotional risk, but there is an excellent starting point in a pamphlet put out by The Hartford called Family Conversations With Older Drivers. Check it out at www.thehartford.com.

Crash rates start to increase when people reach 60 and soon after their fatality rates go up even more, partly because they're in as many crashes as teen drivers and partly because their bodies are less capable of withstanding trauma at that age.

But it's better to pay attention to aging drivers in case their personal situation changes sooner. One of the most common signs of declining faculties and skills involves a near-crash situation that caught the driver by surprise.

If you or someone you know has recently had a "near-miss" that came out of nowhere, it's time to consider the risky situation you or your family member might be in.

A couple of tips for older drivers:

-Try walking more, since that would help you keep the physical skills you need for driving.

-Avoid making left-hand turns, since the biggest risk to older drivers comes in failure-to-yield situations, of which the left turn is the most dangerous.

# Avoid Attacks In And Around Your Car With Planning And Technology

Safety and security is a popular topic on the internet, and here are a few auto-related tips that seem useful:

-Have a look in the trunk of your vehicle to see if it has an emergency release tab. If you do, it might serve you well if you're ever grabbed and thrown into the trunk. If there isn't one, or it doesn't work, you can always try to smash the tail-light cover with your shoe. Once the light cover's broken you should be able to stick your hand through and wave for help. It's also possible that you might be able to remove the rug on the floor of the trunk and whatever else covers the spare tire. Assuming the whole jack apparatus is there (which you should check when you're looking for the emergency release lever), the jack handle could serve you well as a weapon. It's a long, thin piece of metal that should be easy to hide until you want to do some damage with it.

-If you're the type who tends to get in her car in a busy parking lot and sit there for a time while you look for something in your purse or check your list to see what chore's next or whatever, you may want to change your behavior patterns. You maybe want to lock your doors immediately and drive away, or at least start the engine so you can drive quickly away if you need to. Go somewhere in the parking lot that's not busy so you can do that purse- or list-checking in a safer setting.

-Car park behavior begins with parking as close to a well-lit and well-traveled area as possible, and not pulling up next to the big, window-less van (the type used for delivery and service purposes) that seems to unnerve so many women and indeed would be the perfect vehicle for hiding a woman that had just been grabbed. If you're nervous at all, go to another spot. You could also wait in the car until another woman or a couple walks by and get out and stay close to them.

When you return to the car, look around before you get into the car. If you see broken glass, or the door ajar, do not assume it's a robbery and go to see what's happened. You're going to need the police or building security in either case, so move away from the vehicle as you call for help. If there are no signs of a break-in, it's still a good idea to look inside the car first, on the floor of the front passenger seat and the back seat.

If that van's there, or there's a man sitting alone in the seat nearest your car, or anything else makes you nervous, move away or go back into the store. Ask someone from the store or whatever to watch while you get into your car. Better to look paranoid than not live to regret it later.

And don't forget to call someone on your cell phone the moment you feel unsafe. Tell them where you are and keep them on the phone until you're out of danger.

## Take Care With Personalized Messages

People pay more for personalized plates because they want to say something about themselves, but saying something about yourself may give a crook a key piece of information.

If you were a bad guy looking to mug someone, for example, would you stake out the car with a "NRAChamp" plate or the car with the plate that said "BestGrandma"?

On the other hand, if you were a bad guy looking to steal some extra guns, which of those two cars would you pick?

The same thing applies to bumper stickers, of course, and could extend to things you believe to be utterly positive. By proclaiming your religion, for example, you might become a target for someone who resents your church. Sometimes it pays to look harmless or threatening and sometimes it doesn't. Maybe the safest course is not giving the bad guys any information at all.

# Women Benefit More From
# Better Use Of Head Restraints

When it comes to saving lives in car crashes, the auto companies have pretty much hit a plateau until they work out how to get our vehicles to talk amongst themselves and, as a result, stop running into each other.

So the safety emphasis has shifted to things that reduce injuries, and on that front there's maybe nothing more important than their work with head restraints. This is of particular importance to women, since studies have shown that women (because they are usually shorter) are more likely to suffer the kinds of injuries that better head restraints can stop.

Thinking about those cushions at the top of the seats as "head restraints" rather than "headrests" is a good step to making yourself safer, since they are primarily there to stop your head from whipping around in certain crashes and damaging your neck. This is of course a "whiplash" injury, and for many people that description suggests a dubious medical condition concocted by greedy doctors and lawyers. The term became wildly popular in 1964 with Walter Matthau's Oscar-winning performance as a lawyer called "Whiplash Willie" Gingrich in The Fortune Cookie and became something of a synonym for lawyers seeking payment for injuries that couldn't be easily traced by modern medicine.

In some instances this may still be the case, since a search of this subject on the web will almost always direct you to a website for a personal injury lawyer. But there's also a scientific study that claims that 10 to 20 percent of the population has limited mobility because of neck pain and that 35 percent of those injuries could be eliminated if people had better head restraint systems in cars.

There's no denying that a neck injury is the most common and most serious injury when you're in a car that's crashed into from behind. The speeds involved don't even have to be that great -- 5 mph can do it -- but the greater the speed the worse a neck injury's likely to be.

If nothing else, you need to reposition the head restraint on your current vehicle so it provides you with better protection. In general terms that means putting it as far forward as it can possibly go, to allow as little movement of the head. There may even be some aftermarket devices available that can make your head restraint protect you better, but take care to examine all claims for these products carefully. On that point, some of those lawyer-sponsored websites about neck injuries have lots of helpful data.

If you're in the market for a new vehicle, the best product to protect your neck is called an "active head-restraint system." Such systems reformat the front seats in the event of a crash, repositioning the head restraint and moving the seat to counter the physical forces that can cause the injury.

Because neck injuries cost them a lot of money, the insurance companies are actually leading the way on bringing information about how different vehicles perform in a rear crash, through their wholly-owned research group -- the Insurance Institute for Highway Safety.

Look to www.iihs.org for information on how different vehicles fare on the institute's tests, and be prepared for some surprises. Consider that out of all of the models Toyota sells in North America today, only one of them (the full-size Tundra pickup) earns a Good overall rating (out of Good, Acceptable, Marginal and Poor).

Paying more is not always a solution, since Toyota's most expensive model (Avalon sedan) scores an overall rating of Poor. That score suggests that this is one of those rare times when vehicle size may not play that big a role in safety.

The IIHS website shows the test scores for all models of all brands of recent vintage, new and used.

## Traditional Cars For School
## Aren't The Best Bet For Your Kids

When you consider that most college students are in the age group for whom car crashes are the leading cause of death, it's amazing how many parents want to send their children off to school in some of the least safe cars on the road.

But you see it all over the continent -- kids from 16 to 20 years of age going to and from school in small cars without the full complement of safety features, either on a daily commute from home or half-way across the country to attend college.

Roughly, licensed drivers of this age group make up about 6.3 percent of all drivers in the country, but they account for about 12.6 percent of driver fatalities, and male drivers die about three times as often as female drivers. Overall, young drivers are involved in 16 percent of all police-reported crashes, with male drivers again making up the majority of that number.

In 2005, the last year for which hard numbers were available at press time, 3,467 15- to 20-year-old drivers (2,575 boys and 892 girls) were killed and an additional 281,000 were injured in motor vehicle crashes in the U.S.

On top of that, young drivers get more speeding tickets than other groups, largely because the experience of driving is new to them and they are more prone to do things on the road "for fun" than their parents. This is one of those times when parental concern for their children actually comes close to reflecting the reality of the situation.

In the face of this fearsome truth, parents who plan to procure cars for their kids to drive to high school or college ought to be rethinking the traditional choices, which usually involve small cars.

Small cars may seem appropriate for school because they

don't use as much gas and are easier to park on crowded campuses, or they look like starter cars, or they're cute, or something, but they are simply not the safest cars for young drivers. In truth, small cars are probably not the smartest cars for anyone to drive (see Pages 18 and 20 for supporting information), but statistics make it clear that they are particularly ill-suited for young people since they are more likely to get into a crash than their parents are, and at a greater speed, which increases the chance of injury or death.

In almost every case there is, the larger the car the lower its mileage, but each parent has to think about how high the price of gas has to go before they're willing to compromise their children's safety.

There is also the matter of putting your children in a vehicle with crash-notification technology, which can call for emergency help if the occupants cannot (they could be unconscious, or have no cell phone service, or any number of things) and send the paramedics and police to the precise location of the crash.

In our view this is a critical service for anyone who is genuinely concerned about safety, since it provides the quickest possible call for help in a situation where time without first aid or medical treatment can determine the difference between life or death. How important is that to you? (For more information on this, see Page 38.)

At the moment and for the foreseeable future, that pretty much restricts parents to vehicles from General Motors or Mercedes-Benz, since they are the only firms that supply crash-notification – OnStar and Tele-Aid, respectively.

The GM connection is especially good news for parents concerned about price and safety, since many of the U.S. firm's models are getting long-term dependability scores that match those of the Japanese firms famous for quality but that fact isn't widely known in the used car market. Today's used car market still largely believes that a second-hand Honda or Toyota is worth a lot more than a car from another brand for quality reasons, and all kinds of studies show there really isn't a quality difference.

This means parents will be able to get a larger car from one of the GM brands for their school-going kids that provides more safety than small Japanese models that cost more, which will negate the extra fuel costs. Depending upon how much money you want to spend, there's a full complement of models from various GM dealerships that are OnStar equipped.

In terms of quality, Buick recently tied Lexus at the top of the JD Power three-year dependability study, but then all the brands on the market are within a shade of each other on the survey (see Page 150) so you can go for the best deal, or even the vehicle your son or daughter wants.

In general, keep them away from any kind of SUV from any company, since they tend to roll over more easily than traditional cars and that's a whole other dimension of danger you don't want to consider.

If all this scares you, see the story on the next page about how you can avoid the costs of financing a car and the insurance for your kids.

## Girls Behaving Worse At The Wheel

Young men are still a lot more reckless behind the wheel than young women, but a 10-year study shows the behavioral gap is closing. More young women than ever are binge drinking and then driving home without their seatbelts, so more of them are dying or being injured.

That's the primary result of a study by the emergency room doctors at University of California Irvine Medical Center, using statistics gathered from 1995 to 2004.

The risk seems to be greatest for women aged 21 to 24, and there's surely no need to give the safety lecture again.

# Consider Extended Chauffeur Duties Or Limo Or Taxi Service To Keep Teens Alive

Since a car crash is THE most likely cause of death for people aged 16 to 19, lots of parents are struggling for ways to protect their children while they're behind the wheel.

But many parents are going the extra mile -- literally -- to keep their children safe by simply keeping them from getting behind the wheel. The percentage of teens getting their license at 16 has been falling for years as parents expand their chauffeuring duties for as long as they can. Those endless trips to the mall may be tiresome, but they help to get them through the prime danger years for teen driving.

The thing to remember is that the older a person is when she or he starts to drive, the less chance there is of them dying in a car crash. It's that simple and that cruel.

If a chauffeur's duties become too much or there's some event you just can't make, consider professional help -- taxis and limos. That may sound extravagant, but if you ask your car insurance agent about how much it costs to add a 16-year-old to your policy, you're likely to learn that you would probably save money by giving them cab fare or arranging a limo instead. And since kids tend to run in groups, there's likely to be one or more teen willing to share the cost.

You might also try talking to the parents of your teen's friends, to see if there isn't some way to work together to cut down on the chauffeuring duties or the cab-limo expenses.

Whatever you do, make sure that your unlicensed teen is NOT riding in a car driven by a teen with a license, especially if they're both boys. Studies indicate that teen boys riding together get into more crashes than a teen boy driving a girl, or girls driving girls, or girls driving boys.

Just do what you can to keep them out of cars driven by anyone under 19, whether it's them or someone else.

# Devices Will Let You Watch Kids
## (Or Anyone) While They're Driving Cars

While most parents want to treat their teens like the responsible young adults they probably are, they also worry like crazy about what they might be doing when they're out in the family car. After all, who can forget that almost 4,000 teens die in car crashes in Canada and the United States every year, and many thousands more are injured.

So there are lots of companies offering devices and services to help parents bridge the gap between trust and concern when it comes to cars.

The most obvious may be the DriveCam, which attaches to the rear-view mirror and starts recording when it senses the kind of physical stresses that come with hard driving, such as rapid acceleration, sudden braking or speedy turns. One lens faces the road ahead and the other faces the driver. The system then records the 10 seconds before the event and 10 seconds after it, providing 20 seconds of irrefutable evidence for the post-drive trial.

Early reports suggest DriveCam has a salutary effect on the driver's behavior if that person has to report to someone after-the-fact.

American Family Mutual Insurance has been making the system available in certain packages for some time now, but DriveCam can also be purchased directly.

More details about the system can be found at www.drivecam.com.

But there are also lots of GPS-based products to keep track of where the teen and the car are, or even when the teen and the car are doing something risky. There's another system that uses multiple cameras to record everything going on in and around the car.

You only need to web-search "teen driving monitor technology" and a flood of alternatives will be put before you.

You can look to see where the car is at any moment using a GPS tracking system, or be alerted by another system that the car is being driven hard, if the seatbelts are being worn, and so on. There are also record-keeping devices that tell you after-the-fact where your child and the car were and when.

On top of the peace-of-mind associated with these devices, there might also be a chance for a break on the amount you pay to insure your teen drivers. In fact, it might be a good idea to start with your insurance company to see if they have any programs that might apply, or even suggestions to make.

This stuff is of course not free, but it's not overly expensive either and might even be recovered by a lower insurance rate. What you're willing to pay for the lowered level of concern is up to you.

### Distractions Used To Steal Purses

Keeping your hands or your eyes on your purse is excellent advice, but there are situations when that's not possible and loading/unloading your car is one of them.

Clever thieves seem to be taking advantage of that by creating distractions (car alarms going off is a favorite) that give them enough time to snatch your purse while you're not watching. So anytime something distracts you while you don't have your purse under control, it could be time for extra caution.

Once you're in the car, of course, make sure the windows are closed enough so that a thief can't reach in and grab your purse. It wouldn't hurt to lock the doors, either.

### Restrictions For Young Drivers?

Norway is considering an outright ban on youth driving after dark and on weekends in the aftermath of one of those late night crashes that killed several young people.

# There's A Chance You May Weigh Too Much For Your Car

If you travel with all of the seats in your vehicle occupied by adults, there's a good chance that you might be surpassing the maximum weight level for its safe operation. That applies to seven-seat minivans as well as two-seat sportscars and everything in between, excluding large pickups and SUVs.

It's a safety issue because each vehicle is set up to handle a specific maximum weight, which means the tires and the suspension won't operate as well if you go beyond that, which can result in handling problems. It might also present you with an issue if you've over-loaded your vehicle and are in a crash, the dealer might void your warranty, and there's no doubt many insurance companies would be glad for a reason not to cover your losses as well.

Sure, none of these legal problems might occur, but it's always wise to use a little judicious paranoia in such matters.

The passenger weight limit should be posted on the door pillar of cars from the 2006 model year and on, and it might be worth a look before you buy, or before you offer to take four friends somewhere in your five-seat sedan.

You might be surprised by the weight limits, and perhaps not pleased. You probably couldn't take the average starting-five from a boys high school basketball team to the game in a seven-seat minivan and stay below the weight threshold.

## Japan Wants Seniors To Give Up Driving

Around the world, people over 65 tend to get in more crashes than any other age group. But the situation with Japan's vast seniors' population is so bad that the police and government in Tokyo are offering discounts on meals and amusement park rides for anyone over 65 who turns in their license and stops driving.

# What To Do When The Babbling Brook Starts To Speak A Little Deeper

If your only experience with a vehicle's ability to go through more than a little water comes from what you see in TV ads, you may not have all the facts about fluid dynamics.

And we're not going to give all the facts to you because who wants to have fluid dynamics explained to them in depth?

The important thing is that you need to be careful if you're driving towards a body of water, particularly if it's flowing. If your car stalls in a stream that's moving at even a moderate pace, there's a chance the water could float the car and wash it downstream, where the depth might be greater and more dangerous.

The higher and/or faster the water, the greater the danger. Two feet of water moving at a jogging pace will lift most small sedans off the ground and float them away.

This may sound like an unlikely event, but people in cars account for about half of the drowning deaths during a flood.

Cars as well as SUVs are able to cross a standing or moving body of water at a shallow place (i.e. "ford") in safety, but the specifics vary from vehicle-to-vehicle and, accordingly, so does the level of danger.

The key issue is keeping the water from getting at the engine and making it stall, so the higher the vehicle's clearance (the space between the road and the bottom of the vehicle) the better.

The other danger in a flood is that the water may have worn away the normal road surface, which could mean it won't grip the car's tires as well, which increases the chance that traction will be lost and you'll float away.

There's no easy answer for any of this since each situation is different, but extra caution is never a bad idea when the creek's rising or the rain's falling hard.

# Danger From Aging, Low-Mileage Tires Even If You Don't Drive On Them Much

If you have a car that's been using the same tires for more than six years, you should strongly think about replacing them no matter how many miles they've been driven.

It's now widely accepted that the chemical composition of the tires -- even if their tread is not worn down that much -- simply breaks down over time, sometimes to the point where they can come apart when the car is moving.

The situation may be exacerbated by a hot climate or by frequent high-load conditions, such as hard driving.

Unfortunately there seems to be no way to tell that this is an issue until the tire fails. So a tire that looks good, has a healthy-looking tread depth and hasn't covered more than normal distance (about 12,000 miles a year) can still be dangerous. Replacement's the only solution.

## Stores Fight For Safe-Parking Awards

By handing out awards to stores that develop and maintain parking lots with low-crime rates which in turn draw more customers, the UK is encouraging even more stores to take up the challenge to make their premises safer for customers.

The award is given out by the Association of Chief Police Officers in Britain and is intended to create parking lots with good standards of safety and security so they will have lower crime levels than the streets around it.

As far as we can determine, no such program exists in North America. Pity.

## Concern About After-Crash Care

To make sure your health care goes as you want, carry copies of a living will and a power-of-attorney in the car.

## Apparently You Can Be Too Thin
## When It Comes To Car Crashes

Heavy people are twice as likely to die in a crash than people of average size, studies repeatedly show, but that's mostly because they don't do up their seatbelts as often as other people. That problem can be solved to a large extent with the purchase of a seatbelt extension and regular attention to using it.

People who are really thin, on the other hand, tend to get more broken bones in a crash because they have less body mass to protect them when they get hit by something or are thrown into something. No easy answer for that, unfortunately, except to stay as far away from any outside surface of the car as possible, but particularly the steering wheel. Thin people not wearing a seatbelt are as likely to die as the obese.

There might be other causes for the death count of obese people, including a predisposition to sleep apnea, heart conditions and diabetes, all of which can create physical symptoms that might create a loss of control.

## Is Drivers-Ed A Bad Thing?

Everyone assumes that formalized driver-training makes for safer drivers, but there has been precious little empirical evidence to back that up.

Now comes an extensive study that shows a "significantly higher" collision rate for people who take the voluntary beginner driver education program in Ontario, which is Canada's largest province.

According to this study, 55 percent of first-time drivers enrolled in the program crashed their cars about 62 percent more often than the people who didn't take part in the program.

No one at the Ontario government has so far been able to explain why this is happening.

# Your Car Airbags May Be Fakes
# Or Simply Installed Incorrectly

If you're driving a vehicle that has previously been in a crash that deployed the airbags, there's a chance that you have what can only be called "fake airbags" because they won't do what they're supposed to in a crash.

This could be an extremely serious problem if you are one of those people who refuses to wear seatbelts, but it's much less serious if you always buckle up. The seatbelt is after all the primary restraint system, which is why the airbag's proper name is SRS, which stands for "supplemental restraint system".

It seems that many auto body shops are replacing deployed airbags with airbags that simply do not work, or the wrong airbag, or no airbag at all, or whatever they can get away with. This allows them to put in a fake or no airbag at all while charging you or your insurance company for the real thing. Your safety is apparently not an issue for them.

On top of that, even auto body shops may not do the job right because putting in a replacement airbag is one of the most sophisticated repair processes going.

Airbags are not generic, they are instead created for specific vehicles. You may not even be able to use a bag from a 2005 model in your car if it's a 2004 model.

If your car's been in a crash with you or a previous owner at the wheel, you should strongly consider getting it checked by a qualified mechanic.

This is particularly important if the car's airbag warning light does not operate correctly. The light should come on when you start the car and then go out. If the light doesn't come on at all, or doesn't go off at all, get the system checked by a technician qualifed by ASE to work on airbags.

Most important of all, always wear your seatbelt.

# Crash Frequency Differs
# Depending On Your Location

A car crash every 10 years is what the average American driver can expect, but the timetable can shift dramatically (from 13.7 to 6.6 years) depending upon your location.

That's the chief finding of the third annual Allstate America's Best Drivers Report, based on traffic statistics from every state but Massachusetts, where the company has not sold car insurance for some time.

According to this survey, the ten cities with the lowest crash average are

1. Sioux Falls, S.D., every 13.7 years
2. Fort Collins, Colorado, every 13.6 years
3. Flint, Michigan, every 13.4 years
4. Warren, Michigan, every 13.3 years
5. Huntsville, Alabama, every 13.1 years
6. Knoxville, Tennessee, every 13.0 years
7. Chattanooga, Tennessee, every 12.9 years
8. Colorado Springs, Colorado, every 12.7 years
9. Milwaukee, Wisconsin, every 12.7 years
10. Des Moines, Iowa, every 12.6 years

Rather than list the municipalities with the worst crash frequency scores, Allstate chose to list the 10 big cities with the worst crash frequency scores. They are:

78. Phoenix, every 9.8 years
116. San Diego, every 9.0 years
160. San Antonio, every 8.1 years
163. Houston, every 8.1 years
169. New York, every 7.9 years
178. Dallas, every 7.7 years
183. Chicago, every 7.4 years
185. Los Angeles, every 6.9 years
190. Philadelphia, every 6.6 years

# Consider Car Travel Organizer
# For Safety While Driving And In A Crash

Travel organizers may look like a gift you buy for the person who has everything else, but in truth they perform a couple of really good safety functions.

They keep everything together, so you don't have to be too distracted looking around on the floor, the glove box, or anywhere else for a pen or CD or whatever.

If they have pockets or flaps, organizers can also keep things restrained so that they don't go flying all over the place hitting people in the event of a collision or a rollover.

The organizer bag itself can be a safety hazard in a crash or rollover, so it's best to get one with straps that tie around the seat or attach to the seatbelt.

Only leave those things lying around that you wouldn't mind hitting you in the eye when they're bouncing around inside the car at 30 mph.

## Value Of Newest Safety Technology

The Insurance Institute for Highway Safety (IIHS) recently took a look at some crash-avoidance technologies that are showing up in cars and was enthusiastic about two of them.

That would be forward collision warning (also known as active cruise-control) and lane departure warning.

The former alerts a driver to something on the road in front of her and can even be set up to slow or stop the car without her help. In our view this is by far the most useful safety technology to come along in some time.

The IIHS is less enthusiastic about lane-departure (and so are we) because it's hard to set up so that it isn't constantly crying wolf when it's not important.

Blind-spot detection, brake assist and headlights that turned with curves in the road aren't likely to be as valuable.

# Cell Location In Emergency
# Proves Not Reliable In Tests

There's no doubt that cell phones have had a tremendously positive affect on getting help for people injured in a car crash more quickly, but a recent study makes it clear that they're pretty bad at leading emergency workers to your location if you can't give it to them yourself.

(Cell phones are also no good at all for getting help when you can't get a signal or can't use the phone for some other reason, but that's another story. It's on Page 38.)

The study showed that a bunch of cell providers across the U.S. did a very bad job of meeting the targets for finding a customer that are set out by the government, which are themselves not very encouraging.

The rules state that a provider using network technology needs to be able to locate a customer within about 328 yards 95 percent of the time.

At that distance across a flat, open surface a rescue worker wouldn't be able to recognize the type of car it was, let alone if you were inside it needing help. And if there were trees, hills, building or some other object they wouldn't see your vehicle -- let alone you -- at all.

But even that kind of pinpointing seems beyond the regular reach of cell providers that try to triangulate a position from cell towers to get a fix on a customer needing help.

The head of the study would only say that the group was "very disappointed" in the results, and that was being kind. More than half the time the service providers couldn't meet the minimum distance.

Providers of phones with the new "handset" technology use global positioning satellites to find their clients have stricter rules (165 yards 95 of the time) and they did a lot better on the study. Not real close, but it could make a difference.

## Brake-Interlock Doesn't Trump
## Common Sense For Maximum Safety

Despite the best efforts of 60 Minutes back in the 1980s to prove that "unintended acceleration" could happen in a car even if the driver was pressing down hard on the brake pedal, truth and sanity eventually won out.

Yes, there are conditions in which a car may move ahead without the driver pressing the gas pedal, but it's virtually impossible for a car to do that if the driver is also stepping on the brake pedal. You can prove this to yourself quite easily. Put your car in gear, press down hard on the brake pedal and then press down hard on the gas pedal. The anguish from the engine will be great, but the car will not move.

You will not be able to do that test in that exact order if you have one of the best but most unsung safety devices available today -- the brake-transmission shift-interlock, since it won't let the transmission come out of Park and into a drive gear if the brake is not being pressed.

This technology is widespread across new vehicle models, though there are still a handful of products that don't have it, so be sure to ask about it if you're shopping for a new vehicle. Shift-interlock will be mandatory by 2010, but there will still be lots of old vehicles that don't have it, and as long as they're still on the road the safety threat is still there.

Brake interlock also makes it hard for children to put the car in gear by mistake, or in an attempt to mimic an adult.

It's always a good idea to press the brake pedal first.


## Truman Capote On Cars And Shrinks
The author of In Cold Blood and Breakfast At Tiffany's wrote that he should have skipped the one bout of therapy he had and gone for a long drive in a convertible instead.

# Take Care With Keys When
# Dealing With Valets Of Any Type

The day a friend of ours returned home after a business trip to LA, the police called to ask why his car had taken part in a robbery while he was away. It turns out that the car had been borrowed by the folks at the valet parking centers near the airport for use as a getaway car.

Similar things have happened when people leave their cars with the valet at a store or restaurant, and it's not always the parking staff who are responsible since the keys usually dangle there invitingly in an open box.

It's often more than just the car that's at risk, since professional thieves have driven the stolen car to the victim's home and let themselves in with the house key to rob the place.

Giving up valet parking at the airport in favor of lock-and-walk places or limos is straightforward, but for shorter stays there are other methods of fighting this problem.

Valet keys limit access to the car and some of its technologies and can be had new or aftermarket. But never leave anything but the ignition key with the valet, or indeed whenever you leave the car for service.

Take the driver's license, registration form and insurance papers with you, and make sure you've left no other personal ID papers or credit cards behind. It also wouldn't hurt to keep track of the exact mileage when you leave the car with the valet, perhaps so they see you do it to warn them off.

Make sure you have a copy of your license plate and vehicle identification numbers (the VIN) and keep them with the license and other papers, to help the police recover the vehicle if it is stolen.

And if strange things start happening to your car in a valet parking situation (new smells, missing gasoline, inexplicable trash, strange radios station) consider going someplace else.

# How Anti-Theft Protection
# Can Put You In Danger

In a bitter irony, it looks like the people who have vehicles with immobilizers on their car engines are actually putting themselves more at risk of personal injury. This seems to be especially true of people with high-end products, most particularly imports from Europe and Japan.

Because cars with engine-immobilizers are much harder to steal, thieves are starting to grab the car's keys and use them to take the car. This involves one of two methods – a carjacking on the street in which the driver is threatened unless she gives up the car right then, or a break-and-enter into the home to pick up the keys and then the car.

Above all else and no matter where something like this happens, the only sensible move is to give up the keys and the car and get away with your life. Your car can be replaced, your life can't.

The classic carjacking that happens on the street is more familiar to most people, since it occurs more than 30,000 times a year all across the continent and is often the first step in a series of crimes. It also often features death or injury for the car owner because she's right there when it happens, usually at the end of a gun or other weapon. This kind of crime is mostly random, depending more on the opportunity to take any kind of vehicle to sell for drugs or to take on a joyride or whatever rather than a specific type of car, but who knows what goes through a crook's mind at such a time?

There are considerable tips for dealing with and even avoiding the classic carjacking, which we'll get to in a moment. But first let's consider how to deal with the second type, in which the crooks break into your house to take the keys to your car, almost always because it's a model they specifically want.

On that point there's very little advice beyond call the cops if you realize there's someone in your house, and stay away from them. We might add that you should probably also leave the keys somewhere that they're easy to find, since you certainly don't want the thieves hanging around longer than necessary searching for the keys and getting upset. This is the home version of turning your keys and car over to a street hijacker without delay.

Prevention plans for key thieves would include whatever you'd do to stop a regular house-breaker (deadbolts, security doors, alarm systems and so on). Unfortunately, while home thieves prefer breaking in when you're not there, car thieves need your car to be home, which usually means you're home as well, so there's more danger.

This reality should perhaps make you think about what kind of car you're going to buy. If you're thinking about a luxury import (say a BMW), you should consider that you're buying a popular target for car thieves looking to meet a specific demand in a global market. Someone in Moscow really, really wants an SUV that he saw in a rap video but it's not legally on sale in Russia, but there it is in your driveway or garage.

Owning one may also be making you a personal target as well, for street carjackings or break-ins or a mugging in the parking lot or at drive-through ATMs and the like.

The notion of showing people you are rich and successful enough to have a big BMW, Land Rover, Lexus, Mercedes and so on is one of the key reasons people buy such cars. Drawing attention to the fact that you have a lot of money also suggests that you're likely to have a bunch of it with you. Maybe you should start carrying more cash so you won't disappoint the armed mugger.

That may sound like a joke, but then maybe it isn't. Who knows how the robber's going to feel if he takes such a big risk and doesn't get the expected reward? Think how upset you get when that happens to you, and you're not strung-out on drugs looking for a fix.

Because carjacking is a crime of opportunity, it can usually be avoided if you don't allow the opportunity to happen. On that front, the accepted advice includes:

-watch for suspicious people that you think might be a danger and stay away from them if you can, especially if they're waiting somewhere that you have to stop, like an intersection

-avoid any parking lot or garage, bank machine, mall parking lot, phone booth and any other place that allows someone to walk up to you and your car in space with no other people or traffic around

-have your keys out and be ready to go with the doors locked and windows closed as soon as you get in the car, even if it means waiting a while to do up your seatbelt

-call a trusted friend on your cell to tell them precisely where you are and keep them online until you get to a more secure place

-have an escape strategy in mind at all times, so you can react immediately if you sense a threat

-leave a gap between you and the car in front so you can pull around it to escape

-if you can get away by breaking the law without putting yourself and others at risk, then do it and explain what happened if you're lucky enough to have a police officer see you.

Bear in mind that you run a greater chance of finding a pair of jeans that fit than of being carjacked, but it never hurts to keep your eyes open for situations that put you at risk.

## Comic Drive For Three Women
If you need a great laugh, try to find a copy of Flip Phone, an 8-minute short film about friends headed to a wedding.

# In-Car Heartbeat Sensor Could Save Lives Of Kids, Pets, Drivers

Develop a technology that directly addresses two of the darkest fears many women have about cars and it's treated as an afterthought by the auto media, which, to be fair, reflects the way the company that's bringing it to market treats it. The technology was revealed in concept form six years ago and has only just recently come on the market. It's amazing that this isn't deemed to be more important, and so is the technology in question.

That would be a heartbeat sensor inside the car. The original application from Volvo on some of its new models is meant to tell you if someone is hiding there waiting for you, but it could easily be adapted to tell you if you've forgotten someone in the car, such as a baby or a pet.

The idea of not remembering that you've left an infant in a car is truly horrendous but sadly not unknown, so a heartbeat sensor can address that if it triggers a warning signal to the person with the keys.

For now, Volvo's Personal Car Communicator key fob only advises you if someone's inside your car from about 100 yards away.

Other companies have been working on similar technologies for some time now, and if there's enough demand either or both uses of the heartbeat sensor technology could be in widespread use in a couple of years, and aftermarket systems for existing models won't be far behind.

Women will have to pressure the car companies for this, of course. One male web blogger said he thought the Volvo's commercial for the "pointlessly paranoid heartbeat sensor" was a "parody or a joke of some kind" and he couldn't understand who the "core demographic group" could be, even though the ad showed a woman walking up to the car.

# Getting Safely Out Of A Sinking Car
# Requires Thought And Preparation

Though rolling into the water and sinking is something that happens to cars more on television than in real life, those frightening images following the bridge collapse in Minneapolis prove it can actually happen in real life -- and that people can survive it.

Indeed, it's fairly simple to explain to a calm, fit adult how to survive situations in which her car goes into the water: open a window and get out of the car as soon as possible.

But the degree of difficulty changes dramatically depending on the number of people and their positions in the vehicle, along with their ages, physical conditions and even their clothing at the time.

What do you do with small children who can't really help themselves in the best of circumstances, and then imagine them screaming in a bulky snowsuit that will fill with water and make them sink? How about a large, unfit person wearing heavy winter clothes, who will have a lot more trouble getting out of the vehicle and then staying afloat, or even getting to the surface? What are the tactics for four fit, calm adult passengers getting out in an orderly fashion? Are you fit enough to carry anyone to safety, and perhaps go back to help someone else?

If you don't travel alone all the time, you probably need to work out a drill in advance and be ready to explain it during the crisis, or if danger's near. With kids, you may even want to practice escape methods when you're going on a drive that takes you over or near water. You need to do a greater examination of information on the web world to see what tips there are that fit your particular situation.

But before that, here are some tips for you:

-Stay calm. Sure, advising anyone to stay calm before a crisis happens is usually a waste of time. But knowing that surviving an encounter with deep water is possible if you know what you're doing might help you keep your panic in check.

-Your primary goal is to create an escape route so you can get out of the car as quickly as possible, but definitely before it's totally submerged. If you can't do that, you should still be able swim to the surface from a totally sunken vehicle.

-If you know you're going into the water and you haven't got your seatbelt on, try to do it up. Water's soft when you're in it, but hard as cement when a car hits it, and you don't want to be thrown up against the dash when you crash into the water.

-When going into the water's inevitable, make an X with your arms and grab the shoulder strap of the seatbelt, to stop your arms from flying around. A broken arm's bad enough, but a broken arm that stops you from getting away safely is even worse.

-Resist the temptation to undo your seatbelt right away once you're in the water. In the first place, you'll have more important things to do, and the seatbelts will keep you in place and provide you with leverage if you have to force a window or door open.

-Your first responsibility is to open at least one window and unlock all the doors so you can escape through them. This is especially important if you have power windows and locks, since the water will short the power in your car and that could trap you inside the car under water. The power likely won't short out for a couple of minutes, but it's crazy to count on that happening if you don't have to. This is an extremely important issue. If the car's leaning to one side, consider opening only a window that isn't underwater at all. If your windows are manual, of course, you can almost always crank them open, even under water.

-If you have a sunroof, you may also be able to get out that way before the water's over the roof of the car.

-If you're in a car with a hatch door (minivan, SUV, etc) you may also be able to get out through that opening, since vehicles tend to sink nose first because of the weight of the engine. It may even be possible to drop the rear seat and open the trunk from inside.

-Whatever kind of vehicle you're in, getting through the window, sunroof, or hatch should be done before the car windows go below the water line and the water pours in.

-Each situation will be different, depending on the type of vehicle, the crash angle, the clothes you're wearing, and so on. This is why you need to stay calm and think it through before you act.

-As soon as you feel confident about what you're going to do, unlock the seatbelt, take off any bulky clothes, and go out the window. Taking things with you, even a purse, can increase the degree of danger, but that's your call.

This is a basic primer on a sinking car situation, but the careful or paranoid person will want to look at the huge amount of information available on the web and see how it relates specifically to her car and her personal situation.

Consider the safety risks for you and create a plan that can minimize your risk.

## Getting Help To Where You Are

OnStar's the best system for getting help to where you are even if you're unable to use a cell phone. But if you don't have a GM vehicle there are devices called personal locator beacons that were created to save those folks who go adventuring in the wilderness and get lost or hurt or caught by bad weather. They cost several hundred dollars, you have to register with a group that promises to send help to your location, you have to have it on you, and, again, you have to be conscious and able to work it.

# Escaping In An Emergency
# Might Require Ingenuity And Planning

Movies and TV shows notwithstanding, cars aren't really that likely to burst into flames after a crash, no matter how severe. But sometimes getting out of a vehicle after a crash is the smartest thing you can do, and that can often be as straightforward as opening one of the doors.

But if all of the side doors are unavailable, you could consider going out the back. In minivans, SUVs, crossovers, hatchbacks and station wagons the rear door is obvious, and a sunroof also makes a handy pre-packaged exit point.

In a sedan, where the cabin and trunk are separate, it may also be possible to get out through the trunk, though it might require some work and a special tool or two.

Normally, the back of the rear seat and a thin partition in the trunk are all that separates the cabin from the trunk. A regular utility knife should make short work of the fabrics, and a pair of pliers with a wire cutting feature should help with opening up the coils in the cushions.

Once you're in the trunk, there's likely to be an emergency handle that will open the lid and let you out. These devices were made mandatory a few years ago to allow children who climb in there to play a way to get out, but they will work for adults as well. It could be smart to check your trunk to see where the release handle is located.

If you have a pass through in the back seat for skis, you can maybe reach in and pull the emergency trunk opener. Look for that release handle beforehand, and perhaps run a cord from it to the seatback in case that emergency does arise.

You can also try going out a window if the doors are jammed, but you'll probably need a special hammering device to help you with that; they're sold in auto supply stores and on the web.

**Alexander Law & Susan Winlaw   77**

# New Seats Promise Greater
## Side-Impact Safety For Kids

Though there are no government guidelines on their design or value, child safety seats designed to protect their occupants in side-impact crashes are turning up on the North American market, usually with European labels and the higher prices that usually come with imports from that continent.

Before we get too far in this discussion, however, a reminder of general child safety: the safest place for anyone in a vehicle is as close to the middle as possible. That means the second row, as far from the doors as they can get.

If the child seat's there, there's still good reason to pay as much as $250 for one of those safety seats, which resemble wing-back chairs.

They are designed to keep the child from being struck by a side airbag in the car, and to prevent the child from flopping around from side-to-side in the aftermath of a collision.

There's no hard data to back up the importance of either danger, but common sense suggests that keeping the child encased in a protective package and from whipping around in the seat is a good thing.

This is particularly true when there's an adult in the back seat with the child, since they can serve as an object to hit against.

If nothing else, these seats probably fall in the category of "it can't hurt and might provide some benefit, so buy it if it makes you feel better and you can afford it."

## Jacks Useful For More Than Flats

If you're ever in a situation where you need to raise something heavy, the jack from your car might be useful. It was designed to lift the corner of a two-ton car, but it can also be used to lift many kinds of heavy objects.

# Many Safety Benefits From "Active" Cruise Control

"Active" cruise control provides considerable occupant safety and is finally starting to arrive in different brands.

Regular cruise control keeps a vehicle going at a pre-set speed without any help from the driver, but as well as doing that on a lightly-traveled highway it will do that right into the rear of the car in front or through a red light or into a wall. Maybe "blind" cruise control's a better name for it.

"Active" cruise control can be pre-set at a certain speed, but it will also slow the vehicle if it senses something in front of it, like another car or vehicles crossing its path in an intersection. This is the part of the technology that really brings rewards to the consumer, though it won't help if you are heading for that cliff edge. In any situation, you should still be paying attention.

If it's set up right by the manufacturer, active cruise can allow a vehicle to keep up with stop-and-go traffic without the driver having to do much more than pay attention to what's happening in front of her. This is what Nissan's after with the Distance Control Assist program, and it is the key ingredient in Volvo's over-hyped City-Safety auto-brake system. Setting up the car to bring itself to a stop without driver involvement is fairly simple with today's technology. The big problem is legal, since you know lawyers are going to make a big deal of it when a Volvo with City-Safety crashes into something.

Active cruise control also helps you "see" better in bad weather or limited visibility situations -- particularly fog (see Page 27) and could very well keep you out of all kinds of trouble. It's primarily available only on more expensive cars and will be sold under various names, but you should look for it when you do that pre-dealer online research session that's so important when buying a car.

**Alexander Law & Susan Winlaw** 79

# Looking After Pets Correctly Should Start With The Type Of Car You Buy

For people concerned with keeping their pets safe in a car, the same rules as apply to the safety of humans should be followed:

-If you're buying new, get the largest vehicle with the most safety systems (with a particular eye to stability control, which can prevent many rollovers) that you can afford.

-Whatever the age of your car, keep your pet restrained (in a cage or attached to a seatbelt), since flying around in a car that's in a crash or rolling over is worse for your pet than it is for you.

-Put your pet in the middle of the vehicle, which keeps it as far away from the danger zone if another car crashes into it.

-Keep your pet out of the cargo bay of a station wagon, a small SUV or the back of a hatchback car. Remember that those areas are also called "crush zones" by companies looking to talk up the safety standards of certain models.

-If you plan to travel with a pet, consider a car from General Motors that has the OnStar system. Not only is OnStar incredibly good for looking after you in a crash or directing you to the nearest emergency center if you need help, it will do exactly the same thing for your pet.

You can be in the middle of nowhere without cell phone service and OnStar will likely be able to tell you precisely where you are and how to get to the nearest veterinary facility. And we're talking a catalogue of vet specialists that would cover every need your pet might have, not just emergency treatment centers. This can be also be useful if you find an animal on your travels that needs help and you're looking for a place to take it.

For more help on looking after your pets on the road, there are about 158,304 websites willing to help you.

# Litter Can Be Dangerous For You As Well As Bad For The Environment

In the mid-80s most of the trash on the road was "deliberate," meaning soft drink cans and burger bags and what have you tossed out of passing cars.

But now most of the trash on our highways is "negligent," which means it fell off a vehicle by mistake and is usually big and hard enough to pose a direct threat.

And make no mistake, something that falls from a vehicle going 65 mph doesn't have to be very big to be a direct threat to you. It's unlikely to come through the windshield but it might shatter the glass or startle you enough that you make a mistake that causes you to crash. Or if it's on the road it could cause your vehicle's tire to blow out and that can easily result in a crash. There's also the risk involved in making an emergency maneuver to avoid stuff on the road.

The best advice here is to keep your eyes open for any vehicle carrying objects that you can see, working on the theory that if it's visible (i.e. not covered by a tarp or in a box) it's more likely to come loose and create a hazard. Being in front of vehicles like that is the best choice.

Being way, way behind such a vehicle is a poor second choice, since you might get caught in a pile-up that results when someone else crashes into that litter.

You might also consider reporting something you feel to be a hazard to the police. As you might expect, there are rules about how you can transport things in a vehicle.

Finally, you should take extra care if you decide to transport something yourself, since it's the responsible thing to do and, if that's not enough, the legal system is starting to get tough with people who cause grief on the roads.

So if you must put people in danger like that, be sure you dump trash that the cops can trace to you.

## Let's Not Be Blind To The
## Danger Of Silent Cars

Back in the 1990s, when society was considering and rejecting electric vehicles, we got to spend a lot of time behind the wheel of many noble efforts to save the planet.

Each electric vehicle was different, but without fail each and every driving experience featured the same expression over and over -- the look of unhappy shock on the face of a pedestrian as she wondered where in the blazes that car had come from.

More than you imagine, vehicles that run on electricity are surprisingly quiet, which means they scare a good number of people with their unannounced appearance in the personal safety zone we all build around ourselves. The reaction can be kind of funny if you're at the wheel of silent car and making sure the pedestrians are not in danger, but not many of them find it amusing, it must be noted.

Here we are in the late Oh-Ohs with hybrid SUVs from GM that will run on their batteries around town coming onto the market and the silent vehicle's about to become a serious issue for more people than ever.

Now, most people would say the risks are all on the part of the pedestrian, and in a physical sense that's true. But who wants to live with the emotional cost of running someone over, as well as the possible legal cost?

The problem is that many new and upcoming vehicles will run constantly, or for long distances, on electrical power, which means they don't produce the kind of clatter and roar that comes from the internal combustion engines that have powered all our vehicles for so long. Sure, they still create some noise from the tires and perhaps the stereo, but in relative terms they are essentially silent vehicles.

Vision-impaired citizens have already made their concerns

about this known, since they must listen for a vehicle's approach, and vehicles running on electrical power don't always register with them.

But there are also lots of sighted people who have developed a mental safety system that starts with listening for the approach of a car and then moves to looking to see how far away it is. The risk is that they will be relying so much on an aural pre-warning that they won't make a visual check.

Experience also suggests the issue of silent vehicles might be a particular concern with children, which raises the stakes even more. There are already reports of that happening.

This has been pretty much a small-scale problem so far, since EVs still aren't selling in serious numbers and fuel cells are mostly a science project. But now comes the first of the lineup of two-mode hybrids from a consortium of companies that includes BMW, Chrysler, General Motors and Mercedes and the issue is no longer moot.

Early reviews suggest that the two-mode is the best hybrid system in the world in terms of fuel efficiency, and a lot of that comes from the fact that the electric motor can push a vehicle around town at speeds of up to 25 mph without using internal combustion propulsion.

This means we now have vehicles weighing more than two tons rolling around our streets in almost complete silence.

We need to consider some type of legislation that requires that vehicles make a certain amount of noise, or broadcast a special tone, or who knows what. But for once it would be great if we could get ahead of a developing safety issue rather than waiting until a lot of people are dead.

## Playing Blind For Fun In Films
Al Pacino won an Oscar for playing a blind man who drives a car in Scent Of A Woman, but the scene in Cousin Cousine where a character pretends to be a blind is funnier.

# Leave Nothing In Your Car To Steal

And when we say "nothing" we mean literally that, not just stuff of traditional appeal like briefcases, suitcases or even knock-off designer bags. If an identity thief sees a piece of paper that might -- might -- give him access to your personal and financial life it would take him about 10 seconds to break a window, pick everything up and disappear.

So never leave anything inside the car where a potential thief can see it. Put the stuff you have to leave behind in the trunk, or the cargo space of an SUV or minivan and cover it with that rollup-up plastic screen or anything you can.

Be rigorous about removing or hiding identity-theft material. That means no personal files, bills to pay, credit car receipts, mail or anything else. Even a pile of unimportant paperwork in a storage bin or somewhere visible might cause thieves looking for some identity data to break in.

## Driving Tired Like Driving Drunk

If you've been up for 18 straight hours (a not unusual state for most of us), it's like having a 0.5 blood alcohol level. Stretch the time limit to 24 hours and your impairment level reaches 1.0. So your chances of being in a crash or hurting someone or even yourself have increased.

## Five-Year-Old Steals Car

Something else for parents to worry about: a five-year-old Czech boy recently took the keys to the family car, put cushions on the driver's seat, and went for a short joy-ride before crashing the vehicle into the wall of a house. The local social service agency was asked to discover how a child that young knew how to start and drive a car. From a video game would seem to be the logical answer, but who knows?

# Floormats In Your Car Can
# Cause A Serious Safety Problem

If the notion of "killer floormats" sounds like a joke, consider Toyota recently recalled the floor mats in a bunch of its Toyota and Lexus models because they might jam the accelerator pedal and cause the cars to go forward by themselves.

This came as no surprise to the folks at Transport Canada, who investigate claims of sudden vehicle accelerations and stuck throttles and "frequently discover that the problem relates to some interference between the vehicle floor mats and the pedals."

This can be a big deal, since the inability to release a gas pedal has resulted in many crashes, some of them deadly. It usually involves a set of aftermarket floor mats used to protect the original mats during the winter.

Says Transport Canada: "Typically, the interference occurs when non-original equipment floor mats are used without properly being restrained to the vehicle floor. The floor mat can then move under the driver's feet and become lodged either between the pedals, on top of the pedals, or under the pedals. Another common problem occurs when consumers install multiple floor mats on top of each other, reducing the clearance between the vehicle floor and the pedals."

If you have installed aftermarket floor mats in your vehicle, Transport Canada advises, make certain they cannot move while you're driving. If you are going to install rubber mats for the winter or any other reason, be sure that you remove the originally equipped factory floor mats.

Hard braking should bring any vehicle to a stop even if the accelerator's jammed, but many people forget about that as they attempt to release the gas pedal. The best advice in such a situation is to put the car in neutral and apply the brakes as hard as necessary.

# Kids And Pets Still Being
# Left Alone In Cars To Suffer Or Die

This is going to seem like an old and unnecessary story to anyone whose seen recent media coverage about parents being charged with leaving their children alone in cars, but the fact is that about 30 very young children a year still die from heat stroke after being left in a car too long.

The number of pets that suffer the same fate is unknown, but it's undoubtedly even greater.

It must first be noted that hyperthermia does not actually require southern-states-in-July temperatures, that it can happen anywhere that temperatures go above 70 degrees Fahrenheit.

The best and most straightforward advice for parents of young children is to never leave a child alone in a car, regardless of their age, but particularly if they're young.

The temperature inside a vehicle can go up to more than 19 degrees higher than the outside temperature in about 10 minutes, with the heat continuing to rise as time passes. In an hour, the temperature differential between outside and inside the car can rise to 45 degrees. If you start at 70 degrees of outside temperature, that puts you way past the level at which heat stroke occurs inside the car -- 104 degrees.

And leaving the windows open "a crack" won't help those temperatures from occurring, and leaving the windows open even more creates other dangers to unprotected children.

While conditions like this would be unpleasant for adults, they can be deadly for small children because their bodies warm up three to five times faster than adult bodies. That means it takes less time for them to reach a core body temperature of 107 degrees, which is considered lethal.

So parents should never leave their children alone in a car, and passersby should always call for emergency aid if they see children -- or pets -- alone in a car.

# Putting Pets In Danger
## By Showing Too Much Affection

It's hoped that even Britney Spears has learned the dangers of driving with a child on your lap, or even riding with one on your lap if you're in the front seat.

But the same dangers from exploding airbags apply just as much to animals and that knowledge doesn't seem to be getting through.

Make no mistake -- if an airbag deploys and crushes a dog against you, the dog will almost certainly be injured and possibly die, and it's not going to do you much good either.

This doesn't even address the fact that having something live and erratic on your lap while you're driving is a textbook definition of a distraction.

You see drivers -- women mostly -- holding small dogs on their laps in places where carrying lapdogs around in a purse is becoming a common habit.

It's more than ironic that what they would call a display of affection is really a grave threat to the pet's life.

Any pet in a moving vehicle should be restrained -- preferably in the back seat -- if for no other reason than they pose a risk to humans in the car if there's a crash and the pet is tossed around in the vehicle.

A 20-pound dog has the same physical force as an NFL player if it's tossed about in a 30-mph crash.

## Make Sure Spare Is Inflated

When you or the service guys are checking the tire pressure in your car's tires, make sure you also look at the condition of the spare.

There are few things more irritating about owning a car than having to stop to change a tire only to find that the spare is also flat.

**Alexander Law & Susan Winlaw**

# Quick, Where's The Nearest Emergency Health Care From There?

Location, location and location are said to be the three most important things in real estate, but they're also very important should the time ever come that you need help in your car.

If you're going to have a crash, the best place would be the entrance ramp to the emergency room of a large hospital, preferably one staffed by doctors and nurses as smart, caring and good-looking as the ones you see on TV.

It follows that your chances of surviving a car crash or a heart attack or some other health crisis decrease the farther you are from emergency care, since they are directly related to the time it will take for help to get to you, or you to get to help.

As obvious as this point may sound to you now, it's probably not something you consider as you go about your life. But maybe you should think about it, especially if someone you normally drive with has a medical reality that might need emergency care in a hurry, like a heart condition or an allergy to peanuts or one of a thousand things.

If you live in a big city and never leave it you don't have to worry so much, though even then it might be wise to give a thought to how your route relates to hospital location, traffic conditions, and so on.

Once you wander away from your normal stomping grounds, of course, the situation can become more acute. And you don't have to go too far outside of some major urban areas before emergency services become a dream more than a reality.

You can spend a day driving up Route 1 beside the Pacific Ocean between LA and San Francisco, for example, and pass through long stretches where it's hard to find gas or a washroom, let alone serious emergency assistance.

Sure, this all sounds like paranoia, but wait until you're with someone who has a heart attack and you don't know whether it's better to head for Town A or Town B, both of which are more than an hour away. Who's paranoid now?

A little time with a good DVD-based map service from the AAA or Delorme or someone like that before you travel could give you the information that could save someone's life, even maybe yours.

## Ratings Compare Child Restraint Installation Ease, Not Restraint Value

The most important thing to remember about NHTSA's new five-star child restraint ratings is they do not -- NOT -- measure the relative safety of the various systems.

The US government's road safety division does not measure the safety levels of each system because the assumption is that they all meet the required safety standards.

What the new five-star rating program does measure is the Ease of Use of child restraint systems, which is critical since an improperly used system can be dangerous to the children sitting in them and it turns out to be easy to install a child restraint system incorrectly.

To get a good look at the restraint system ratings guide, check out www.nhtsa.gov or call 1-888-327-4236.

On balance, then, it's probably worth reviewing a new child restraint system with one eye on these ratings. From that starting point, it's easy to get lots of help with the installation process.

The manufacturer's instructions should be your starting point, but there's also lots of web-site help and it's quite fashionable for service groups and police forces and other groups to put on clinics to check the installation for anyone who's interested.

## Protect Personal Information
## When Your Car Is Parked

Many people know it's not a good idea to leave anything in their car with personal information on it (home address, credit card number, etc) lest someone break in and steal it, but not everyone extends this wisdom to the ownership and insurance papers in the glovebox.

But a recent story about a family whose home was robbed and set on fire while they were at a hockey game should make that point clear. The thieves broke into the family car at the game and got the home address from the insurance papers.

There's also the likelihood that more sophisticated thieves could use the information to help them perpetrate an identity theft, which has chilling consequences of its own.

You're likely required to have a certain amount of paperwork with the car at all times, so you can't leave it all at home. Learn to carry it with your wallet all the time, or find a clever hiding space in the car. This latter idea will probably work best, unless you're really bad at hiding things or are really bad at remembering where you hid them.

## Get Ready to Rumble

Tired of people not noticing their sirens and flashing lights, some police departments are adding a device called the Rumbler to their cars. This would be a device designed to make the ground vibrate beneath your tires, courtesy of an amplifier hooked up to a pair of high-output woofers that can alert you to the presence of a cop car from 200 feet away. The low-frequency signal vibrates everything in its path, including the rear view mirrors of cars in its general vicinity. So if you're in Washington, DC, and some other big city and the car starts to vibrate, look in your mirror for a police cruiser.

# That Car Color May Not
# Suit You Or Keep You Safe

Comic Rita Rudner's act regularly involves the differences between men and women, often with regard to their feelings about cars.

In a Palm Springs show, for example, she asked a man in the front row what kind of car he had. She listened and nodded politely as he gave a lengthy answer involving torque and oversteer and all that and then she said: "Now ask me what kind of car I have, and why?"

"What kind of car do you have, Rita," he dutifully replied, "and why?"

"I have a black car, because it goes with everything."

Good a reason as any to buy a specific type of car, many people will say, and it's hard to argue with that given the excellent quality and abilities of today's new vehicles.

But it turns out that black may not be the smartest color choice from a safety perspective. According to recent research, black cars have a 12 percent greater risk of being in a crash than white cars, with grey and silver being 11 and 10 percent, respectively, riskier.

The big problem is that darker cars aren't as easy to see, particularly in times of limited visibility, like dusk or when it's overcast. Turning on the headlights will help to overcome that, though buying a car with daytime running lights offers a more comprehensive solution.

## Think Of Something Smart

When their car's headed for a crash, most people tend to tense up and let it happen. But there may be time to spin your car so it's hit in the rear or the side where you're not sitting, or something that puts you at less risk. To protect you before a crash happens, think about avoidance moves to make.

# Convertibles Have Security Risks
# Unique To The Segment

Ask a man about the safety standards of convertible cars and his answer will likely begin and end with crash test results. Women tend to understand that safety -- and security -- extends far beyond how much damage a particular convertible model sustains in a pre-determined crash situation.

But if you're looking for a car with a convertible top, those ratings are a good place to start, since they make it clear that a car with a folding roof does about as well in NHTSA and IIHS crash tests as a car with a hardtop roof. This was not always the case, so this is definitely a positive development.

Another positive safety/security development in the convertible market is the recent introduction of the folding hardtop roof, which means the car has the security of a real metal roof when it's parked along with the pleasure of the droptop experience when you're driving. This started within the last year, but the idea has taken off and now a folding hardtop is part of many brands, with more likely as time passes.

Having a hardtop to put quickly in place provides the cautious driver with much greater security in many situations. You can't cut through a hardtop roof, after all, the way you can cut through a cloth one, and that has anti-theft as well as personal security benefits.

But driving with a top down has safety and security issues in any model, since your property and person are more exposed to people who might want to do you harm. There's also increased danger from things that might fall off another vehicle or get knocked up by a passing car or whatever, and don't even think about what happens if a convertible rolls over. That's a whole new chapter in safety concerns.

It seems to us that the superior safety features that come with OnStar make the Pontiac G6 a segment leader.

# Signal Boosters Can Help
# Your Cell Phone Stay Connected

As emergency room physicians will tell you, the sooner you get an injured person to medical attention the better his or her chances are of surviving a car crash.

That means you need to be able to call for help following a crash, and if you don't have a GM vehicle with OnStar (See Page 99) to provide crash notification for you, then your cell phone will have to do.

Assuming you're conscious and able to use the phone, it might help you reach emergency services if you had a passive antenna in the car helping your cell service along. It can even find a signal where you phone can't on its own. It might also improve your general use and enjoyment of the phone when you haven't been in a crash.

These things aren't very big and should plug into the antenna portal in your cell phone. They usually cost less than $50, are easy to set up, and work with virtually any cell phone sold on this continent.

They will also work with some wireless handsets (you have to have the right frequency), so you better check on that first if it's an issue.


## Online Financing Fades

Fewer customers are looking for automotive financing online, it seems.

A survey by J. D. Power and Associates found that fewer than one in four of the respondents to the survey looked for online financing in 2007 when they were buying a car, down about a third from 2004.

The smaller number of people who did use online financing did have slightly more success, since 14 percent of them found financing online last year, up from 12 percent in 2004.

**Alexander Law & Susan Winlaw** 93

# Safer Cars Can Make It
# Harder To Rescue You In A Crash

The good news is that the car companies and emergency rescue units across the continent have come up with a way to lessen the problem to some degree, but the bad news is that changes to vehicle design that are supposed to protect you also make it harder to rescue you.

For example, those pillars that were strengthened to stop the cabin from crushing in certain crashes are also harder to cut through to allow patient extraction.

Essentially, this means that you're more likely to survive a crash, but the time it takes to get you out of the vehicle and on the way to hospital might be a lot longer. In general, it seems that it's taking about twice as long to get people out of vehicles made after 2005 than it did for older vehicles -- from 10 to 15 minutes to 20 to 30 minutes or longer.

All of that eats into what the folks in the emergency services business call the "golden hour" that you have to get a person medical help after they're injured.

Various emergency services have been struggling with this for years, trying to fit bigger and better extraction equipment (like the Jaws Of Life) into smaller and smaller budgets (your tax cuts at work).

On top of the changes to existing models from all the car companies, there are all those new models from the Europeans, Koreans and Japanese as part of their ongoing effort to grow their market share to make the emergency rescue business more complicated.

A long-term solution is more sharing of the vehicle assembly information with the rescue teams, and that will begin in earnest this year. But the extremely cautious buyer might want to consider staying away from the newest models and going with a big-selling car rescue teams already know.

# Roadside Assistance Safety Net
# Not Offered On All Brands

If you hate the idea of having no one to call if you need help with a flat, an empty gas tank, a car that won't start or any other roadside emergency like locking your keys inside the vehicle, then be extra cautious if you're thinking of buying any type of car, truck, SUV or minivan from Honda, Scion or Toyota.

Those are the only brands in the U.S. that do NOT offer roadside assistance warranties.

If you buy one of their products and get stranded on the side of the road, you're on your own unless you spend some more money.

That means you have to join the AAA or some other commercial road service organization, but you should do that before you find yourself stranded with no one to help you.

You might also want to consider AAA coverage even if you have roadside assistance from your vehicle's manufacturer, since the car companies often prefer to reduce their costs by buying the cheapest, spottiest service that provides nominal coverage.

Indeed, it's an excellent idea to consider the details of the brand's roadside assistance plan before you buy, to see if it omits any service that seems particularly important to you.

## Probably Wise To Avoid New Brands

Several companies are hoping to cash in on the move to greener or alternative fuel cars and are promising they will be selling different models before long.

They may well be doing that, but buying one of them will almost certainly come with great risk to the buyers. The new firms have no experience, little service capability and problems we can't imagine now. There will be tears.

# Toll And Bridges Said To
# Be Safer Than Regular Roads

Toll roads are apparently safer than the regular old free roads, according to a recent study, but especially toll tunnels and toll bridges.

In 2005, the number of fatalities per 100 million vehicle miles traveled in the U.S. was 1.47, which is pretty low when you consider how much angst is spilled on the subject of vehicle safety. It only looks bad when you view it as around 40,000 deaths a year.

Most of those deaths take place on roads that don't have controlled access, which means the ones with stoplights, parking lot entrances, left turns and so on. On the controlled access roads (which includes toll roads) things are better.

The fatality rate per 100 million vehicle miles traveled on rural interstates is 1.21, and on all urban interstates it's 0.55.

On all toll facilities the fatality rate is 0.50.

## Nader Claims NHTSA Is Compromised

Ralph Nader has brought the issue of auto safety into the run for president by charging that the federal government's chief car safety branch (NHTSA) "has now become a pathetic consulting firm for the motor vehicle manufacturers."

The chief reason for Nader's ire is what the Independent Party candidate calls "a weak auto-industry-approved roof crush safety rule." Studies have shown that some people (especially if they're not wearing a seatbelt) might be saved in a rollover if the vehicle roof was sturdier.

Nader virtually created the idea of automotive safety in the 1960s with a book called Unsafe At Any Speed, which was the primary motivation for the creation of NHTSA. But now he will rail against the "the auto industry's takeover" of the organization during the presidential election.

# Towing Any Brand Of Trailer Brings Great Risks

There's been a lot of coverage recently about possible safety problems related to one famous trailer rental company, which might be worth checking into if you're thinking of renting one. But the broader issue involves safety issues related to towing trailers in general, no matter whose name is on it.

Simply put, towing a trailer of any brand, vintage and condition can put you in situations that you will not have encountered in decades of regular single-vehicle driving, and in a severe situation -- such as turning or braking hard -- this can be especially dangerous.

When you attach a trailer the first time, the immediate difference is how much more slowly your car pulls away, thanks to the greater weight.

Once you get rolling and inertia takes over, the difference is less noticeable, unless you're pulling enough weight on a bumpy road and you can feel the trailer tugging on your car.

If you remember to swing farther out to make a turn, you should also have no trouble in the city.

In all circumstances -- but particularly when it's raining or snowing -- you need to be more conscious of your speed and braking distance.

If the wheels on the trailer let go during a hard stop or sharp curve, you'll have serious problems bringing the trailer and the vehicle back under control. This is a lot more dangerous a situation than losing control of a car by itself.

## Using Group Power For Safety

If you're amongst a group of women heading to their cars after leaving a building at night, ask them to walk you to your car in exchange for a ride from your car to theirs.

# Traffic is The Real Risk
# When You Travel Overseas

While a terrorism attack is probably what most North Americans fear during foreign travel, followed by infectious diseases and robberies, the truth is that dying in a car crash is the biggest statistical risk for travelers.

Many developed countries have safety laws and emergency services to match those in North America, but many countries have developing traffic and road systems and limited ambulance or medical care. This means the inexperienced locals might not be as adept at driving as you are, and good emergency services may be a long way away.

But even the places with excellent safety records and support services can be dangerous, which is why many North Americans who die in crashes overseas die in Germany. The unlimited-speed autobahn may have something to do with that.

So the trick is to drive even more carefully when you're in a foreign country than you do at home.

A good place to go for more local information if you plan to travel is www.asirt.org, for the Association for Safe International Road Travel.

Even some place as familiar as Great Britain has its unique risks. Consider our favorite British road sign and try to imagine that you have two seconds to figure how to handle it: "Oncoming Traffic May Be in Middle of the Road."

## Video Shows Reality Of Auto Safety

For a look at what a massive crash is like and how it's possible to survive it, check out the YouTube posting of a 2003 Ford Explorer rolling over about 10 times, from which Emily Bowness of Michigan walked away. Her seatbelt was done up. At www.youtube.com/watch?v=eZICPgRpyWE.

# OnStar A Necessity For People
# Who Are Really Serious About Safety

For anyone with a comprehensive view of safety, the array of features that come with GM's sophisticated GPS-based telemetrics system should be a top priority.

We strongly urge you to investigate the service yourself, at www.onstar.com, to see the full extent of its features and how they would apply to you and yours.

Basically, OnStar goes beyond a vehicle's ability to withstand a crash (which is the current unfortunate understanding of safety) and beyond your cell phone's workable range to help ensure your well-being in any number of ways, including:

-sending help to your precise location if you're in a crash and unable to call for help yourself

-honking the horn and flashing the headlights to help you find the car

-unlocking the doors remotely if you've misplaced your keys or left them in the car

-advising you of possible technical problems that might cause your vehicle to break down

-giving you specific, turn-by-turn directions based on your precise location so you can stay out of dangerous areas

-allowing hands-free calling, which cuts down on the kind of distraction that leads to many crashes

-providing a system that will let OnStar (under police supervision) carefully disable your vehicle if it's been stolen, which would reduce those dangerous police pursuits

-letting your children send for help if you're not able, and

-providing a specific location for your stolen vehicle.

Various features of OnStar are explained throughout the site, but the best thing to do is consider the service from your own perspective.

**Alexander Law & Susan Winlaw**

# Don't Let Gas Prices Force You Into A Bad Financial Move

Lots of people are unhappy about gas being around $3.50 a gallon or more, and that's causing many of them to take action that may be out of proportion to the problem and presenting them with new issues to worry about.

A common response to big ticket fill-up costs is dumping the big vehicle in favor of something smaller, often without regard to the overall economic sense of such a move.

Another response is just to pick the model with the best fuel economy standards from the segment you're considering regardless of any other considerations, and that is really a dangerous move.

But before we get to that, a few words about the reality of a smaller vehicle. Most importantly, smaller and lighter vehicles put you more directly in harm's way, as every bipartisan expert in the scientific world will tell you. (See Page 20 for that evidence.)

The extra risk alone ought to make you reconsider the move to a smaller vehicle, particularly if you have children. But there's also the reality that smaller vehicles have less room to carry people and things, might not be as comfortable as you're used to, and quite possibly are noisier than large cars.

These are big steps to take for what is, in reality, not that big of a financial hit when you compare it to the likely costs of getting out of a lease early or selling a big vehicle at a loss in a market that is starting to turn its back on big vehicles.

As the accompanying chart shows, going from a vehicle that delivers 20 mpg to one that gets 40 mpg with gas at $3.50 a gallon will save you $875 for every 10,000 miles you drive. For the average driver, that works out to something like a weekly saving of $17. With gas at $4 a gallon, going from 20 to 40 mpg will save you $1,000 every 10,000 miles, or less

# What Different MPG Rates Will Save You

Cost of gas to travel 10,000 miles at various fuel economy rates

| $ / G | $3.50 | $3.75 | $4.00 | $4.25 |
|---|---|---|---|---|
| **MPG** | | | | |
| 45 | $777.78 | $833.33 | $888.89 | $944.44 |
| 44 | $795.45 | $852.27 | $909.09 | $965.91 |
| 43 | $813.95 | $872.09 | $930.23 | $988.37 |
| 42 | $833.33 | $892.86 | $952.38 | $1,011.90 |
| 41 | $853.66 | $914.63 | $975.61 | $1,036.59 |
| 40 | $875.00 | $937.50 | $1,000.00 | $1,062.50 |
| 39 | $897.44 | $961.54 | $1,025.64 | $1,089.74 |
| 38 | $921.05 | $986.84 | $1,052.63 | $1,118.42 |
| 37 | $945.95 | $1,013.51 | $1,081.08 | $1,148.65 |
| 36 | $972.22 | $1,041.67 | $1,111.11 | $1,180.56 |
| 35 | $1,000.00 | $1,071.43 | $1,142.86 | $1,214.29 |
| 34 | $1,029.41 | $1,102.94 | $1,176.47 | $1,250.00 |
| 33 | $1,060.61 | $1,136.36 | $1,212.12 | $1,287.88 |
| 32 | $1,093.75 | $1,171.88 | $1,250.00 | $1,328.12 |
| 31 | $1,129.03 | $1,209.68 | $1,290.32 | $1,370.97 |
| 30 | $1,166.67 | $1,250.00 | $1,333.33 | $1,416.67 |
| 29 | $1,206.90 | $1,293.10 | $1,379.31 | $1,465.52 |
| 28 | $1,250.00 | $1,339.29 | $1,428.57 | $1,517.86 |
| 27 | $1,296.30 | $1,388.89 | $1,481.48 | $1,574.07 |
| 26 | $1,346.15 | $1,442.31 | $1,538.46 | $1,634.62 |
| 25 | $1,400.00 | $1,500.00 | $1,600.00 | $1,700.00 |
| 24 | $1,458.33 | $1,562.50 | $1,666.67 | $1,770.83 |
| 23 | $1,521.74 | $1,630.43 | $1,739.13 | $1,847.83 |
| 22 | $1,590.91 | $1,704.55 | $1,818.18 | $1,931.82 |
| 21 | $1,666.67 | $1,785.71 | $1,904.76 | $2,023.81 |
| 20 | $1,750.00 | $1,875.00 | $2,000.00 | $2,125.00 |
| 19 | $1,842.11 | $1,973.68 | $2,105.26 | $2,236.84 |
| 18 | $1,944.44 | $2,083.33 | $2,222.22 | $2,361.11 |
| 17 | $2,058.82 | $2,205.88 | $2,352.94 | $2,500.00 |
| 16 | $2,187.50 | $2,343.75 | $2,500.00 | $2,656.25 |
| 15 | $2,333.33 | $2,500.00 | $2,666.67 | $2,833.33 |

See www.caradviceforwomen.com for higher gas price updates.

than $20 a week.

Those are not insignificant amounts of money, and the change in vehicle size may suit you if the current lease on your SUV is about to expire and your kids are now in college so you're not ferrying them around any more.

But the costs you may incur with getting rid of a bigger vehicle before its lease or loan has matured, and in a chilly market, are going to be significant. These factors could easily negate the lower costs of the greater fuel economy levels.

On top of that, there really is a significant safety, utility and comfort difference between the vehicles that now get 20 mpg (many large SUVs, minivans and crossovers) and the compact cars that get 40 mpg. The difference will come as a surprise to you if you've spent the last two decades in minivans and/or SUVs.

If you are in a situation where it's a good time to change cars and you're thinking of going to a different type of vehicle altogether, it's wise to consider more than just the fuel economy ratings of the models involved.

Any vehicle that's in the same general category will likely offer fuel economy levels that are close, and a quick look at a gas cost chart shows the exact differences at various prices per gallon. With gas at $4 a gallon, for example, a car that gets 29 mpg costs about $130 more over 10,000 miles than a car that gets 32 mpg. That's about $2.50 a week.

If everything else between the two vehicles were the same, that might be the deciding factor, but everything else is never the same between two vehicles -- the car companies and dealers work overtime making that happen.

(The only exception to that rule, of course, involves the initial quality levels, which are pretty much a 350-way tie for first. See Page 150 for details.)

Almost certainly you will be in a better bargaining position with the dealer whose model in a certain segment does not get the best fuel economy, because a lot of buyers who aren't as smart as you are simply buying the vehicle with the top mileage figure and don't have much leverage.

If you're paying $1,000 more for a model that gets 32 mpg over what you'd pay for a model that gets 29 mpg, you're actually losing money. Saving gas for sure, but also definitely losing money. Feel free to do that if you want.

And there are other non-product items that should be considered -- roadside assistance, dealer availability, service intervals, and all the other things the smart buyer should think about. Why pay for slightly better fuel economy and lose those other benefits, some of which are costly.

Grumble all you want the next time you visit the pumps, but don't jump to a smaller vehicle until you've crunched some bigger numbers, and take the time to consider all the cost factors if you do make the jump.

## Check Insurance Costs Before Picking Car

If the overall cost of operating a car is more important to you than owning a particular model, it makes terrific sense for you to check the vehicles you're interested in for their insurance rates before you decide on one. You will almost certainly find cost differences in the models you're considering, even if they seem pretty similar on paper.

This is now a fairly painless process, thanks to all of those car insurance quoting services available online. You just open one of them up and enter all of the pertinent data -- your address, age, driving record and so on -- and then the type of car and range of insurance coverage you're considering. Then do the same for the other models that you have your eye on.

That should give you a more precise idea of what the different cars are going to cost for a year, and since all cars are essentially on the same level of quality now, a monthly saving on insurance might very well be the deciding factor.

# It's Not Hard To Save Fuel Now If
# You're Willing To Make Necessary Changes

If you'd like an immediate 15 percent (or even more) increase in your vehicle's fuel economy levels, there's a quick, zero-cost solution we can share with you:

Drive slowly and gently to the nearest air pump, inflate your vehicle's tires to the maximum recommended level, and continue to drive slowly and gently everywhere you go (while making sure your tires stay inflated) until you are no longer upset by fuel prices.

Yeah, it's that simple and it's that effective, and it will absolutely, positively reduce the amount of fuel you use right away, by more than you would imagine.

Here's another quick and easy method to save fuel and help the environment in the process: if you're about to enter a line-up for a drive-through that will take you more than a couple of minutes to get through, park the car and go inside to get whatever it is you want.

In fact, avoiding any situation that causes you to sit motionless in your running vehicle is smart for a very simple reason: 0 MPH = 0 MPG. You're using gas, in other words, but not covering any distance. Idling can use up to a gallon of gas an hour.

By driving gently, we mean that you should make the vehicle engine work as little as possible. As a general rule of thumb, the less noise the engine makes the less it's working and the less fuel it's using.

If your vehicle has a tachometer, watch the needle and try not to let it go above 2,000 rpm in the city and 3,000 rpm on the highway.

If you have a manual transmission, put it into the highest gear as soon as possible, even if it means going from first to fifth.

On the highway, set the cruise control at a slightly slower speed than you would normally cruise at and leave it there as much as possible.

Driving gently and going slow may be frustrating for you, but it will save you money on fuel.

As for the tires, the harder they're inflated the less rolling resistance is created, and that means you'll need to use less fuel to get and keep the vehicle moving. Your vehicle's tires are almost certainly under-inflated now, so bringing their pressure up to spec will have an immediate and pleasing affect. (See Page 110 for more details.)

From there on the tips on saving fuel won't have anywhere near as great an impact, but they're worth pointing out just the same.

-If you do a lot of driving that involves looking for new addresses in unfamiliar neighborhoods, using a GPS navigation system can cut down on a lot of unnecessary fuel use and wasted time. (See Page 238 for more on those devices.)

-Remove everything from the vehicle that you don't need to carry, since every kilogram of weight the engine has to pull around uses more fuel. In the winter, be sure to remove the snow and ice because they disrupt the car's aerodynamics as well as add weight.

-Don't make a trip unless you really have to. Consider car-pooling, the public transit, walking, or cycling. The last two will even make you feel better.

-Take off any cargo carrier and roof racks, as they detract from the vehicle's ideal aerodynamic shape.

-Clean out the engine air filters so the engine can get its ideal air/fuel mix.

-Get a tune-up, unless you've been faithful about keeping your car serviced. You can get another tune-up if you want, but that costs money so be sure you need one.

-Ask a technician you trust if you need a wheel alignment,

since unaligned tires can also require more engine energy and that means more fuel.

-Stay out of traffic as much as possible (remember the 0 MPH = 0 MPG rule), and getting the vehicle moving again after it has slowed down or stopped really uses fuel. It's possible that covering more miles in lighter traffic and spending more time on the road can actually use up less gasoline than a shorter, quicker drive in heavy traffic.

-Do up the seatbelt, adjust the mirrors and check your teeth before your start the engine, since new vehicles don't need much warm-up time. Today's cars are designed to be driven almost immediately; 30 seconds of warm-up time is probably more than enough.

-Don't use the air conditioning unless you really have to, and then keep it as warm as you can stand. At the same time, do not open the windows (or sunroof) when you're moving because that creates drag and ruins the car's ideal aerodynamic package which increases fuel consumption.

-The smoother the road, the less fuel you'll use. Dirt or gravel roads require more fuel than a paved surface.

-Even if your car is built to run on premium gas, you can still put lower octane fuel in without causing any harm. All that will happen is that you'll lose a little off the top of your maximum power ratings, and since you're driving gently that doesn't matter. This won't give you better fuel economy, but it will save you a significant amount of money on the price between regular and premium gas.

-Don't overfill the tank, since a few drops of spilled gas can take you farther than you would imagine. Make sure the fuel cap is screwed on tight, to ensure the fuel doesn't evaporate.

-Gasoline prices can vary considerably, so get used to stopping for fuel where the price is low, rather than where you always stop because they know you and they're friendly and yet still charging you more per gallon. On the other hand, avoid places that don't get that much traffic, since their fuel could be old and flat and that's not helpful.

-Park in the shade if you can, or keep an eye on where the sun will be when you come back to the car and position the car so it stays as cool as possible, since cooling a car requires energy. In the winter, park in the sun, since warming a car requires energy.

-Park where you can drive straight out rather than backing out, and look for a slope to park at the top of so the car's weight will move it forward from a stop.

-Consider paying for your fuel with a credit card that has some kind of rebate program or gives you a discount or allows you to earn frequent flyer miles or something similar.

-Consider paying for your fuel with cash if the service station offers a discount for that.

-Do not assume that self-service is always less expensive than "full-service," because they may be expecting you to think that and charge more for self-service.

-Plan trips so you do more than one errand at a time and you take the best route.

-Shift the fuel cost to someone else -- instead of going to a store to buy something, order by phone or on the internet and see if they'll deliver.

-And again, drive less and go slow when you must drive.

## Smog From Logs And Paint

While we have to keep doing our best to make vehicles emissions-free, it's worth noting that smog comes from other sources as well. Burning a cord of wood creates more smog than driving a 2007 Chevrolet Trailblazer around the world 37 times, for example, and using a gallon of water-based paint generates more smog than the same vehicle going from Chicago to LA and back again. Don't get us started on the pollution from lawn mowers and charcoal barbecues.

# Hybrid Value Low And Could Get Worse
# As Times And Technologies Change

The financial benefits to consumers from hybrid vehicles have never been good except under extremely rare conditions, and recent developments make it seem even less likely that their chances of saving you any money will improve. In fact, there's now a very real possibility that hybrids could turn into a major financial mistake in the near future.

But before we get to that, a review of the current situation. Simply put, at today's gas prices it's unlikely that owning a hybrid will save you any money on gas unless a) you pay a lot less than the car companies are currently charging for hybrids or b) you're driving waaaaay more city miles than the average person, since that's where today's hybrids do best. But that would use up your warranty coverage in much less than three years and that would make you liable for repair costs sooner. Not a cheery picture for the average buyer.

If you're going to lease a hybrid for the length of the warranty so you can get rid of it if circumstances change, the key is to pay as little as possible for one over the cost of a similar model with a traditional engine. At this moment, your best bet there is likely going to be the new Saturn Vue crossover with the existing hybrid, not the upcoming Saturn Vue with the new two-mode hybrid as it will be a lot more expensive. Other good choices would include the Chevrolet Malibu (or any other GM model) with the same "light" hybrid as the current Saturn Vue.

But if you can find any dealer of any brand that's willing to give you a hybrid for close to the cost of a similar non-hybrid car, it could be a good move.

No matter what hybrid you get, it's always been difficult to figure the financial prospects of a hybrid because there are three major variables that are hard to predict -- the price of gas, the cost of repairs, and the resale value. Proponents of hybrids like to say that the answers to those questions will be high gas prices, low service costs and high resale value because that is what you must have to make them economical for the average consumer. For the most part, then, the positive economic views of hybrids reflect wishful thinking.

But something's come up recently that could change the entire dynamic of the hybrid car market and turn the current hybrids into the automotive version of the eight-track sound system.

This game-changer is of course the plug-in hybrid as personified by the Chevrolet Volt.

As envisioned by General Motors in the Volt, a plug-in hybrid would essentially be an electric vehicle that can be recharged at your house overnight, or as you drive along by a small gas-powered engine in the car if the driver takes it beyond its regular range.

This means the Volt would be virtually emissions-free for the average driver and much less expensive per mile than gas. On top of that, the need to stop for fuel would be reduced dramatically or perhaps eliminated altogether. You may not have to burn or buy gas with a plug-in hybrid. That's the kind of game-changing technology that almost never comes along, and if GM can make it work in the Volt and other vehicles, and other manufacturers follow suit, then demand for the current crop of hybrids -- Prius et al, new and used -- would pretty much collapse.

We should see the Volt in 2010, with competitive models to follow in quick order. If they live up to their promise, they should be all the rage by 2011 or shortly after, but their affect on Prius and the others would be more immediate. Why would you want a vehicle that was a slight improvement on a traditional car if you could wait a year and have a vehicle that was a huge improvement on a traditional car?

If you didn't have a hybrid at that time none of this would matter, but if you had a Prius or any other current hybrid your economic case would go down as quickly as the vehicle's re-sale value. Remember that a high resale value is key for you to save money with a hybrid.

Gas pricing going up is another key to the economic case for a hybrid since the higher a gallon or liter of gas the better the case for you earning the extra purchase price back. But if there were plug-in hybrids that used little to no gas, higher gas prices would work against an existing hybrid.

In light of all that, it seems harder and harder to make a case for buying (as opposed to leasing) a hybrid vehicle the closer we get to the end of the decade. The exception to this would be if you can get a hybrid for the same price as a traditional vehicle and you do almost nothing but urban driving.

On the subject of hybrid pricing, there's really no need for Toyota and Honda to charge as much as they do for their hybrid models. Both firms earn most of their global profits from selling cars to Americans and Canadians, so they could quite easily sell hybrids for the same as regular models, or at least a lot less. Moreover, there's evidence that Japan funded hybrid development. The fact that they don't sell these vehicles for less speaks directly to how much more committed they are to profits than to helping you use less gasoline.

## Health Concerns About Hybrids

There's a discussion going on about the safety risk from the electromagnetic fields (E.M.F.) in hybrids like the Toyota Prius. At the moment there aren't many facts to consider, but the people with credentials (engineers and so on) say there doesn't seem to be anything to worry about. Hybrid users with their own testing equipment tend to maintain otherwise. If you're considering a hybrid in the future, it might be wise to check the avaiblable information at that time.

# Checking Tire Pressure Can Save Your Life As Well As The Environment

By far the most important safety and fuel economy technology in some time, tire pressure monitors have been added to all new vehicles sold for the 2008 model year and beyond.

Unfortunately, the means to take action on the information the device delivers to you is no easier or more appealing than it ever was. That is of course the tire-filling air pump devices that are usually found in the least charming corner of a service station.

The good news is that the tire-filling thing may not actually be as messy or mechanical as you might have thought, and there are ways to deal with it, including some that won't put your nails in harm's way.

This is a good thing because, without the new warning device you were able to pretend that there was nothing wrong with the air pressure in your tires and go on your merry way. Now there'll be a little reminder on the dash telling you there is a problem, and it will stay on until you deal with the offending tire(s).

The tire-pressure gauges were ordered into new vehicles by the federal government, which understands that under-inflated tires increase the amount of gas your car uses and make it less stable, which means more danger to you.

According to various experts, your car's fuel economy drops one percent for every three PSI (Pounds per Square Inch) of pressure a tire is down, which means an extra fill-up of gas a year for the average driver.

It's not uncommon for some tires to be under-inflated even more than that, so the fuel economy will drop even lower while the cost to you will rise.

As for the danger from soft tires, they simply don't deliver the grip they're designed to give and that can mean a loss of traction at a critical moment and that can mean a loss of control, which too often means a crash or a rollover or some other unpleasant event. In extreme circumstances, it can even mean a tire blowout, which is usually worse.

Once the car alerts you to the fact that you've got a problem with a soft tire, you should consult the owner's manual for general information.

The guide telling you what the tire pressure should be is on a sticker on the car's door, sill or edge. Don't know why it's not always in the same place, but it really shouldn't be hard to find.

Translating this information into action involves figuring out those air pumps in the service center. In general, these things are easy to work:

-Turn the dial to the pressure the sticker says,

-remove the little black plastic cap from the top of the small metal valve that sticks through the metal wheel on every tire, and

-put the nozzle at the end of the tire pump's black hose onto the valve and press down.

If the pump hisses while you're pressing down, you're not pressing hard enough and letting air out. So press harder.

It should ding or make some sort of noise while it forces air into the tire until its pressure matches the pressure number that you dialed in. When it stops dinging, remove the nozzle.

You can buy a tire pressure gauge for not much money that will check you've got the right pressure, if you want to, but the car will tell you if you haven't succeeded.

There are about 35 websites (at least) that will be happy to show you all this in great detail if you search "putting air in tires".

If doing it yourself doesn't appeal, you could ask someone at the service station to show you, or tip him a buck or two to do it for you. It's worth it if the tire pressure warning light is on. You might also look around for one of those lube places that include a tire check with an oil change.

The only problem there is that you probably don't need to change your oil as often as they'd like you to, so you'd be spending money and wasting oil to save money and gas made from oil.

Whatever method you come up with, you should find a way to take advantage of the warning that new gauge is giving you.

If you want to see the bureaucratic perspective of all this, go to www.checkmytires.com.

## Mileage-Based Fees Replace Gas Taxes

If consumers are really serious about moving to smaller, more fuel-efficient cars it's going to leave the agencies responsible for highway construction and maintenance with a serious budget shortfall.

After all, less gas consumed means less gas purchased means less taxes paid.

So some states are looking at the possibility of charging cars a per-mile fee to keep their revenue base up.

To make this work, vehicles would be outfitted with GPS devices that count how many miles they travel, with the owner then getting a bill for the miles covered at whatever rate the government sets. The per-gallon gas price would go down because the tax portion would be removed.

The GPS systems would not keep track of where miles or when miles, just how many miles.

Cars with out-of-state plates would presumably be charged a per-gallon price that was higher, to make up for the per-mile taxes they're not paying.

No advice to offer; just wanted to let you contemplate what might be your tax-paying future in advance.

# Saturn Vue Hybrid Saved Money
# In Long-Term Real-World Test

When we decided to test a hybrid for a year to see what it was actually like to live with one, particularly in terms of its ability to use less fuel and save money, there seemed to be only one model with a decent shot at doing the job -- the Saturn Vue Greenline crossover/SUV/wagon from General Motors.

None of this will matter, of course, if you are a member of that tiny, tiny group of folks who are so concerned about the environment that they're willing to shell out whatever it takes to make a tiny dent in the emissions problem. If that's you, buy whichever hybrid (or subcompact car) you like and thank you on behalf of humanity.

But if you're a member of the vast majority of folks who have repeatedly gone on record as saying you won't pay any more to help the environment, you need to know that the Vue Greenline's primary appeal is that it's not much more expensive (about $1,500) than a regular Vue. The lower price is possible because its hybrid setup isn't as complicated or expensive as the hybrid setup in something like a Toyota Prius or indeed even the other, more expensive hybrid Vue that Saturn will be selling later this year. That means the Greenline doesn't deliver the same kind of fuel use reductions as any of the more expensive hybrids.

But Saturn has struck a nice balance between price and fuel economy gains with the Vue Greenline, assuming that most of the miles you cover are in the city rather than on the highway. Like virtually all hybrids, Vue Greenline delivers better fuel economy gains when you're stopping and starting your way through traffic and stoplights and so on.

Based on the strength of our fuel savings over a year's driving at about $3 a gallon on average and the number of miles a year we drive (a little higher than average), we would have been able to recover the extra cost for the hybrid model in about three years.

Your own results will vary due to the amount and kind of miles (city's better than highway) you drive a year, and the cost of gas per gallon. The more miles you drive, but especially in the city, and the higher the cost of the gasoline, the greater your chances of recovering the extra cost of the hybrid vehicle.

If you're driving enough so that you're using, say, 150 gallons less a year than you would with a normal vehicle, at $3 a gallon you'd be saving $450 a year, or $1,350 over three years. With gas at $4, 150 fewer gallons a year means you're saving $600 a year or $1,800 over three years. At $4.50 a gallon for 150 gallons, it would be a saving of $675 a year and $2,025 over three years.

The other way to make your money back on a hybrid is to do lots more miles a year than the 12,000-mile norm. The risk here is that you'll be driving the car out of its warranty faster (it is 12,000 miles or 12 months, after all) and that presents a set of risks that are too complicated to consider here, including repair costs, resale value and so on.

Your best chance of recovering the extra cost of a Saturn Vue Greenline (or any other vehicle that carries an equally modest premium) is to stick almost completely to city driving. That will deliver the best fuel economy and probably keep you under the warranty limit.

There's an economic component to hybrids (and indeed any more fuel-efficient car) that's rarely talked about, but should be because it's meaningful to most people: The less fuel you use, the less time you have to spend in gas stations filling up. Every response to this is different, depending upon where you are in relation to a filling station, where you drive (gas stations are getting harder to find in city centers), and how you feel about the process in general. Do you hate having to stop for gas, do you worry that you might run out of fuel, or is there another feeling at work? How much having that angst reduced is worth to you is a personal issue, but there likely won't be many women who'll miss having to visit a service station to pump gas.

As for the Saturn Vue Greenline itself, it's an excellent package for the kind of family demands that are so common across North America. It seats five people quite nicely, with easier access than a traditional car, and it has lots of space in the back for regular cargo or, by folding down the rear seats, the bulkier items that come along now and then.

It's also easy to steer through traffic and around parking lots or school driveways.

As with all hybrids, the Vue Greenline runs and sounds a little (a very little) different from the way a vehicle with only a regular internal-combustion engine does. But there's nothing different about the way it drives or the way you have to treat it, except of course putting less gasoline in it.

On top of all that, it's a GM product and that means it comes with OnStar, which should be mandatory in every vehicle used to transport children. For more information on that, consult the sections on crash notification (Page 38) and OnStar in general (Page 99).

## Nissan Car For Young Japanese Women

To make its brand more attractive to young Japanese women, Nissan has created a concept car called the PIVO 2 to address their concerns. The car has a "robotic agent" with two eyes that speaks to the driver in a soothing voice to help her deal with the stress of driving and can be driven sideways into a tight parking space.

Car sales are down about 30 percent in Japan since 1990, partly because more young people there find cars boring.

# Buy A Better House To Help You Save The Environment

People looking for a new place to live on all those TV shows never, ever seem to connect the price of the house with the cost of commuting to their workplace or wherever it is they drive the most. They have a maximum to pay for a house and will face awful commutes to live there. The idea that they could have more money to spend on the house if they lowered their commuting costs never seems to occur to them.

This is very odd, since house value and location can be improved if you pay more attention to the economic costs of commuting. That is to say, the less distance you have to commute the more money you can spend on a house. The monthly payments for gas, maintenance and insurance will all drop, and if you're one of those people who keeps a car until it stops running, you won't have to replace it as soon. In all, it can add up to a considerable pile of money, which you can put into a better home, which almost always appreciates in value, if not year-to-year then historically.

You will also reduce the time that you're putting yourself at risk by being out on the road, or at gas stations filling up.

On top of all that, you get to spend more time at home or the gym or the office or anyplace other than your car, since your commuting time is reduced.

Oh, and the planet has fewer emissions to contend with.

Live closer to work, get a better house, spend less time in the car, and help the planet.

## Any Kind Of Oil Is Better Than None

If your car's engine is down a quart of oil and you have to do some long and/or hard driving, putting in any kind of motor oil is better than waiting until you find the perfect choice.

# Diesels May Use Less Fuel
# But They Have More Issues

Bar none, the best part of a car with a diesel engine is that it gets a lot better mileage than the same car with a gasoline engine, since that means fewer stops at the service station.

But anyone who remembers diesel-powered cars from the past will perhaps wonder what those service station visits will be like now, since stations with diesel pumps were hard to find. When you did find one the diesel pump was off in the corner so big trucks could use it and there was much less consideration given to things like cleanliness or convenience or even a paved surface. We can only hope that the gas companies have made some effort in this regard, since there's a growing desire from the car companies to offer more diesel-powered cars, along with all the diesel-powered trucks they've sold for years.

But if you're thinking about choosing a diesel you may want to have a look around where it's convenient for you to fill up to see if they sell diesel and what the conditions are around the pump. It also wouldn't hurt to see what the stations that do sell diesel as well as traditional gasoline are charging for it. Since diesel cars usually cost more to buy, recovering that cost is sometimes only made possible if the diesel fuel is cheaper, which it certainly is not right now.

The fact is that diesels don't have an immediate economic value unless you drive a lot more in a year than the average driver, and even then it's tricky. Diesel-powered cars cost at least a couple of thousand dollars more than a similar car with a gas engine, so that wipes out a lot of the joys of their significantly higher (25 to 40 percent, depending upon the driving conditions you encounter) fuel economy levels. And for the car companies to meet future emissions regulations, the costs are likely to go up even more.

There's also the noise factor, since diesels still clatter like a truck making a delivery. If it helps, it's mostly other people who'll hear it, since the car companies have done a good job blocking the sound from getting into the car itself.

There's also a long history of diesels requiring what you might call emergency repairs, even though they are all scheduled for fewer regular service stops than a gas-powered car. But there's also the risks associated with getting service of any kind with a new technology (see Page 179) and that can be a problem. Sure, diesels aren't new, but when the market grows the dealerships will be slow to add service capability.

There are also issues with the kind of diesel that will be available, and the fact that some states may ban the sale of many diesels for environmental reasons.

On the plus side, if you really care about performance, the new diesels have been cranked up to be as good or better than gas-powered cars. Their torque numbers in particular make many men drool since they provide improved launch.

It's hard then to see a solid economic case for buying a diesel unless you regularly do a lot of long-distance highway driving with welcoming service stations and reliable manufacturer service support.

## Revisions Make Cobalt An MPG Leader

By making various modifications to an existing model, car companies can do quite a lot to improve their fuel economy ratings. For example, GM's Chevrolet division has created a new version of its Cobalt compact called the XFE (for Xtra Fuel Economy) that gets 9 percent better mileage than the current model, which puts it ahead of the other cars in this category -- Honda Civic, Mazda 3, Toyota Corolla, etc.

With its new tires and various engine modifications, the XFE registers 25 mpg in the city and 36 mpg on the highway.

# Partial Answer To Reducing Our Oil Use Could Be E85 Fuel

It couldn't be easier for you to switch from gasoline to the E85 fuel that's environmentally-friendly, North America-sourced, and often less expensive than gas the next time you need a fill up. All you have to do is pull up to the E85 pump at the service station.

The problem with E85, which is the nickname for a renewable fuel that's made up of 85 percent ethanol and 15 percent gasoline, is that not many vehicles have been equipped to use it, and it's not widely available. It is however easy to find out if your current vehicle or your future vehicle is already set up to run E85, and even easier to find out where the E85 stations are.

Don't bother looking if you own a vehicle from Acura, Audi, BMW, Honda, Hyundai, Infiniti, Kia, Lexus, Mini, Mitsubishi, Subaru, Suzuki, Toyota or Volkswagen, and most vehicles from Isuzu, Mazda, Mercedes and Nissan.

If you own a vehicle from Chrysler, Ford, or GM, on the other hand, your chances are better of it being E85-ready since the fuel's meant to be a renewable, low-emissions alternative to foreign oil that can be sourced in North America. Things like that just don't seem to be a priority for firms from Asia or Europe.

The list of existing E85-capable vehicles and much else that you need to know about this fuel can be found at www. E85fuel.com. But bear in mind that more will be added as the technology advances and as the world grows more determined to reduce its use of fossil fuel, so be sure to inquire about something you may have in mind.

There's a lesser chance that you'll be able to find a station that pumps E85 ethanol, though the list of such stations at e85fuel.com has been growing quite steadily in recent months, and increasing demand should result in increased supply.

As for price, E85 is usually less expensive in the Midwest, perhaps because that is also largely the source of the fuel.

You don't have to settle on either gas or E85, by the way, since you can use one or the other as you see fit.

The primary downside to E85 at the moment is that it doesn't deliver the fuel economy of gas, but if it's less expensive that could still come out in your favor.

But it certainly puts out a lot fewer emissions and that point seems to gain in consumer importance all the time.

You can actually run E85 in a regular vehicle without too much trouble but no one in a position of responsibility will flat-out say this because they don't know how much damage it might do to the engine. Today's engines are incredibly sophisticated and finely-tuned to deliver the best performance and the best fuel economy and that requires gasoline with certain precise characteristics. E85 does not have all of those precise characteristics so it's possible that some amount of damage will result, usually in terms of reduced engine performance. But, again, the experts are largely guessing here.

The e85fuel.com website has more information on E85 than a normal person could ever imagine needing to know, including the creation of E85 from the "biomass portion of municipal solid waste."

Looks like we're getting ever closer to the dream engine of all men -- one that runs on urine and can be refilled from inside the car.

## We Need Doc Brown More Than Ever

The holy grail of alternate energy has never been better described than it was in Back To The Future, in which the time-travelling DeLorean returns to 1985 having been altered to run on common household garbage instead of plutonium.

# Use A Toll Road If You Want
# To Save Money On Gas And Repairs

If traffic is moving quickly on a freeway and a toll road covering the same ground, the freeway makes better economic sense every time.

But the more the real-world situation deviates from that ideal, the more appealing the financial case for the toll road becomes. If traffic on the freeway is so heavy that you get into that famous stop-and-go rhythm, your fuel economy starts to go down. As soon as you stop moving at a steady speed on the highway and get into a situation where you're going brake-gas, brake-gas, brake-gas and so on, your fuel economy drops, and the more brake-gas, brake-gas then the more fuel you're using.

And when you're stuck motionless in traffic, remember this equation: 0 MPH = 0 MPG.

You must also consider the cost associated with the wear and tear that stop-and-go traffic brings to your vehicle, most significantly its brakes and tires. A vehicle that stops and starts all the time suffers a lot more duress than a vehicle cruising smoothly along, and that will eventually cost you in repairs and maintenance.

On top of all that is the increased damage to the environment caused by the increased use of gasoline and the extra oil changes and so on that are required.

Since a toll road can also save you time, you have to judge the value of that for yourself. As strange as it may seem to some of us, there are people who actually like sitting in a car going nowhere for an hour every afternoon because that's the only chance they have all day to spend time alone.

A cost-analysis of using the toll road could show that it's actually the smarter economic choice, and might be the smarter emotional choice as well.

# Dust-To-Dust Costs Show
# Real Energy Usage Of New Cars

For consumers genuinely concerned with the total environmental damage their next vehicle choice will cause, there is no more important source of information than the Dust to Dust survey produced by CNW Marketing.

This survey provides consumers with a remarkably thorough overview of the total energy cost to society of planning, building, selling, driving and disposing of a vehicle from initial concept to scrappage. This includes such minutiae as plant to dealer fuel costs, employee driving distances, electricity usage per pound of material used in each vehicle, police enforcement, road maintenance, fuel transportation, even car washes and more than 3,000 other data points. It took CNW two years of research before it was able to put the first Dust to Dust survey online in 2005, and now every year the company does an update to include all of the vehicles available for sale in the U.S.

While the whole survey is interesting, for consumers the primary information can be found on the Energy Cost by Model per Mile chart. It and the 450-page Dust to Dust study are available to read or download at www.cnwmr.com.

What the survey is not is a comparison of the costs to consumers operating specific vehicles. That's a personal expense, rather than a societal expense.

One of the most interesting results of this study is that the fuel-economy darlings of the moment -- hybrids -- do not come off looking too great, while others that don't normally generate any public enthusiasm for their energy efficiency come off quite well.

The results were compiled to create a "dollars per lifetime mile" figure paid for directly or indirectly by society for every single model that goes on the road, which is represented in the survey as the Energy Cost (EC) per mile driven. On average, the CNW survey shows, a new vehicle cost society $2.946 in energy costs for every mile driven. The averages shown are straight averages and do not reflect the volume of vehicles produced or consumed.

As a general guide, here are some of the more interesting results from summer 2007. But check at www.cnwmr.com to see the latest figures when you're looking for a new vehicle. Hybrids as a group cost society $3.652 per mile in 2006, which was more than four times the Budget Segment of cars (such as Chevrolet Aveo) with average $0.874 cost per mile and the Economy Segment of cars (such as Toyota Corolla) with average $0.858 cost per mile. It was also more than twice the average of the Standard Mid Range Segment of cars (such as Chevrolet Impala, Ford Taurus, Honda Accord and Toyota Camry) with average $1.749 cost per mile.

Some of the hybrid models with high Energy Cost per mile driven included the Toyota Prius ($2.865), Honda Civic ($3.398), Honda Accord ($3.421), Ford Escape ($3.540), Toyota Camry ($3.618), Toyota Highlander ($3.656), Lexus GS450h ($4.421), and Lexus RX400h ($4.546).

It is interesting to see the vehicles that have both a conventional and a hybrid version. In most cases, the hybrid version's energy costs are about $1.00 more per mile.

Here are some of the most popular selling models in North America:

Toyota Camry ($2.356)
Honda Civic ($2.361)
Honda Accord ($1.960)
Mini Cooper ($1.960)
Toyota Prius ($2.865)
Chevrolet Impala ($1.353)
Dodge Caravan/Grand Caravan ($2.165)
Jeep Wrangler ($0.709)
Ford F-Series Pickup Trucks ($2.381)
GMC Silverado ($2.376)

Here is the full lineup of the listed segments from CNW's Dust to Dust survey, showing the average energy cost per mile in each segment and the vehicle with the lowest cost in that segment. (Note: the categories may not be as logical as you might guess, so look around when you are trying to find a specific vehicle. Also, the list only shows the name of the vehicle model and not the car company.)

Cars: Budget $0.874, with Chevrolet Aveo at $0.744.
Cars: Economy $0.858, with Toyota Scion xB at $0.492.
Cars: Lower Mid-Range Car $2.240, with Pontiac Vibe at $1.023.
Cars: Standard Mid-Range Car $1.749, with Chevrolet Impala $1.353.
Cars: Premium Mid-Range Car $2.028, with Saab 9-2 at $1.625.
Cars: Traditional Car $1.627, with Ford Crown Victoria at $1.377.
Cars: Touring Car $2.061, with Hyundai Tiburon at $1.496.
Cars: Near Luxury Car $1.996, with Saab 9-5 at $1.545.
Cars: Luxury Car $4.457, with Lincoln Town Car at $2.661.
Cars: Prestige Car $3.749, with BMW 7 Series at $2.888.
Cars: Premium Sportscar $3.432, with Chrysler Crossfire at $1.644.
Cars: Upper Premium Sportscar $3.070, with Dodge Viper at $2.355.
Cars: Ultra Luxury Car $5.215, with Aston-Martin at $3.072.
Cars: Ultra Premium Car $13.407, with Rolls-Royce at $10.977.
Hybrids: All Types $3.652, with Toyota Prius at $2.865.
Minivans: All Types $2.225, with Mazda MPV $1.929.
Sport Wagons: Entry $2.002, with Honda CR-V at $1.466.
Sport Wagons: Mid-Range $2.537, with Mitsubishi Endeavor at $2.171.
Sport Wagons: Premium $3.159, with BMW X3 at $2.513.
SUVs: Entry SUV $1.361, with Chevrolet Tracker at $0.665.
SUVs: Lower Mid-Range SUV $2.073, with Dodge Durango at $1.572.
SUVs: Upper Mid-Range SUV $2.426, with Hummer H3 at $2.069.
SUVs: Large SUV $3.989, with Ford Expedition at $3.549.
SUVs: Premium SUV $3.598, with Porsche Cayenne at $2.539.
Full-size Van $2.445, with Ford Econoline at $2.249.
Trucks: Small Pickup $1.369, with Chevrolet S-10 at $0.761.
Trucks: Full-size Pickup $2.588, with Chevrolet Silverado at $2.376.
Trucks: Specialty Pickup $2.293, with Chevrolet Avalanche at $2.250.
Industry Straight Average $2.946.

**Alexander Law & Susan Winlaw**

# GM's Volt And Vue EVs Could Be
# Game-Changers For The Entire Market

When it first appeared at various auto shows and in the media, the Chevrolet Volt concept car was widely seen as a cute and clever addition to the lineup of "plug-in hybrids" that might attract some consumer interest.

But the situation has changed with the Chevrolet Volt from General Motors (and the Saturn Vue with the same technology), since they will actually be electric vehicles (EV) with a portable battery charging unit, and there's an excellent chance that cars like them with the same technology could fundamentally change the nature of the auto industry in general, and your life in particular.

First off, Volt, Vue and cars like them should severely reduce the appeal of hybrids like the Toyota Prius as the plug-in technology is a much better solution to the issue of decreasing the use of gasoline in almost every way.

As for how it might change your life, the benefits to the Volt and cars like it are impressive: your gasoline consumption would be greatly reduced or even disappear completely (as would -- bonus -- your visits to gas stations), your cost-per-mile would be greatly reduced, and you could attain the coveted "zero-emissions" status as a lover of the environment.

The excitement around the Volt and Vue has energized General Motors to the point where it has become a top priority. The American company is now promising production versions of Volt and Vue by 2010 or so, with a whole lineup of similarly-equipped cars of different sizes to follow in short order. In case you're wondering, none of the other major car companies (including Toyota or any of the other Japanese firms) seem likely to beat GM to a real-world, big-volume application of this idea.

Volt and Vue and the other cars GM is promising can be

charged overnight using regular household electricity and, in the right circumstances, can then operate full time as an EV, which is how it reaches that zero-emissions status. This could be especially appealing in urban situations, where smog is a particular issue.

It must be pointed out that, like all EVs, the emissions from Volt and Vue will be transferred to the generating stations that create the electricity they use instead of gas. Since a great deal of power comes from coal, that greatly reduces the overall environmental benefit. Plug-ins might just be marketed to places that don't use so much coal, but that would be a political decision.

Volt and Vue will not have to use power generated by a gas-consuming internal-combustion engine if they're driven less than 40 miles a day, which covers the regular daily travel life of about 85 percent of the continent already.

That range also assumes that you're only recharging overnight at home, when electricity is more available and often less expensive. If you recharge at work during the day, the Volt/Vue EV range goes back up to the max.

If you do get into a situation that puts you over the distance the batteries are able to cover, the small four-cylinder engine that's part of the package starts producing power to recharge them.

In many circumstances, the combination of the pre-charged batteries and the power from the gas engine will keep a Volt/Vue moving for 640 miles before you have to stop for gas, or a recharge. That's about as good as any car gets for range.

The engine in a hybrid engine like the Prius will also recharge the batteries, of course, but it's hooked up to the drive-train system alongside the batteries and won't get anything near the same range at the same price.

Prius will always have to use gas, the Volt/Vue is capable of working without using gas.

Volt/Vue engines only recharges the batteries, which makes them EVs. This is not as ideal as running on the zero-emissions batteries alone, but it's better than anything a regular car or even a hybrid can provide.

As always, individual mileage rates will vary, but Volt/Vue is likely going to deliver a cost-per-mile charge that works out to something like 100 mpg in traditional cars. GM is also planning to have the Volt/Vue's engines run on gas, E85 and diesel.

It's hard to describe how much the idea of the Volt/Vue and vehicles like them have taken off at GM and a lot of the auto industry in such a short time. There's now a widespread sense that this package -- batteries that will look after most daily commutes with an engine to provide back-up juice if needed -- could become a huge part of the world's engine choices and have a significant impact on the use of oil.

The addition of the Volt/Vue and cars like them isn't much help if you're looking for a new vehicle today, but it's something to keep in mind the next time you're in the market and thinking about a regular hybrid.

That will still do a slightly better job of saving gas than a regular engine, but if Volt/Vue and cars like them come out and catch on, it will hurt the appeal of second-hand hybrids and that will worsen the already unpromising economic case for Prius and its ilk.

## Locate Alternative Fuel Sites

If you're thinking of buying a vehicle that runs on alternative fuel (natural gas, E85, and so on), you first might want to search the U.S. Department of Energy's "Alternative Fuel Station Locator" to see where the stations are in relation to your location.

There's no point buying a vehicle to save fuel if you have to drive for miles to find a station that sells it.

# Consider The Gas Station
# Before You Buy The Gas

Though www.gasbuddy.com likes to list gas prices by city or region, it will also give you prices inside those regions by city, zip/postal code, county and so on, and the per-gallon differences might surprise you. Here are some tips from the website that directs people to the cheapest gas virtually any place in Canada and the U.S.

In most places, the cheapest gas seems to be in the outlying suburbs. In places near expensive houses where land is more expensive, taxes higher and the neighbors not so sensitive to price, gas may be more per gallon.

Stations conveniently located near major freeway exits may be more expensive than stations further away, so passing by the first place you come to and going up the road a piece can probably save you some money.

Some stations are always the price leaders in the area, gasbuddy.com says. Grocery stores, wholesale clubs and department stores with gas stations will often sell gas close to cost or at a loss to get people into the stores where they may buy other, higher margin items.

You might have to be a member to take advantage of some of these loss-leaders, but it could be worth it. There may also be discounts on stuff inside the store. As always, the financial results may vary, so do the math on your own situation.

Service stations with an auto repair shop on site, says gasbuddy.com, often have more expensive gas.

Some stations put discount coupons on gas purchases on the back of the store receipt, or in mail or internet coupons. You might also get less expensive gas from some places if you use the car wash, and so on.

As always, all gas stations are not created equal when it comes to pricing.

# Large Hybrid SUVs From GM
# Offer Car-Like Fuel Economy

If you're one of those folks who decided to take a pass on a large SUV because you wanted something that consumed less gas in a $4-a-gallon universe, you might be glad to hear that General Motors has rolled out a pair of extremely attractive hybrid SUVs that score better fuel economy ratings than Toyota Camry and many other mid-sized and large cars.

This means you don't have to sacrifice the size, utility, presence and cachet of a full-size SUV and settle for something as boring and uninviting as a Camry or another model of that persuasion.

It will cost you quite a lot upfront, of course, since a hybrid system as sophisticated as the one that was created by BMW, Chrysler, Mercedes, and GM working together and has debuted on the Chevrolet Tahoe and GMC Yukon is hugely expensive.

The same system will soon turn up on GM's full-sized pickups, and you can expect variations on the theme from the other companies in the near future. For the most part, it will be restricted to large and/or expensive vehicles in the near future, but the economics of technological development will eventually cause it to turn up on smaller and cheaper cars.

For the foreseeable future, however, the car companies will want to pass much of this cost along to you, so it's unlikely you'll be able to recoup the extra cost through fuel savings unless gas goes to beyond $5 a gallon or you drive two or three times as much as the average person.

On the plus side:

-you'll be using a lot less gas than virtually anyone with a regular full-sized SUV, so you'll be able to lead the way for others to follow

-you'll be making fewer stops for gas than if you had any

other SUV

-you'll be in a large, heavy vehicle and that increases your safety level beyond that of anything smaller and lighter

-you'll have the world's best crash-notification system (as part of OnStar) working for you should you get into a situation where you wouldn't otherwise be able to summon help

-you'll be able to stay on electric power around town (up to a little over 30 mph), so you won't be emitting bad odors in crowded places

-you'll be able to run electric power only in stop-and-go situations, so if you do a lot of that (hello LA) your fuel economy will be even better, and

-you'll be using the most sophisticated hybrid system in the world, superior to anything from Toyota or Lexus that your friends own, and that's particularly sweet.

As always, individual fuel economy results will vary, but in general GM is talking about a 25-to-50 percent reduction in gas consumption. If you do a lot of urban driving, you should do even better.

## Women Willing To Pay For Clean Air

Sophisticated, mature and highly-educated women on the west coast who read things like the New Yorker, Sunset and Wired are more likely than anyone to pay extra for environmentally-friendly vehicles, but in general our society is not willing to pay much -- if anything -- for better air.

According to a survey by J.D. Power and Associates, only about 11 percent of the population claim to be "very willing" to pay more to help the environment. Most people show their concern by buying cheaper, smaller cars rather than larger, expensive cars with a hybrid propulsion system.

The Power survey shows there's apparently not much enthusiasm for buying environmentally-conscious vehicles in the mid-west, particularly among men.

# Specific Directions By Cell Phones
# Are Now Available In Some Areas

Directions to specific places in various large U.S. cities are now available for people with a regular text-messaging cellphone by dialling Directions (347-328-4667).

Except for the cost of the text messaging and the inevitable appearance of a small ad on your phone screen, the service is free from Dial Directions, at www.dialdirections.com, if you want to eyeball it in advance.

You tell the automated service where you are and what address you're looking for and the service texts the directions to your cellphone, virtually right away.

Not as impressive as the full-color map with turn-by-turn arrows and all the other bells and whistles that you get on more expensive phones with built-in GPS, but better than wondering around wasting time and gas while you look for someone trustworthy to give you directions.

The service was limited to the major metropolitan areas (LA, NY, SF, DFW, etc) to start but is expected to grow with time. It also helps to have a specific street address, rather than just the name of the place, though that is also expected to change with time.

# AAA TripTiks Now Free To All

The American Automobile Association (AAA) is now making its famous TripTik route and roadside guides available to everyone, not just members.

Simply search AAA TripTik and order up a TripTik for virtually any drive on the continent, for no charge.

The results will provide you with a driving guide that knows no equal in road specifics (including construction), especially when it comes to revealing details about sites and services along the way.

# New Mileage Grades Better Reflect Real World Driving

To more realistically measure the gasoline consumption in new cars, the U.S. government has changed the way it creates those famous EPA fuel economy ratings.

It looks like mileage has dropped across the board, but what's really happened is that the new figures more closely reflect real world consumption. In the long term this will be good for consumers, but right now it will probably just confuse a lot of people.

The best place to go for a comparison of the old and new fuel economy figures is www.fueleconomy.gov, where you will also find geek-level explanations of how and why the testing works and lots of really useful consumer information about costs, consumption and emissions.

Even with the new way of testing, the official fuel economy figures won't likely be the same as those you achieve in the real world -- your real world, that is, since everyone's driving style and situation is different.

But they will provide you with a list of all the new vehicles' tested in the same circumstances, which should give you an idea of how various models compare and those differences should suggest the mileage rates you'd achieve in them. Not a perfect system, but better than before.

## Gas Gadgets Score Badly In EPA Tests

Whenever the U.S. Environmental Protection Agency (EPA) tested 93 gadgets over 30 years, none of them earned that group's seal of approval.

An EPA spokesperson said "These products often are found to have little or no savings in terms of fuel economy and can damage your engine or increase emissions."

# Will The Sun Ever Shine
# On The Future Of Solar Cars?

The traditional favorite in dream fuel sources is still solar power, which is probably more realistic since the energy load from the sun is there for everyone to feel. It is even fairly easy to use the sun to power a car. As ever, the trick seems to be in getting solar energy to propel a vehicle that people would want to use and could afford.

Some progress is being made, since the vehicles that take part in those long-distance solar-powered competitions look less like lunar-landers and more like cars you might see in a sci-fi movie set in 2020. But there's still little in the way of interior creature comforts and usually only enough room for one person.

The best use of solar power might be in putting the energy-collecting panels on the roof of the garage and using them to charge the batteries in a plug-in hybrid (see Page 126). That would effectively take the vehicle off the regular power grid, with a gas-powered engine of some kind in reserve for when the trip surpasses the range of the batteries. Indeed a French firm will market a test model of that sort sometime soon, for more money than most people can afford in dollars or euros or any other currency.

There are also some solar-powered boats being tested in countries around the world, but the widespread use of the technology is generally not expected to happen without some major technical breakthroughs.

## Book Helps Women Negotiate Better

Women Don't Ask covers the general topic of the female attitude to negotiation, but there's enough about getting a good deal on a car to make it worthwhile reading. Women of all ages are still paying more than men for cars, it seems.

# Are "Stick-shifts" Going
# To Save You Gas And Money?

Once a favorite of men looking for a sportier driving experience, the manual transmission -- aka the "stick-shift" -- fell drastically out of favor over the past 20 years.

But the stick-shift has regained a little consumer popularity over the last couple of years, propelled by women hoping to pay less for their car while getting better fuel economy.

In 2007, 12.49 percent of the people who responded to a survey by CNW of Portland, Oregon, said they were interested in a car with a manual transmission. That's down considerably from 31.6 percent in 1985, but is the third straight increase from the 10.3 percent of 2004. That was the year that more women than men said they were looking for a car with a manual gearbox, for economic reasons.

A manual transmission in a vehicle appealed to many women because those models usually sold for less and got better fuel economy to boot.

As for manuals costing less than automatics, that's at least true if you look at the list of sticker prices on ordinary, everyday cars. But it's an ironic fact that the sticker price is just about the only price that people don't pay for a new car. If you're going up against most dealers, you have to negotiate a price and that means all bets are off. Indeed, as soon as the dealer senses that you actually want something in particular (like a manual transmission) he or she will try to use your desire to get you to pay more for it.

As for a manual transmission providing better fuel economy than an automatic transmission and letting you save money on gas, that's not as true as it used to be because automatics are much more sophisticated these days. Look at the nearby chart to see how the difference plays out on the EPA tests.

An automatic will always deliver close to its best fuel econ-

# EPA Estimates Outline Manual-Automatic Differences

| Model | Engine | Transmission | Fuel Economy | Fuel Cost per year * |
|-------|--------|-------------|--------------|---------------------|
| Chevrolet Aveo | 1.6 | A - 4 speed | 23/32 | $1,958 |
| | | M - 5 speed | 24/34 | $1,881 |
| | | Savings | | $77 |
| Mazda 3 | 2.0 | A - 4 speed | 23/31 | $1,958 |
| | | M - 5 speed | 24/32 | $1,881 |
| | | Savings | | $77 |
| VW Rabbit | 2.5 | A - 6 speed | 21/29 | $2,120 |
| | | M - 5 speed | 22/29 | $2,120 |
| | | Savings | | $0 |
| Toyota Corolla | 1.8 | A - 4 speed | 25/35 | $1,754 |
| | | M - 5 speed | 28/37 | $1,642 |
| | | Savings | | $112 |
| Ford Fusion | 2.3 | A - 5 speed | 20/28 | $2,212 |
| | | M - 5 speed | 20/29 | $2,212 |
| | | Savings | | $0 |
| Kia Spectra | 2.0 | A - 4 speed | 24/32 | $1,881 |
| | | M - 5 speed | 23/30 | $1,958 |
| | | Savings | | -$77 |
| Toyota Camry | 2.4 | A - 5 speed | 21/31 | $2,034 |
| | | M - 5 speed | 21/31 | $2,034 |
| | | Savings | | $0 |
| Chrysler PT Cruiser non-Turbo model | 2.4 | A - 4 speed | 19/24 | $2,420 |
| | | M - 5 speed | 21/26 | $2,212 |
| | | Savings | | $208 |

* Annual Fuel cost is estimated assuming 15,000 miles of travel (55% city & 45% highway) and average fuel cost per gallon of $3.39 (regular unleaded). Www.fueleconomy.gov/feg/FEG2008.pdf

Engine Size is in litres and all samples listed have 4 cylinders. Transmission lists whether it is Automatic (A) or Manual (M). Fuel Economy is listed as city/highway miles per gallon.

Visit www.fueleconomy.gov to calculate annual fuel costs for a specific vehicle based on your own driving conditions and per-gallon fuel costs.

omy if you let it go about its work without too much aggressive accelerating. A manual gearbox delivers better fuel economy if it's used correctly, which means shifting up as quickly as possible, and of not accelerating aggressively.

The trick to using a manual involves keeping your eye on the tachometer (if your car has one) and making sure that you keep the needle on that as low as possible. The tachometer measures the revolutions of the engine per minute (RPM), and the higher the revolutions the more gas you're using.

The way to get the best fuel economy out of a manual transmission is to shift it into its highest gear as quickly as possible. Use first to get going and once you're moving put it directly into fourth or fifth. This will mean some extremely lack-lustre performance, but better fuel economy. Use all the gears if you're anxious to get up to speed quickly, but otherwise put up with the slowness of it all.

If you don't keep shifting when necessary the car's engine will rev higher than it needs to, and that means you'll actually be using more gas.

Buying a manual can indeed save you money, but it requires more attention than driving an automatic.

## Finding The Cheapest Gas On The Web

There are several sites on the web that try to deliver a comprehensive view of gas prices for specific areas, and the smart thing to do is try several to see what best reflects your own area and your own requirements. If you're looking for premium gas prices, for example, you might not have much luck.

In general, the site operated by the AAA (www.aaa.com) seems to have the best reputation across the board. If the local chapter where you live doesn't have such a site, the AAA's California branch probably has prices for your area.

There's also gasbuddy.com, mapquest.com, gaspricewatch. com, and others that hook up with your cell phone.

# The Awful Truth About The
# New Car Buying Process

Much as we regret saying this, there's really no way for us to give you all the advice you're going to need to navigate the car-buying process quickly and economically.

As well as being intensely complicated and different in each state or province, the new car market is also always fluid, which makes it hard to keep track of the newest developments on a daily basis, let alone explain them in print in a book like this.

You're also up against professionals whose whole life is dedicated to making money for themselves by taking it away from you through the business of selling cars and related products, and they are extremely clever at coming up with new ways to make that happen. They make the process confusing so you can't find out the reality of pricing or anything else, and many of them will distort reality, withhold facts or flat-out lie to you if they think it will do the trick.

On top of that, the people who own car dealerships spend a lot of money to earn the loyalty of local politicians and they use their enormous political power to enact laws that favor them and disadvantage you.

Most of the people who own and manage new car dealerships are honest and decent people, but that's not likely going to stop them from taking as much money from you as they can using techniques that are legal, if not created to help the consumer. That's the nature of the current business ethos in cars and pretty much everything else.

In every way you can imagine, then, the odds greatly favor the car dealer. As a result, it's highly unlikely that you'll be able to come away with the lowest price possible, but if it's any consolation it's also unlikely that anyone else will either.

We wish it weren't so, but it is and it's better to acknowledge it up front.

There are ways to help you get a better deal and we'll tell you about a lot of them, but before you go too far into the process it's important to think about how much time you want to spend on it.

Putting half a year's income into a new car is a pretty common thing for consumers to do, so that means you shouldn't treat the process lightly. But there's also some point at which the principle of diminishing returns kicks in, so maybe it's not worth your time to spend, say, an entire Saturday driving from dealership to dealership trying to save an extra $10 a month on a lease payment. You have to figure out what your time's worth, and then you have to factor in the irritation value. That is to say, how much do you hate the prospect of shopping for a new car and what are you willing to pay to avoid the exercise altogether?

Only you can answer those questions, and you should know your feelings before you start the buying process. If nothing else, you might be able to budget your time better.

Having said all that, we're glad to give you our best advice on how to take the irritation out of the car buying process and get yourself a good deal:

Hire someone who knows what they're doing to find a car for you. Really, buying a car is a specialty process and you probably wouldn't consider spending $15,000 to $150,000 on anything else without some professional help -- a lawyer, a realtor, a home inspector, whatever, so why should this be any different?

The best part of having someone who knows what she or he is doing help you buy a car is that (unlike other advisors) he/she will probably save you enough to pay his/her fee, and maybe a little more.

If you can find a person who does it for a living (a broker), that's probably your best bet. But those folks can be hard to find because most dealers hate them and often won't work with them, which ought to explain their value to a consumer.

Failing that, look for a knowledgeable amateur. These folks are around everywhere, and your research time will probably be better spent finding one of them than looking into double-secret factory rebates and stuff like that.

If it looks like they know what they're doing, be willing to pay them a decent amount of money for their time. If you pay them, say, $250 a day to talk to you about what kind of car you want and then go with you to car dealers and talk to salesmen and what have you, it will likely be money well spent, especially if you're looking for something other than an entry-level car.

That raises an interesting point: the more expensive the car you want, the more room there is for dealers to jack you around on the final price. If you're at the bottom end of the price ladder in a basic car, there isn't as much room for them to hide extra profit in the final price.

You could also consider something from Saturn, which is still the industry leader in no-haggle, no-hassle sales and is building up a nice selection of products as well. This pretty much guarantees that you won't run into someone with the same car as you who paid less money for it.

The AAA also runs a car-buying program that arranges fixed prices for various models, which means you'll likely get a decent bargain with a lot less angst on the side.

Finally, when you settle on a car and a price, don't open yourself up for heartache by asking everybody you see with a similar car how much they spent. This is as risky as asking the person sitting next to you on an airplane how much she paid for her ticket, or the person behind you in the checkout line how much she paid for her hotel room. This is the down-side of a free-market economy.

# Try Out And Consider As
# Many Cars As You Can

Maybe you think all vehicles are the same so it makes no difference.

Maybe you don't want to spend that much time looking at different models.

Maybe you haven't been warned.

No matter the reason, we kindly advise you to put yourself in as many vehicles as you possibly can before making a decision on a new car.

Experience shows us that many people abandon their original choices for a new vehicle because they find something unexpected that suits them better.

It's like dating a bunch of guys who fit some vision you have for the perfect man and not finding anyone worth hanging on to and then falling for someone with few if any of the traits you thought you wanted. Only it's easier to dump the wrong guy than it is to get rid of the wrong car.

Auto shows are the automotive equivalent of those speed-dating events and there are no feelings to hurt. Just sitting behind the wheel of a car at an auto show can give you a good idea of how a car will be to live with.

Get the seat in the right position (see Page 8 for info on how close you should sit) and then pretend to use the car the way you will in real life.

Can you see out of it okay, can you reach stuff, is there a good spot for your favorite beverage, are you comfortable, and all that.

Sit in every vehicle in your general price range and see how they all feel. You might be surprised at how different two cars that seem to be the same thing can feel.

Buying the first car you look at is like marrying the first guy you date, and you know how well that's going to work out.

# The Essential Ingredients
## For Buying A New Car

The three things that are absolutely essential to buying a car from a dealer yourself and getting the best deal are:

-Time. You must have a good deal of time to spend on the process, since pressure to meet a deadline puts you at a disadvantage and can lead to you making a bad deal.

-Research. Look at the market you're buying in (the dealers you're considering and so on) and the type of vehicle you need (note we didn't say "want") to a degree you might think borders on the obsessive-compulsive.

-Determination. At any stage of the process (right up to the "I do" moment) you must be willing to walk away the second you think you're being pressured to do something you do not want to do.

If you're not willing to commit this deeply to the traditional haggling process, it might make more sense to consider an alternative method of buying -- brokers, car-buying service, or a no-dicker dealer.

Your commitment to these three demands should grow in direct relation to the general price of the vehicles you're considering. The higher the MSRP, the greater the risk of your paying too much and the greater the reward if you drive the price down.

There's a smaller markup on a $15,000 vehicle than there is on a $25,000 vehicle, and more on a $30,000 vehicle and so on. Plus, it's harder to hide a big profit lump in a $15,000 car.

Bearing in mind that getting the holy grail of price reductions takes a lot of time in research, preparation, driving around and talking to sales people, and that there are other ways to save some or all of the money on a purchase, you need to decide if the commitment is worth it.

# The Essential Strategy
# For Buying A New Car

Once you've decided on the vehicle you want, here's what you have to do to get the best price:

-Check Edmunds.com and KBB.com to find out what the dealer wholesale prices of your vehicle are, with any company rebates for the dealer factored in.

-Decide how much you're willing to give the dealer over and above his cost.

-Arrange your financing for that amount in advance.

-Go to a dealer that sells the car you want and offer him your maximum figure, which will cover the vehicle cost, any factory transportation charges, "dealer fees" and anything else except what you're legally obligated to pay -- taxes, license fees and whatever else some level of government requires.

-Make the offer upfront so you don't waste anyone's time, which might be enough to make the dealer see the value of a quick sale for less than he really wants. This also shows him you're ready to deal and to walk if necessary.

-If he accepts your offer, say no to extended warranties, rust-proofing and everything else he tries to add.

-If he declines the offer that you're determined to stick to, walk away.

-Go to other dealers who sell the car you want until one of them agrees to your offer. (You don't have to return there for servicing, so don't worry about ever going back.)

-If you keep going to dealers and they keep refusing your offer, it may be time to reconsider your original offer.

-If you decide to raise your price, repeat the dealer-visitation process until you get the vehicle you want.

-Keep track of the hours you spend making this work. If you're burning up a lot of time to save $250 or something, you might want to be flexible on your top price.

# Post-Deal Transport Charges
# Are Not Mandatory Fees

By far the biggest trick played on consumers by the auto industry is the notion that somehow the "transportation" or "delivery" or "preparation" fees that they add after you've agreed on a purchase price are mandatory.

This is absolutely not true. There is no legal requirement for you to pay anything other than government-mandated taxes or fees after you've agreed on a price with the dealership. Those fees are nothing more than efforts to get more money out of you after you think you've come to terms.

Dealers count on you being so tired of the whole bargaining process that you'll just let it go as one of those unfortunate but unavoidable extra costs of doing business. They know that, and that's why they present the extra amount as some kind of compulsory charge over which they have no control. In truth, it's a subterfuge carefully designed by the car company and the dealership working together to get more money from you.

The process of fooling the customer begins when the car company announces an MSRP for a new car and a delivery charge as a separate item. These numbers are duly passed on without comment by the media, who don't care enough about their readers' interests or are worried about upsetting the dealers who advertise with them.

The delusion on this point is so fixed and widespread that even people who should know better (the Canadian Automobile Association is a recent example), haven't figured out it's a mass delusion.

If you decided to buy a coat from Nordstrom's for, say, $500 and then the clerk told you there was also a $50 "destination" charge even though you'd carried the coat to the counter and you planned to wear it home, what would you do? Agree to pay the fee or tell the clerk the deal was off unless the store waived it? That is exactly the same situation you're in with a new car and a destination charge. You can agree to pay the fee or tell the salesperson the deal is off. The dealer can then decide if he wants to sell you the car for the agreed-upon price.

As always, your best move in a situation like this is to walk. The dealer may or may not agree to stick to the agreed on price without the destination charge, but there is no reason in the world that you have to pay it.

## Get A Personal View Of Dealer On The Net

By and large shoppers tend to use the Internet for general information about what kind of cars to buy and how to get the best deal, and that's good.

But you might find a whole other level of enlightenment if you use the net to search for references to individual dealers, dealer-principles (the owners), managers, service managers, or sales people, particularly if you also include words that suggest consumer dissatisfaction in your search terms.

We discovered the usefulness of this when we searched "contractors" and "criminal charges" in our area and found a renovations firm we were thinking of hiring.

Searching that way on the net might help you to tap directly into the real-life experiences of other consumers with that dealership and its staff, and that might cause you to rethink your opinions.

For example, if you were thinking of buying a car in northern California and came upon the website that we found by accident you would want to reconsider buying from the dealer that is the subject of a scathing indictment until you got more details about its history.

Get creative and specific in your search terms and the net can be an extremely useful resource for the smart shopper.

# Paying Invoice Price Or Less
# May Be Harder Than It Sounds

It's widely believed that getting as close to the "dealer invoice" price as possible is the holy grail for new car shoppers, since any price below that means the dealer's losing money.

Leave a couple of hundred dollars above invoice on the table so the dealer makes a little profit -- that's only fair, isn't it? -- and walk away thinking you've done well by yourself.

Well, you probably have done well by yourself, but you almost certainly haven't gotten to the bottom of a dealer's profit margin.

This is because the relationship between the dealer, the auto manufacturer and whatever financial institutions are involved is usually quite complicated.

The primary aspect of that relationship that concerns profits for the dealer involves what the industry calls "holdbacks," which are essentially incentives for the dealer that vary by the amount of time a vehicle's on the lot. The less time a car's on the lot, the more the dealer gets.

So if you're really aggressive and are looking at a car that's newly arrived on the lot, you can certainly try to push below "dealer invoice" for an even lower price. The salesman may not have any idea of what the "holdback" is or even if it exists, but someone in authority will if you press.

This may not get you any more savings and they may deny the existence of "holdbacks" or the moon or even themselves if it makes them some extra money, but there could be an opportunity for you there if you're willing to put the time and emotional effort into it.

For everyone else looking for a new car, the key point might be that the process of buying is more complicated than you ever thought and is undoubtedly designed to give the dealers more of an advantage than the customers have.

# Pick A Dealer You Like
## Rather Than A Car You Like

If you're simply looking for an appliance that allows you to be mobile and you don't care about image or brand or whatever, the smartest move could be to buy the best dealer you can find rather than the best car.

After all, virtually every vehicle on the market today is of similar quality and content to the others in its segment (GM models with their OnStar safety and security system being the significant exception). So if you don't really care what brand you drive and the models in the segment are pretty much in a tie, maybe you ought to put more weight on the issue of dealing with the dealer.

That is to say, if there's a dealer who has a reputation for treating people well, offering fair prices, raising money for charity, supporting community events, offering exceptional service treatment, or whatever floats your boat, consider buying what he or she has on offer that suits your needs.

It may not work in your particular situation, but it could be a great way to cut down on the aggravation that often comes from dealing with a dealer.

## Not Going To Dealers For Service

Contrary to widespread belief fostered by dealers, the owners of vehicles under warranty do NOT have to use that dealer or any other dealer representing the company that built the car for the required maintenance. Warranties remain valid if scheduled maintenance is done by any qualified service facility or person who is skilled in automotive service. You just need to make sure all the required maintenance is done and keep the receipts for the work and have the service person complete the maintenance record.

# Why You Should Ignore
# Those Famous Quality Studies

In general, if you're trying to decide which vehicle to buy, those famous product quality studies from JD Power and other consulting firms should play no -- NO -- role in your thinking. Yes, these studies are extremely important in helping you get a high-quality vehicle, but there's no reason for you to consult them first.

The only Power study you should examine is the Sales Satisfaction Study, which charts consumers' experiences at the dealerships, since picking the right dealer (regardless of the brand) for sales and service is more important to you than the quality rankings of individual models. As for the initial quality study, here's why you should pay it no heed:

According to the study, the average consumer who buys a new vehicle today -- regardless of price, brand, country of origin or anything else -- will have about 1.25 issues with that vehicle in the first three months. That's right, you're likely to have only one thing that displeases you no matter what kind of car you buy. Virtually no one will have more than two issues with that vehicle in the first three months, and many people won't even have one. (See accompanying chart for specifics by automotive brand.)

If they do have an issue with a new vehicle, it will most likely involve things like not liking the feel of the volume knob on the stereo system, or being disappointed with the real-world fuel economy, or noting a difference in the color match of two interior pieces, or hearing too much wind noise. It is possible that these issues may include serious mechanical failures but statistically, those studies make clear, that's more unlikely now than ever before.

These surveys also make no effort to weight these issues differently, so the engines in Toyota's expensive new Tundra pickup self-destructing are judged to be no more of a problem than those regarding the texture of those volume control knobs.

Furthermore, these results are not scientifically determined through the use of precision measuring equipment or some pre-determined standard, nor are they the seasoned findings of trained engineers. They are instead the completely subjective opinions of the car buyers themselves, most of whom have little to no experience in the comparative value of various vehicles. So if you were to look at a vehicle that was judged harshly for some reason, you may love the way the volume knob feels, not notice the color mismatch or the wind noise, and be delighted with the real-world fuel economy. You may instead have an issue with the texture of the sun visor or the sound the trunk makes when it opens remotely or who knows what, which concerns no other person in the universe. That's the kind of subjective feelings the survey takers record as "problems".

It's also important to point out that the studies of J. D. Power and the others have been reporting these kinds of results for years, with companies floating up and down the ratings for no apparent reason and to no great effect. More importantly, the industry-wide commitment to quality will almost certainly keep things going like this for a long time to come.

If you do have a "problem" that requires care, the car dealers and manufacturers will likely be delighted to fix any issues or complaints you might have as soon as you point them out, usually for free.

All of this adds up to an annual report that should not get the media attention it does, and the results of which should have zero affect on your buying decision.

The primary lesson for the consumer from this truth about the various quality surveys is that there is essentially no difference in quality in a new vehicle, so you should not worry

# J.D.Power and Associates

## 2007 Initial Quality Study Nameplate

## Ranking of "Problems" per vehicle

| | | | |
|---|---|---|---|
| **Porsche** | **0.91** | **GMC** | **1.31** |
| Lexus | 0.94 | Nissan | 1.32 |
| **Lincoln** | **1.00** | **Saturn** | **1.32** |
| Honda | 1.08 | BMW | 1.33 |
| **Mercedes-Benz** | **1.11** | **Pontiac** | **1.33** |
| Jaguar | 1.12 | Saab | 1.33 |
| **Toyota** | **1.12** | **Subaru** | **1.33** |
| Mercury | 1.13 | Cadillac | 1.35 |
| **Infiniti** | **1.17** | **Audi** | **1.36** |
| Ford | 1.20 | Chrysler | 1.51 |
| **Scion** | **1.23** | **Suzuki** | **1.53** |
| Hyundai | 1.25 | Mitsubishi | 1.55 |
| **Kia** | **1.25** | **Dodge** | **1.56** |
| *Industry Average* | *1.25* | Volkswagen | 1.60 |
| **Buick** | **1.27** | **Jeep** | **1.61** |
| Chevrolet | 1.29 | HUMMER | 1.62 |
| **Volvo** | **1.29** | **Mazda** | **1.63** |
| Acura | 1.30 | Land Rover | 1.70 |

Insufficient responses from Mini and Isuzu owners to quantify so much about buying a new vehicle because you're afraid it will give you grief. This means that you can instead concentrate on the vehicle's appeal to your heart more than your head, or simply pick the best price.

If this all comes as a surprise to you, that's because the people doing the quality surveys and the media reporting them tend to ignore this reality for their own reasons.

The survey takers insist on presenting their findings as "things gone wrong" per 100 vehicles, which tends to make things look more serious than "things gone wrong per vehicle" would. It's not in their best business interests to tell you that all of the car companies make vehicles of essentially the same quality. So they tend to present the results like sports scores, lumping the teams from the U.S., Asia and Europe together so they can make totally useless comments about one group catching the other.

Unfortunately most of the media falls for this and that's why you see stories with a "first past the post" angle. So you get headlines like "U.S catching Japanese in quality" or "Japanese still ahead of US vehicles in quality" or whatever. That's apparently of more interest to them than the reality that gives the consumer some helpful information.

To be fair to the media, those stories do serve a useful consumer function because the executives of all the car companies are afraid that their firm will slip a little (to 1.24 issues per vehicle, say, from 1.22) and some reporter will write "Toyota slips in the quality standings" or something like that.

This connects directly to the real value of the Power quality study and others like it -- the very real desire of the car companies' executives to come out on top, to not be embarrassed in print, to qualify for a bonus, to not have to explain to an irate boss why they failed. The fear of reading similar headlines continues to be a primary motivation in the fight to maintain the highest quality standards, and we should applaud that.

As for those ludicrous accusations from various websites and bloggers that the Power rankings are cooked -- well, no one would ever believe that if they were ever in the company of a senior auto executive the moment he or she learns the results. The shock, joy, disappoint, fear, whatever is obviously genuine and is repeated regularly around the industry. Whatever else they may, the J. D. Power results are honest comments from real people and that pulls weight with the car companies.

So when the time comes to pick a vehicle you have to live with for the next three or four years, ignore the quality findings of J. D. Power and the others and just get the car you really like, or can best afford, or matches your luggage, or brings out the color of your boyfriend's eyes, or makes you feel successful, or whatever you want a car to do. There's an excellent chance it will treat you as well as any other model you might pick.

## Online Video Of Cars At DriverTV.com

If you want to look over the possible choices for a new car to prepare you to buy/lease one, you might want to check out www.driverTV.com.

The web channel broadcasts extensive video tours of most of the new models sold in North America, with lots of helpful data (specs, prices, etc.) in support and gives you links to dealers and insurance companies for quotes. There's an audio guide, pause, rewind and fast forward controls, and many other functions.

While the car companies pay to prepare the videos to a format and to keep them on the air, the overall tone is pretty straightforward, with a soupcon of boosterism. It's the kind of comprehensive overview you rarely get at a dealer, and there are no polyester sports coats to be seen anywhere.

# Cars That Drive Themselves Are Coming
# Really, This Time It's True

Recently the chairman and CEO of General Motors presented a car to the public that has been a favorite dream of sci-fi writers, futurologists, engineering geeks, traffic planners, safety advocates and multi-tasking mothers for decades -- a vehicle that drives itself.

Yes, you've heard that before, but this time the auto world really means it, and it's probably closer than you can even imagine.

Something like a GM concept vehicle called "The Boss" could be on the market in a decade or so. One of the key technologies to such a vehicle -- active cruise control -- is already available on many production models and is coming on more. Many of the other technical elements to a drive-itself vehicle (such as lane-departure warning) are starting to appear on new cars, and others are being developed in laboratories, basements and garages all around the world.

The results of this work have been on show for the past couple of years in a contest run by the U.S. government to build a vehicle that is capable of driving itself, and there has been astounding progress in a short time. In the first contest in 2004, none of the vehicles made it through 10 miles of desert terrain. By the third event, late in 2007, a half-dozen cars found their way around a 60-mile traffic-filled course without incident.

The government's intent is to have vehicles that can do dangerous armed services work without having to risk lives, but the real world application speaks directly to the desire of ordinary people to have more time to do something more productive or amusing instead of driving a car through stop-and-go traffic.

This is technology that everyone can appreciate.

**Alexander Law & Susan Winlaw   153**

# Buying The "Best" Car In A Category
## May Be The Worst Choice

If you're one of those people who absolutely, positively has to buy a product or service widely perceived to be "The Best" of its kind regardless of its price or the reliability of the rating or any other reason, then we can't help you. All we can do is wish you well and hope that you don't live to regret it from some crash site outside of cell phone range in the middle of the night, or when you find you can't afford that perfect new jacket because your car payments are too high.

As for those of you who aren't interested in paying more for appearances sake, take a moment to thank your less self-assured friends for their attitude because they tend to create a market situation that provides you with a chance to save a lot of money from not buying "The Best".

To be sure, it probably makes a lot of sense to go with "The Best" in some situations, such as having your tumor removed by the brain surgeon with the highest survival rate, the lowest insurance premium, and the admiration of all her peers. But buying a particular car because some publication or group finds it worthy of praise is not as smart a decision.

In the first place, such brandings are often flawed or reflect too deeply the specialized interests of the group or agency passing out the hosannas.

In the second place the differences in new vehicles today are so narrow when it comes to quality, performance and equipment that paying a lot more for one particular model doesn't make any sense. But before we explain how that can work to the smart buyer's benefit, it's worth taking a look at those ratings that cause inflated reputations for some brands.

Any blessings bestowed by automotive writers or automotive publications or TV shows almost always reflect the vehicle's skills in the kind of aggressive driving that usually makes passengers sick and/or scared. This applies to family-friendly vehicles like minivans, SUVs, four-door sedans and the new crossovers as much as it does to sportscars, and for many potential buyers of non-performance cars that should make the advice suspect.

You even have to have some salt on hand when you're given recommendations from agencies and groups with good reputations. The Insurance Institute for Highway Safety (the IIHS) has worked hard to promote its crash-test findings through the media, but particularly TV. These reports have driven all of the car companies to make more of an effort to do well on their tests, and for that we should all be grateful. But it's important to remember that the IIHS is an arm of the insurance industry. That relationship forces the IIHS to be motivated by the need to find and promote vehicles that allow the insurance companies to pay out less for crash repairs and medical treatment. If this also keeps the people inside those vehicles safer, that's a bonus. This kind of thinking causes the IIHS to brand vehicles as the "safest" based purely on their abilities during specific kinds of crashes, which represent only a small portion of the kinds of crashes that take place and ignore completely the importance of crash-avoidance and crash-notification.

Finally, there is the kind of praise that banks too heavily on past accomplishments, the most famous example of which is the belief that Honda and Toyota are way ahead of the pack in terms of quality. While that was undoubtedly true 20 years ago when this legend was born, it is no longer the case. In virtually all surveys, all vehicles and brands are so close it's hard for a rational person to separate them.

But over-inflated reputations live on like a bad smell and that's all a lot of people remember when the time comes to buy a car, and that's what creates the opportunity for the smart buyer.

# Buick Ties Lexus In Long-Term Durability And Reliability

The headline of this story should be information enough for people who insist on keeping their minds closed about the current reality of automotive quality.

Actually, it's not the current reality of automotive quality, since the J. D. Power study involved cars bought new in 2004. Since then, of course, Toyota/Lexus quality has taken a dive (the company has been apologizing about it for some time) and the quality level of all of GM's products has gotten better or stayed the same.

The key lessons on quality are:

-there is no more gap for the domestic brands to be closing with the Japanese,

-all of the car companies are essentially in a multi-model tie for the top spot with a range in reported quality so thin the differences aren't worth mentioning, and

-cost has very little to do with how well the car's built.

Quality studies can now be likened to taking a photo of a race that never ends, in which all the cars run in a tight pack and everyone takes a turn at the front.

Who's in front depends upon when you take the picture.

So it is indeed very much like a Nascar race, and just as boring for the enlightened person.

Better to worry about how convenient a dealer will be for service than the quality of his products.

## Dealers May Get You Cars They Don't Sell

If you have a dealership you really like or trust but it doesn't have the product you want, ask them to get you the car you desire. Many dealers will be glad to do this and it may even cost you less than buying the car directly.

# Buying Too Much Vehicle Is A Common Mistake For Many People

Because they want to be hospitable or ready for emergencies or to cover more contingencies, many people buy a lot more new vehicle than they really need, and they almost always pay more for the privilege -- through things like higher purchase prices, greater insurance costs, and increased fuel use.

Just check out the passenger content of other vehicles you see on the road (particularly seven-seat SUVs) and you'll discover that the vast majority of them will have only a driver, and almost none of them will have a full complement, especially the seven-seaters.

In fact, there's a very good chance you won't see any vehicles at all carrying five people, even if some are kids.

Not only aren't you going to see many vehicles carrying a lot of people, you are also not likely to see any vehicles hauling any cargo of any kind, unless they're vehicles purchased specifically for commercial use.

There's nothing wrong with this, of course, and you should never forget that size has a lot to do with vehicle safety. (See Page 18 for more on that.)

But if you're concerned about saving money, perhaps you might want to scale back your thoughts about how big a vehicle you really need. Go with a five-seater, perhaps, or a seven-seat mid-size SUV rather than a seven-seat full-size SUV. You will almost certainly save money if you do go for something a little smaller. If those situations arrive where you actually need more capacity, use a second vehicle, even if you have to rent it.

By all means get the model you want, but give a little thought to what kind of vehicle you actually need in the life you actually lead.

# For Many Consumers Leasing
# Can Be The Best Financial Choice

Before we present an enthusiastic view of leasing and what it can do for you if you're smart, a few words of caution on automotive finance in general.

New vehicles are an enormously expensive proposition and the people selling them are likely to be vastly more experienced than you at getting the best deal possible for themselves out of a welter of conflicting and confusing choices. A great number of those people will be delighted to overcharge you, and there are some who will even cheat you if the situation presents itself.

So enormous caution is required before you sign anything or turn over any money. Take your time and view every single part of the deal in depth. Each deal is different and usually has several alternative financing choices and it is up to you to examine them all to establish the best choice for you. This is where government consumer bureaus can be handy, and where endless websites supply all kinds of technical information. This is the time when the old Latin warning of "caveat emptor" (let the buyer beware) is particularly important.

Our purpose in this section is to point out some positive aspects of leasing, which are often played down or even completely ignored in the typical advice story. Let's start with the most obvious and finish with the one no one ever talks about.

-Leasing provides the easiest way to stay in a car that's entirely covered by a warranty, which is the key method of avoiding the extra aggravation and costs associated with out-of-warranty service work. You lease for as long as the car's covered by the comprehensive warranty (which is sometimes referred to as the "bumper-to-bumper" warranty) lasts (usually three but sometimes four years with more expensive vehicles), turn the car in and lease something new. Along with reducing the boredom factor that comes with having the same vehicle too long, the vehicle you lease in three years will almost certainly be safer, more fuel efficient and deliver much better value for the dollar.

-Leasing allows you to get more vehicle for the money, since lease payments are typically about two-thirds of a traditional finance package. So you could lease, say, a Cadillac for the monthly rate you would buy a Buick, or lease a BMW 5-Series for the monthly rate of buying a 3-Series, and so on and so on. This can be a status thing or a comfort thing, but it's also true that you probably end up with a safer vehicle because more expensive cars are usually larger and larger cars are almost always safer.

-Depending upon where you live there can be tax benefits associated with leasing that do not apply to traditional finance. This one you need to check yourself.

-Depending upon what you do and how you're paid for it, there may be tax deduction values with leasing that don't come with regular financing.

-You may also pay less money in taxes since you're not buying the vehicle at its full price. What you're actually doing with a lease is paying for the vehicle's depreciation.

-Leasing is also the best way to finance a vehicle that you plan to keep for a long time, which is where we take a step beyond traditional advice and get into the part of the leasing-borrowing debate that's rarely if ever mentioned.

Here's how that works: If you buy a vehicle using traditional financing, you borrow the amount you need after a down payment and you pay that back (plus interest) to the bank or whatever in monthly installments. If you lease a vehicle you have to pay monthly installments to cover the amount that vehicle will depreciate in the time you're driving it, which is a smaller figure than the full purchase price. Usually, a lease payment on a vehicle will be about two-thirds of a traditional loan. For the sake of this discussion, let's say the monthly loan payment for a certain vehicle is $650 and the lease payment is $450.

This difference in payments is of course the primary attraction for the lease-em-and-move-on types, but it's not seen as a positive thing for the buy-the-car-outright types, and that's the mistake.

If you finance the whole price of a vehicle up front, you make the payments for three, four or maybe five years and the car's yours. If you lease the depreciation for three years but want to keep the vehicle at that time, you finance the vehicle's remaining value and pay for two or three more years until there's nothing left to pay and the vehicle is totally yours.

Depending upon the precise costs of the loan versus the lease in this scenario, endless studies show that leasing can cost you maybe 3 to 5 percent more than traditional bank financing. As a result of that, most of the common advice maintains, using leases to finance an outright purchase is a bad thing. But if you factor in the principles of cash flow and money management, that advice is wrong.

The element that's rarely discussed but should be is "What did you do with that $200 a month you weren't using for the car payment?" That's $2,400 a year, or $7,200 over a three-year lease.

Maybe you spend it on something else you need or want, like a better place to live, or a nicer holiday, or more upscale clothes, or whatever pleases you. So you have the same vehicle, but your standard of living is better for a very small cost; three percent more on a $25,000 vehicle is only $750, which you can more easily afford three years from now because of your improved earning power.

Maybe you take that $200 a month and put it into something that earns interest or gains in value for some other reason, so that when the time comes in three years to re-lease the vehicle you have at least $7,500 and maybe more to use to make the payments on the remaining cost. If you get into the right kind of investment, it could possibly reduce your total cost to less than what traditional financing costs.

If you have enough money in the bank to make a down payment on a leased vehicle, do not offer it up as a down payment. Negotiate the price with no cash down and use the funds you were going to use for a down payment to make the monthly payments.

The bad part of this plan would of course involve a significant spike in interest rates between the end of the lease and the start of the new financing, but if that happens and it's a strain on you, you're likely going to have bigger problems to deal with than car payments. Indeed, the $7,500 or so you've been saving may be just what you need to solve some other problem, and you can always turn the car back to the dealer and go another way.

Though things can always go wrong for the whole national economy or just yours, you'd do well to remember these two famous financial maxims: Buy what appreciates, lease what depreciates, and try to use other people's money.

## Being "Upside Down" In A Car

If you owe more than your car is worth, the auto industry calls it being "upside down." The big risk is that you'll be in a crash and the insurance company will pay you less than you owe on the car, which can cost you some money.

But you can get pricey insurance to cover that risk, and the only way to avoid being "upside down" at some point is coming up with a huge down payment to cover the severe depreciation that happens when you drive off the lot for the first time.

# Certified Used Vehicles Come With Higher Costs And More Satisfaction

Though you always have to take great care when you're spending that much money, especially when you're doing business with a car dealer, you will probably find that buying a "certified" used vehicle will cost you more but result in a better experience.

That at least is the primary finding of studies of the "certified" used car market that began to blossom early in this century. It has been gaining in popularity ever since, and is likely to be an even bigger part of the car dealers' business plan with the slowing down of new cars sales. Without the profits from a new car sale, they have to push for the bigger profits from "certified used" sales.

Car companies push the idea that they're providing buyers with new car reliability for used car prices thanks to a rigorous examination of each unit before it gains the "certified" label and the limited warranty that goes with it.

More and more people like the very idea of this and sign up for more "certified" used cars every year and, it must be noted, are happier with them than they are with regular used cars and about as happy as most new car buyers.

As a result, buyers do not mind paying more for "certified" used cars, paying about $2,000 more on average than what the same model costs as a regular used car.

"Certified" used cars from the manufacturers are usually units from the last few model years and almost never have more than 50,000-60,000 miles (100,000 km) on the clock. The car companies put them through an inspection process that covers major mechanical items as well as things like windshield wiper integrity.

It's worth mentioning that anyone can call a used vehicle "certified" just like any restaurant can say their coffee's the "best in town," and this is where the consumer needs to be careful. For example, it probably pays to stick with cars with a "certified" status from a manufacturer, rather than a dealer. There's an important difference there; you should not equate the car company and one of its dealers as being the same thing. There have been times with the manufacturer has legally declined responsibility for a "certified" used car because it was approved by the dealer, not by them.

To clear that hurdle, check the paperwork closely to see whose name is on the agreement; if it doesn't look like a contract with the manufacturer, stay away until you find out for sure that it's not a contract with the dealer.

There have also been times when cars that were severely damaged in crashes have turned up as "certified" models, and at least one famous case where the front end of one car and the rear end of another become a "certified" used car. The legality of that is still being argued in the courts. Several groups are suing the federal government to bring some order to this mess.

There are consumer experts who argue that paying more for a "certified" vehicle isn't worth the extra money, but the car companies argue in turn that they are worth more because they come with more warranty coverage than an ordinary used car.

So check the warranty details and check the car yourself, or pay someone to do it, and buy a "certified" used car if you want. The studies do show that you're likely to have a better experience than if you buy a regular used car, and that it will cost you more.

## Leasing Used Can Save You Money

Leasing a car when it's new makes a lot of sense (see Page 158) and for the same reasons leasing used vehicles can make sense. Check out www.FrontRowCars.com.

# All Warranties Are Not Created Equal In Coverage Or Length

For the most part, every new vehicle sold in North America today comes with two types of warranties. On the other hand, three major players (Honda, Scion and Toyota) still aren't offering roadside assistance.

There's the basic or "comprehensive" warranty that guarantees that the company will pay for any faults or failures in the product for a certain time or distance. The exceptions to this are the stuff that suffers wear and tear, like wiper blades, oil filters and so on. Tires and batteries might be covered by the car company warranty or might be covered by the firms that made them.

Then there's the "drivetrain" or powertrain warranties that cover the mechanical system that makes the car move, which includes the engine, transmission, driveshaft, axles and so on. Again, parts that suffer wear-and-tear, like belts and hoses are not covered. For the most part, this is supposed to look after the kind of catastrophic engine or transmission failure that would cost you a fortune to repair yourself. You shouldn't pay too much attention to the warranties if you plan to lease the car and give it up before the basic warranty runs out, but you should if you're planning to keep it a long time.

## Warranty Coverage

| Make | Basic | Drivetrain | Roadside Assistance |
|------|-------|-----------|---------------------|
| Acura | 4/50,000 | 6/70,000 | 4/50,000 |
| Audi | 4/50,000 | 4/50,000 | 4/Unlimited |
| BMW | 4/50,000 | 4/50,000 | 4/50,000 |
| Buick | 4/50,000 | 5/100,000 | 5/100,000 |
| Cadillac | 4/50,000 | 5/100,000 | 5/100,000 |
| Chevrolet | 3/36,000 | 5/100,000 | 5/100,000 |

# Warranty Coverage

| Brand | Basic | Drivetrain | Roadside Assistance |
|---|---|---|---|
| **Chrysler** | **3/36,000** | **3/36,000** | **3/36,000** |
| Dodge | 3/36,000 | 3/36,000 | 3/36,000 |
| **Ford** | **3/36,000** | **5/60,000** | **5/60,000** |
| GMC | 3/36,000 | 5/100,000 | 5/100,000 |
| **Honda** | **3/36,000** | **5/60,000** | **None Available** |
| HUMMER | 4/50,000 | 5/100,000 | 5/100,000 |
| **Hyundai** | **5/60,000** | **10/100,000** | **5/Unlimited** |
| Infiniti | 4/60,000 | 6/70,000 | 4/60,000 |
| **Isuzu** | **3/50,000** | **7/75,000** | **7/75,000** |
| Jaguar | 4/50,000 | 4/50,000 | 4/50,000 |
| **Jeep** | **3/36,000** | **3/36,000** | **3/36,000** |
| Kia | 5/60,000 | 10/100,000 | 5/60,000 |
| **Land Rover** | **4/50,000** | **4/50,000** | **4/50,000** |
| Lexus | 4/50,000 | 6/70,000 | 4/Unlimited |
| **Lincoln** | **4/50,000** | **6/70,000** | **6/70,000** |
| Mazda | 3/36,000 | 5/60,000 | 3/36,000 |
| **Mercedes-Benz** | **4/50,000** | **4/50,000** | **Unlimited** |
| Mercury | 3/36,000 | 5/60,000 | 5/60,000 |
| **MINI** | **4/50,000** | **4/50,000** | **3/36,000** |
| Mitsubishi | 5/60,000 | 10/100,000 | 5/Unlimited |
| **Nissan** | **3/36,000** | **5/60,000** | **3/36,000** |
| Pontiac | 3/36,000 | 5/100,000 | 5/100,000 |
| **Porsche** | **4/50,000** | **4/50,000** | **4/50,000** |
| Saab | 4/50,000 | 5/100,000 | 5/100,000 |
| **Saturn** | **3/36,000** | **5/100,000** | **5/100,000** |
| Scion | 3/36,000 | 5/60,000 | None Available |
| **Subaru** | **3/36,000** | **5/60,000** | **3/36,000** |
| Suzuki | 3/36,000 | 7/100,000 | 3/36,000 |
| **Toyota** | **3/36,000** | **5/60,000** | **None Available** |
| Volkswagen | 4/50,000 | 5/60,000 | 4/Unlimited |
| **Volvo** | **4/50,000** | **4/50,000** | **4/Unlimited** |

Warranties are in Years/Miles format. For more specifics & exceptions see the company website or contact the dealer.

## Alexander Law & Susan Winlaw

## Avoid Last-Minute Sales Pitches
## No Matter What's On Offer

The general rule of thumb involving services the dealer tries to sell you after you've agreed on a price for a new car and are about to sign the contract is to say "No No No No No No" until they give up and finalize the original deal.

Say "No thanks" if you feel the need to be polite, but they might mistake that for a sign of weakness and keep pressing you to buy something else.

And they are certainly going to press you, since the recent collapse of new car sales will have the dealers scrambling to replace lost sales profits with money from things they pitch customers at the last minute.

Saying no is the smart move even if it's something you might actually want or need (though that's unlikely to be on offer), since you can almost certainly get it after-the-fact and almost always for less money from someone else.

The only exception on this point might be some extra piece of equipment that you want to add to the vehicle you're buying, like better wheels, a towing package, a storage bin, whatever. Buying that kind of thing with the car from the dealer can spread the cost of the part across the duration of the financing and perhaps get the part included in the original car warranty and any future resale value. But you should make a decision on that kind of equipment long before you get to the moment of truth in the manager's office.

The favorite proposals from dealers at the contract signing are for rust proofing or extended warranties, but if they can think of something else that will make them extra dollars (lifetime bikini waxes, daily horoscopes for the car, anything) they'll try to sell you that as well.

Make no mistake, dealers are trying to sell you these things at the last moment for two reasons:

-You're probably worn out by the hassle of car shopping and are anxious to get your new vehicle and leave, so your defenses are down, and

-Selling you those items makes good financial sense for them, not for you.

The second point explains why lots of shoppers remark on how extreme the pressure from dealers can be for you to buy an extended warranty for that new car right there and then as you're hoping to get the heck out of there.

They may even flat-out lie to you about the need for you to buy a service before you take possession of the vehicle. This is all meant to pressure you into paying for a service that they are probably buying from someone else and have marked up as high as they think you're willing to go.

As for dealing with situations like this, there really isn't any specific advice we can give except to stay strong and stick to your guns.

If all else fails, you can simply get up and head for the door without signing the contract, which will likely cause them to change their attitude and finish the paperwork so you can have your car.

Being tough with people may not be in your nature, but when it comes to giving someone money for no good reason you should try it.

## Problems With Toyota Prius

Anyone who's thinking about buying a Toyota Prius needs to go to www.consumeraffairs.com and scan the story about buying a used Prius.

It lists a catalogue of nightmares for people who thought they were "living the dream" that should keep any potential owner awake.

It will shed a new light on Prius, Toyota quality in general, and abilities of the Toyota dealer network.

# Extended Warranties From Dealer
# Are Likely A Bad Idea

The irony of dealers selling extended warranties is not lost on many buyers, and the smart ones see it as a warning.

After all, the sales pitch at many dealerships involves relentless claims about the extraordinary quality levels of their new cars and their unmatched reliability and durability.

All of that is supposed to be forgotten when you've agreed to buy the car and are in the sales manager's office ready to sign the contract. All of a sudden you absolutely must have some expensive extended warranty package to stave off financial ruin from the mechanical breakdown that's likely to befall you a month after the original warranty runs out.

This about-face on quality stuns and confuses a lot of people (particularly Honda and Toyota buyers, who usually know little about cars), and causes them to buy the extended warranty right then.

But you should probably not buy an extended warranty from anyone (but particularly your dealer) since they probably won't save you anything in the long run.

A survey by Consumer Reports of thousands of people who bought extended warranties on all kinds of cars in the early part of the decade showed that they wasted their money.

But if you decide to buy an extended warranty (or anything else), you probably don't want to buy it from your dealer during the process of signing the contract.

You can get an extended warranty if you want at any time (not just during the purchase phase) and there are better places to get it. More on all that in a minute.

Sales people push extended warranties to help themselves, not you. They are usually acting as agents for the warranty company and if they can charge you two, three or four times what the warranty company will charge you for the same coverage they will do it. This business is a major profit source for dealers.

To get you to buy the extended warranty when you're signing the contract for your vehicle, it is not uncommon for the sales people to lie to you. They might tell you that extended warranties are only available while the car is still new, that you need an extended warranty to secure a loan, or to get insurance, or whatever else they can think of to force you to buy the coverage.

Don't believe any of this, and if they persist in trying to bully you into an extended warranty you should just get up and leave. Almost certainly they will change their tune and sign the original contract, but if they don't you're probably better off not doing a deal with that dealer in the first place.

As for the value of an extended warranty, it looks like its primary benefit is acting as an insurance policy. That is to say, even if you never have to use it you take comfort from knowing that it's there.

In terms of cost, extended warranties depend greatly on the model you own (some vehicles can't get it at all), when you buy it in the vehicle's life cycle (just like life insurance), and many other factors.

If mechanical issues beyond the standard comprehensive coverage that comes on all new cars concerns you, it's maybe wise to consider a model from a car company that offers longer powertrain warranties so you're covered longer. Not all problems you have will be covered by such prolonged coverage, but none of the problems will be covered if the coverage isn't there at all.

If you decide you want to buy an extended warranty a lot of work is required to find the right program, and there are lots of places on the web to help with that. We can think of no better place to start than the section on that very subject inside www.carbuyingtips.com.

# Avoiding Off-The-Rack Cars In Favor Of Custom-Made Makes Sense

Despite the growing trend in our society to things that are custom-made to suit our tastes and needs, when it comes to buying a new car the vast majority of us still suffer from "spontaneous consumption" disease, which requires you to get something right now as long as it's close to being what you want.

So you're willing to spend $20,000 and up for the model with the exterior color you sort of like because it comes with the interior trim he thinks is okay and the stereo system she wants because they decided this morning that they wanted a new car today and it's already 2 p.m.

While it is possible to spend more money after-the-fact to get a new vehicle closer to what you really want (see Page 230), it probably makes more sense to decide in advance what you really want and get the car company to build it for you.

This is the common way of doing things in Europe and has been promoted several times in North America, to little affect.

It probably means ordering the vehicle at least a couple of months before you take delivery, though there's likely to be a range of waiting times.

This is less of an issue now since a lot of the things that used to be options (remote locking, power windows, etc) are standard across the vehicle lineup and the internet has made it possible to search dealers in your area for a car that comes close to your needs.

Since it's not on the lot, the dealer's not paying interest on a loan that he took out to buy it in advance. You can perhaps make this point to push for a lower price, though the greatest leverage is actually on the oldest car on the lot since the interest charges are adding up.

# Look At Torque Rather Than
# Horsepower For Best Performance

Here's a handy rule-of-thumb about a car's power ratings to keep in mind while you're picking a new car:

Torque is more important when it comes to launching a vehicle from stop, while horsepower mostly matters if you want more speed for passing on a highway.

From that, it follows that most of us should be paying more attention to a vehicle's torque rating than its horsepower rating when shopping for a new car, since pulling away from a stop is a much more common experience for the majority of drivers than trying to get in front of another vehicle on a two-lane road.

You can check out the torque rating first, but the true test will come when you accelerate hard from a dead stop to maybe 40 mph. If you don't like the way the car feels in such a situation, neither its torque nor its horsepower ratings will matter.

For the most part, the car companies have probably already looked after setting up the vehicles' power ratings to suit consumer demand in that category. But it never hurts to look at the posted numbers so you can have a look at the second half of every horsepower and torque rating -- the rpm level.

That four-digit number tells you how many times per minute the cylinders are revolving when each maximum power level is reached.

In general, the lower that number the better for you and the engine, since it means less wear on the latter and fewer gas purchases for the former.

A lower rpm number should also mean less noise in the passenger compartment, if that matters to you. That's why you should keep the radio, the family and the sales-person dialed down to their lowest levels during the test drive.

# Consumer Reports Should Not Be
# The Last Word On Cars For Shoppers

Consumer Reports long ago worked its way to the top of the list of trusted sources for certain automobile information, and it probably deserves that ranking for passing on the experiences of previous owners.

But you're making a mistake if you put absolute faith in the magazine published by Consumers Union when it comes to rating cars and auto-related products, since there's significant evidence suggesting that the group is not as methodical, careful or impartial as it would like you to believe.

The best thing about the publication by far is the vehicle dependability data that it gathers from hundreds of thousands of people who actually own and operate cars in the real world. This is the world's largest collection of word-of-mouth information and it's probably the most critical piece of information available for anyone looking at used vehicles.

On the other hand, the stuff about new cars that comes out of the publication's testing program in Connecticut is not anywhere near as valuable to the consumer.

It's nothing more than the opinions of a small group of staff members who have exhibited an astonishing prejudice against cars and trucks from American car companies in favor of Honda and Toyota products.

They once recommended a Honda product that would cost the average consumer thousands of dollars more than what competitive models would cost, for no good reason.

Worst of all, the magazine has made a few amazing factual errors over the last couple of years, regarding the safety of infant car seats, the costs of operating a hybrid, and ignoring the huge value of crash-notification as a safety system.

A while back, the magazine admitted that it had been giving Toyota good marks on quality because the editors assumed Toyota products deserved them (a classic definition of "prejudice"), but wasn't going to do that any more.

Most recently, the magazine admitted that it had long known that Honda and the other Japanese car companies tend to set their odometers to show that they were covering more distance than they really were but said nothing. Indeed, Honda is by far the brand the Consmer Reports editors like the most. This is interesting when you think that Honda has agreed to pay out millions to redress this problem (it brought warranties to an end sooner, for one thing) and some of the others are being investigated.

On top of that, CR has never given OnStar its due.

Amazing. With all this going on, you have to wonder what other mistakes Consumer Reports has made.

So stick with the dependability reports of owners when it comes to Consumer Reports if you're looking to buy used, but be extremely careful about trusting the magazine's pet picks, recommended lists and everything else. In many ways, they're just like every other magazine in the world when it comes to writing about cars.

## Car-Buying Not Always Rational

After finishing university in the late 1960s, a friend of ours moved to Vancouver for her first job.

Some months later, she drove to the airport in her new convertible to pick up her mother on the occasion of her first visit to her daughter's new apartment. As they were heading into the city in the sunshine, the mother asked what kind of car they were in.

The daughter said: "A Mustang, Mom, a Ford Mustang."

The mother laughed. "A Ford? That's funny. You got your start in the back of a Ford."

To our certain knowledge, our friend has never owned another Ford and never will.

# Buy A New Car And Get
# A Trip To Europe To Go With It

Along with the economic benefits of buying certain European models in the U.S. and picking them up in Europe, there is also the emotional benefit of the unique holiday that goes along with that and, possibly, bragging rights over anyone else who owns a similar model. You will after all have the chance to drive your Audi, BMW, Mercedes, Porsche, Saab or Volvo on European roads, and that includes the legendary German autobahns with their unlimited speeds. Think of how jealous your friends and c-workers will be, but especially the ones who bought similar cars without going to Europe.

So you can tell your friends you saved maybe seven percent on the price of your new car, had a chance in Trollhatten to try the rotten fish that Swedes love, twisted along the Furka Pass through the Swiss Alps, and went blowing by a Porsche at 150 mph on the road from Cologne to Berlin.

These are the possibilities available to you through the European delivery programs operated by the companies that sell European-made vehicles in the U.S. and Canada, though the deal's not as good north of the border. You buy the car in North America and arrange to pick it up in one of several places in Europe, where you can drive it around and fly home when you're ready, with the car company looking after getting it shipped across the Atlantic to you.

These are broad stroke points of the European delivery program, and you will certainly want to think about such a deal if you're interested in buying a European car, have ever wanted to take a motor holiday in Europe, or would like a driving story to top anything your boring brother-in-law has in his repertoire.

You might even be able to get certain models more quickly if you pick them up in Europe than you can here, but you can't get models that aren't normally sold here. You also can't get the models that are built in North America, like that funny-looking BMW roadster.

Each of the programs is operated by the individual manufacturer and each has its unique wrinkles, incentives and methods of operating, so you'll want to look them up on the European delivery sections of their websites.

These are all well-established, manufacturer-backed programs, not some fly-by-night operations looking to make a fast buck. So this is as safe an offer as exists.

## TV Myths About Cars: Gunfire

Cops crouching behind the open doors of their squad car to protect themselves from bullets shot at them by bad guys is an enduring image on the screen, but regular car doors or even an entire car don't offer the police or anyone else much assistance from virtually any gun.

If you're ever in a situation that involves gunfire near you, the best safety feature of a car is its ability to drive you away from it.

Failing that, try running. The farther you are away from the shooter, after all, the lower the chance that a bullet will hit you.

If that isn't possible or doesn't seem prudent, turn the front of the car toward the source of the gunfire and get on the floor under the dash. That will put you behind the only part of your car that will provide you with any cover at all -- the engine block, which is the big metal box at the heart of all that mechanical gear under the hood.

But even the engine block might not be of much help if the bullets coming your way are big enough.

There are doors for police cars designed to work as anti-ballistic shields, but even they won't work if the bullets are big enough.

**Alexander Law & Susan Winlaw**　175

# Cars From China (Or India) Could Soon Be On Sale Here, Or Not

When exactly cars from China will arrive in North American showrooms is still a matter of conjecture (they would already be here if the original plan had come to fruition), but there's little doubt that the cheap cars will be here before the end of the decade or shortly after. The Chinese car makers have the same manufacturing costs advantage that originally brought low-priced Japanese and then Korean cars to this continent, so it seems inevitable. If the Chinese don't hurry to make the move, they might be beaten by companies from India, who have the same cheap manufacturing cost advantage.

The word "cheap" is used in the sense of "inexpensive," by the way, since no one who knows the North American market genuinely thinks auto consumers will sit still for "cheap" cars in the "poor-quality" sense, the way they did when the Japanese and Koreans arrived.

At the time of publishing, Chrysler had plans to sell a small car from China's Chery Automobile in 2009 as a Dodge model for about $10,000 (that's the current plan, at any rate), and a group called China Motors hopes to sell a $20,000 sedan across the U.S. late in 2008. Whatever happens, we can only hope the products will be up to North American standards in every regard, but particularly safety.

The safety issue will certainly be on the minds of North American consumers who recall the poisoned pet food from China. There were also safety concerns about fake drugs and shoddy tires that China has exported here.

In time, we should also see cars from Chinese companies wearing brand names belonging to GM and Ford, since both U.S.-based firms will be looking for an inexpensive place to source the small, low-cost models they will need to stay competitive if gas prices continue to rise enough to force consumers to cars they would previously ignore.

When that might happen is still an open question, but there will certainly be other efforts to use China's economic advantage to sell cars in the U.S. As the China Motors plan makes clear, it may not even be inexpensive cars from China. The Nanjing Automotive Group owns the rights to MG (an English sportscar) and had plans to build new models in Oklahoma. Other plans call for Chinese cars from Mexico.

There are already some Chinese cars on sale in Europe, so it's hard to equate that too closely to North America since there are now several former Eastern-bloc countries in Europe whose consumers aren't as demanding as buyers in Germany, France and other countries.

Whatever happens in the short-term, it seems likely that North American consumers won't be denied the chance to drive Chinese vehicles for long. The richest and most profitable market in the world is just as hard for a car maker to ignore as the prospect of a "cheap" car is for many consumers.

## Speed Traps And Redlight Runners

If you or someone close to you is prone to speeding or running red lights, the future would seem to hold more expensive tickets in store as municipalities all across the continent install electronic devices to keep track of such behavior.

This means more revenue for the towns and cities and perhaps fewer crashes if people slow down. Furthermore, many of these tickets will no longer be the type that register points against your license, which is a bonus for offending drivers.

The best to avoid all of this of course is to keep your speed down and stop when traffic lights tell you to, but if you're looking for advice on how to behave where the risk is greatest, the web may be able to help. At least one company, www.njection.com is hoping to provide locations of permanent and portable locations for such devices.

# Motives For Car-Sharing Are Good
# But Real World Experience May Not Be

In recent years there has been a lot of noise about car-sharing programs, and there are a number of co-op transit companies operating in bigger cities across the continent.

Essentially, car-sharing is a variation on car rental, though with fewer models to pick from, fewer units available to drive, and less service. Either renting or sharing can play an important role (along with transit and taxis) in allowing people to live in congested urban areas without a car of their own to finance and maintain, which means they can save some money.

But it's hard to see any serious benefits to car-sharing beyond what normal rental provides, unless a sense of partial ownership is important to you or your accountant can write off ownership but not rental.

Most media reports tend to gloss over the downsides of car-sharing, probably in an effort to look like they care about the environment. People they interview who are already members are also hyper-enthusiastic, the way people are when they try to justify a questionable decision of their own by being keen and chatty about the experience.

Best to do some serious research on prices, model availability and pickup location before you sign up. It will matter a great deal, for example, how close you live to a car-sharing depot, and how unhappy you'll be if the nearest depot has no vehicles available when you want one. This is the moment when you'll be thinking of all those ads from rental companies bragging about how they'll come and pick you up, usually for free.

The big players in car sharing are Flexcar and Zipcar (which are merging as we write this), but a couple dozen smaller firms are around as well.

# Beware Special Problems That Come With New Technology

For a long time it will likely be hard to get good service for a new technology, no matter what it is or which company sells it. This is a long-standing situation in the auto industry resulting from the way the car companies and their dealers work.

New technologies (hybrid power, run-flat tires, aluminum body parts, you name it) require training and technology in the dealerships, both of which take time and money.

The dealers are normally required to invest in the tools, equipment and service training, but they don't like paying for something without the prospect of a revenue flow to cover their expenses. So they often take their time in bringing their service facilities and technicians up to speed, hoping that demand for the service will appear before they invest.

A good business plan for the dealers, to be sure, but not the best situation for owners looking for someone to service the new feature in their new vehicle. This often means delays in getting service, or possibly a journey (by you or the car) to another dealer in a bigger community where demand may already be greater and the correct technology and service person available.

The easy solution is not to order the technology right away, but that doesn't help if you really want it and, as is usually the case, it can't be added later as an aftermarket item.

All the smart consumer can do is press the dealer-principle or the service manager (not the sales people) on their plans for looking after the wondrous new piece of technology you're paying them for. Try to get a commitment on timing from them so at least you'll have a promise to wave under their noses if you do need service. Other than that, pray that nothing goes wrong.

# If You're Looking To Save Money
# Buying A Gas-Guzzler Could Be Wise

Buying something that everyone else is desperate to sell has proven to be an extremely smart investment decision throughout history. If the circumstances are right, the principle can work today with those big gas-guzzling vehicles that people want to get rid of so they can buy something smaller and more fuel-efficient.

Many people who've paid a lot for a large vehicle get extra upset when they have to shell out more money at the gas station and all they can think of is reducing their monthly expenses. So they want to get out of the lease for the guzzler and into something smaller that consumes less gas.

Bear in mind some key math on fuel economy: if gas is $4 a gallon and you're driving 10,000 miles a year, you need to go from 20 mpg to 40 mpg to save $1,000 a year in gas.

So if you can get, say, a $5,000 reduction in the cost of a gas-guzzler (which shouldn't be hard) you'll come out ahead.

This creates a situation that allows buyers in the right circumstances to get a vehicle that's bigger (which usually means safer, roomier, quieter and more comfortable) and better than they could normally afford by taking over the lease or buying it used.

The ideal circumstances would include:

-Lower-than-average annual driving distances, especially if they're highway miles. Steady highway miles at a reasonable speed deliver a vehicle's maximum fuel economy, after all.

-A lease that's going to expire in a year or so and allows you to walk away from the gas-guzzler into a new deal. (See page 190.)

-A seller who put a lot of money down to keep his monthly payments down who's now desperate to save on gas.

-A seller who is desperate to reduce his monthly expenses

right away, or who is so agitated by the cost of fuel today that he's not thinking straight.

-An insurance company that charges you less to drive a larger and safer vehicle than they're charging you now.

-If you're going from a car without a warranty to one with a warranty, you could save money on service and repairs.

-If the car's big enough, you might be able to start a car pool and charge people a small fee to ride with you.

The big IF in all this would of course be the cost of gas. If it balloons out of sight in the next year or so it could upset the economics, but there's usually a risk when you make an investment to make money.

You need to add up all the costs of this deal (lease assumption cost, monthly payments, insurance rate, expected fuel cost, possible service costs, etc.) and see how the numbers shake out for you.

It may not work in your favor, but you won't know until you do the math.

## Premium Gas Not Worth The Cost

Unless you have a job that requires regular test sessions on race track there is no legitimate need to ever put premium fuel in your vehicle.

The only time premium gas is really necessary is when the car is reaching for the last few percentage points of its maximum power range, and those moments only occur while you're going at highly illegal speeds or driving extremely aggressively.

Also, modern engines have management systems that let them run without risk on fuel with any octane level, and that should mean gas from any gas station in North America.

To test your vehicle, use regular fuel and see if you can tell the difference. It is possible that there might be some slight decline in everyday performance, but at what cost?

# Upgrades Across The Market Leave Little Value In Pricier Luxury Brands

Nothing puts the question of the intrinsic value of "luxury" car brands into sharper focus than a recent side-impact crash test of pricey mid-sized sedans that ranked the BMW 5-Series worst of the bunch, behind a group of cars that included the Kia Amanti.

Yes, that's right, while the Amanti from Korea's low-cost brand was getting the Insurance Institute for Highway Safety's top score for the side-impact test, the BMW 5-series scored worst. To make matters worse than worst, the 5-Series was upgraded for 2008, and the general idea behind such upgrades is to make a model better.

So what is a buyer considering a new 5-Series supposed to think now that her first choice for a tricked-up sedan gets a worse side crash score than a car that costs a little more than half as much? Perhaps the answer to that is, is there a good reason to spend a lot more money for a BMW or any of its luxury ilk?

Twenty years ago there were good reasons to pay the extra money to get the premium brands, including features that weren't available on lesser models, greater quality, more performance, and maybe better safety results.

About 10 years ago those luxury-ticket advantages began to fade, and today there is not much of real worth in a car that can't be had at every price point in the auto market.

Whatever quality advantage you got by paying more for a car is long gone, with entry-level models and low-priced brands regularly beating or tying the luxury marques.

This turn of events has lead the premium brands to look around for features to add to their vehicles (usually as pricey options) that have offered little real value or actually made the experience worse for consumers.

On the former point, consider the neck-warming system from Mercedes and the "self-parking" system in the Lexus that requires the driver to do most of the work.

On the latter point, those of you who've never tried to work BMW's iDrive function-control system will just have to consider yourselves fortunate.

Some of this stuff most sane people would actually pay more to do without.

On top of all that, the upscale brands have also been chipping away at their "exclusive" nature by adding new models like crazy and running cut-rate discount advertising on their entry-level models.

This reduces the possible motivations for buying a big-ticket model to what has always been the key impulse -- declaring economic status. All this means is that more and more people will understand that you're simply trying to show everyone how much money you make when you buy something from Audi, BMW, Cadillac, Infiniti, Lexus or Mercedes.

Not everyone grasps this reality, however, and that can be entertaining. For example, the marketing manager of BMW USA was surprised to discover that a large percentage of luxury buyers would not consider being a BMW owner because those folks were widely known to be "shallow and lacked substance." He actually thought his brand's buyers were famous for wanting "fun-to-drive" cars and he said "we own fun-to-drive."

To be fair, it's probably easier for him to believe that Ultimate Driving Machine stuff than the real reason for much of the success of BMW and other luxury brands -- they cost more than other cars and that allows their buyers to show strangers how well they're doing financially.

This impulse can overcome a lot of rational thought in the buying process, and it will probably even overcome those poor side-impact crash scores.

# Blind Loyalty To Honda And Toyota
# Could Cost Their Faithful Buyers

An exaggerated loyalty to the Honda and Toyota brands has existed in millions of consumers over the years, causing them to put too much faith in those Japanese brands and to spend too much money as a result.

Nothing showcases the hyper-devotion to the Honda and Toyota brands more than the regular result of decades of consumer clinics involving the use of different car company badges on the same vehicles.

In a recent survey, the participants offered to pay $2,000 to $3,000 more for a particular vehicle they were told was a Toyota when it actually wasn't.

This has been going on for at least two decades. The U.S. car companies have been showing the same vehicle (a sedan in 1990, for example, and then an SUV in 1995, and so on) to different groups of people before it was launched while it was wearing different badges -- say Chevrolet, Ford, Honda and Toyota.

Every single time, the U.S. vehicle gets a much higher score from the clinic participants if it's wearing a Honda or Toyota badge than if it's wearing a Chevrolet or Ford badge. That is to say, the exact same vehicle with different brand badges gets four different scores, with the Japanese brands always doing best.

CNW Research of Portland, Oregon, did one of these tests recently, involving a 2006 Scion xB and a 2007 Chevrolet Cobalt wearing Chevrolet, Fiat, Honda and Toyota badges at different times in front of four different groups. What's particularly interesting about this test is that it involved cars that have been in the media and on the public roads for some time using their real names, and the fact that the consumers were allowed to inspect the vehicles at length and to drive them up to 50 miles. Yet the consumers went on to score the Scion xB 6.3 as a Chevrolet, 8.4 as a Toyota, 8.9 as a Honda, and less than 5 as a Fiat.

With a Toyota badge on the Cobalt during the CNW test it scored much better (8.6) than it did with its real Chevrolet badge (6.9). As a Honda, the Cobalt scored 9.1, the highest grade recorded for any vehicle with any badge. All scores are out of 10, by the way, if you haven't already guessed that.

In a similar test that CNW did in Europe, consumers tended to give the two vehicles pretty close to the same score no matter which of seven different badges they were wearing. In a telling turn of events, Cobalt scored best and Scion second best while wearing GM badges.

As interesting as this is on a theoretical level for all smart consumers, it should sound a loud warning bell for Honda and Toyota devotees.

Clearly, many of you folks tend to have exaggerated beliefs about the ability of those two Japanese firms to turn out better cars than any other company. In a market as hyper-competitive as today's, that probably means you're going to pay more for a high-quality vehicle than you need to, at least if it's wearing a Honda or Toyota badge.

## Locking Gas Caps May Stop Thefts

Anecdotal evidence suggests that more people are stealing gas from cars as a cheap way around today's pump prices. It's not that hard to siphon gas from a car into a can or even right into another vehicle, and it's not that hard to pop open that little door over the gas cap. With a little care for the flip door and a decision to keep the theft small, it can be done so that you don't even know about it. So it might be worth paying a few bucks for a locking gas cap from an auto parts store. That, too, can be beaten, but it takes more effort and time, and that can often deter thieves.

# Volvo's New Reality:
## Sexier, But Maybe Not Safer

"Volvo: boxy, but safe" is the way most people remember the famous line from Crazy People, the 1990 movie in which a stressed out advertising executive prepares a bunch of commercials that tell the truth about certain products.

Actually, the line was "Volvo: boxy, but good" and it was preceded by "Be safe instead of sexy."

The image of Volvo that applied then applies to this day, though Volvo has struggled mightily to make its public image "Sexy, but safe." Or, as a Saab executive once remarked: "Volvo has always been a safety nanny, and now it wants to be a safety nanny in a short skirt."

Throughout this effort to change its image, Volvo has continued to hold a strong appeal for women looking for an upscale car that's particularly safe.

Well, anyone who thinks Volvo has the lead on safety the way it did 20 years ago needs to step back and reconsider. In truth, Volvos are not exceptionally safe any more. In general, the Swedish-based company builds products that are in a solid group of cars in the entry-luxury segment with tier-two safety status, no better or worse than most when it comes to crash standards. But there are cars in the segment that have better general safety standards than anything Volvo builds today, and in a decision the company says was unjust a French court found it guilty of manslaughter in the death of two children in 1999 because of faulty brakes.

In large part, Volvo isn't the same company it was when it was earning its reputation for safety and hasn't been since it was bought by Ford about a decade ago.

Consider what happened with a safety technology that Volvo officials said just a few years ago was essential to more complete safety -- crash notification. This system acts alone to call for help if the car's in a crash and the driver's unable to act because she's unconscious or whatever, and directs rescue teams to the car's precise location using GPS, which a driver might not be able to do in any situation.

Volvo engineers spoke eloquently about the value of crash notification at the time, since Ford was planning to make such a system available in Volvo and its other brands. But when Ford went into a sharp financial fall shortly thereafter, it decided on a "back to basics" cost-cutting strategy and one of the costs it cut was development of crash-notification for Volvo and all its other brands.

There are many crash situations where any delay in getting medical help can mean the difference between life and death. Since it's designed to work without driver involvement, crash notification can virtually guarantee that help will be sent to your precise location as quickly as possible. Lots of GM cars (including Saabs) that are just as crash-worthy as a Volvo have crash-notification, and so do some Mercedes models. But no Volvos do, so that gives the famous Swedish brand second-tier status in safety, even against less expensive cars.

When it was run solely by those earnest Swedes, Volvo really did care about safety above all else. But since Volvo was taken over by Ford, the commitment to safety has become more of a marketing strategy than a prime directive.

Ford's very commitment to Volvo was recently in question, as the Detroit firm planned to sell the Gothenburg operation to the buyer with the biggest wallet to help with Ford's ongoing financial crisis. But now Ford has decided to hang on to Volvo so that it can push it even further upmarket, which means future products will cost more primarily because Ford wants to make more money from them.

Designing cars so they make a lot of money isn't necessarily a bad thing, but it's a long way from designing cars so they can keep their occupants as safe as possible.

Current owners and potential owners should also be wary of Volvo's recent promise to slash the number of its dealers in North America. This is being done to raise dealer profitability, which means they'll be taking more money from owners by giving them fewer places to look for a better price on a new model or a cheaper place to take the car for service.

Buy a Volvo if you like, but don't believe that it's still the leader in safety, or even that worried about the customer's buying and ownership experience.

## TV Myths About Cars: Fires

More often than not, cars in TV shows and movies that crash or are hit by a bullet or go over a cliff or you name it burst into flames or send bits and pieces of the car flying in all directions. Good video, but lousy science. In truth, it's extremely hard to start the explosive kind of fire that involves the gasoline necessary to make a car blow up like that.

Cars do catch on fire (though not so often as you'd imagine), but often it's because of some electrical issue in the wiring, such as an overheating part. If a fire does start inside a car it can be quite dangerous, so getting away from it is usually wise. Leaving the doors open to supply an ongoing stream of oxygen to feed the flames is not so smart.

## Female Racers Entertain Non-Fans

A bunch of young women are starting to become serious challengers in various forms of racing, and even more are expected. But we shouldn't forget their foremothers; one had a good movie made about her (Shirley Muldowney, Heart Like a Wheel) and another wrote an excellent book about her life (Denise McCluggage, By Brooks Too Broad For Leaping). Both women are leading interesting lives, but Denise has a biography that many women would truly envy.

# First-Year Cars Not So Risky For Consumers Now

One of the classic Old Husbands' Tales is that you should never buy a new vehicle in its first year on the market because the company doesn't have all the kinks worked out yet.

For various reasons that's not so much of an issue any more with most new cars, but there's still a distinct risk with new technology or large departures from the mechanical norm. Create a hybrid powertrain, for example, or replace the piston-driven engine with a rotary and there's likely to be trouble ahead for the consumer, even if the technology works.

Car companies have to create the equipment to service new technology and train the people to operate it, and then the dealers have to pay for that, sometimes before they earn money from selling the car. Let's just say this is not their favorite part of operating a car dealership.

So if you need service on the exciting new feature you might not be able to find it, or you might have to wait, and they may not be sure how to fix it. Let's just say this would not be your favorite part of patronizing a new car dealership.

The bottom line is that, if the geeks in your life and the auto enthusiast magazines get all sweaty over something because it has pulsating flux-capacitors or something like that, stay away from it for at least two years. If you're still interested at that point, check the blogs of people who already own the car to see what their experience has been.

## Interest Differences By Credit Ratings

Buyers with the best credit ratings borrowing money for new vehicles can expect to pay only about a third of what the people with the worst credit ratings have -- about 5.7 percent rather than 18 percent.

# Assuming Lease Can Be
# A Good Business Deal For You

Copious amounts of caution need to be on hand when you approach the prospect of taking over someone else's car lease, but there's no denying that such a move can be a smart financial move for the right consumer.

So far, the idea of a "lease exchange" has appealed almost totally to the folks who want to get out of an existing lease for whatever reason. That means that the advantage is almost completely on the side of consumers willing to assume the lease and the car that goes with it.

This means you might be able to get a vehicle for even less than the original consumer was paying every month. If nothing else, the original lessee probably made a down payment to lower the monthly cost of the vehicle, which would make the payments less than if you'd been the original lessee. But you might also be able to bargain a cash payment or other concession from the original lessee, which you can use to help with the remaining payments on the lease.

That is by far the best reason to assume a lease, especially if you enjoy the notion of driving a greater variety of cars. You can look for short-term leases only and go through maybe two, three or four different low-mileage vehicles a year.

You need to examine your personal situation to see how you can play this to your advantage. Suppose, for example, you wanted to take a leisurely, maybe aimless drive across the southern states this winter. You could look for someone whose vehicle was well under the allowed mileage, take over its lease, go on the drive and not have to worry about having to pay for extra miles.

Taking over a lease might also be helpful if you're transferred from, say, Miami to Minnesota, where a hot convertible might not be as attractive as a small all-wheel-drive SUV.

Or you could marry a studly divorced guy with three kids and a dog to haul around on the weekend and the sporty coupe's not useful any more.

Don't forget that arrangements must also be made to get the vehicle from its old home to its new one. That can involve going to get it, or perhaps having a trucking firm ship it. This is the biggest variable in the whole scenario and shouldn't be forgotten when you're looking for a lease to assume.

Again, it usually depends upon your individual situation.

In general, the process starts with the original lessee making an offer on one of the websites and the potential customers looking for something that interests them. The potential customer contacts the original lessee by phone or e-mail, and if they agree on terms the website then steps in to make it happen -- as long as the car company or financial institution that holds the lease approves it.

For the most part, the financial organizations (the lessors) who hold the paper on leased vehicles are willing to go along with this if they like the look of the new lessee and they get their monthly payments. They may also charge a flat fee for letting the swap happen and/or demand aggravating amounts of adminstrivia, but apparently even they are starting to come around to the notion and are trying to make things easier.

At the moment, the vast majority of leased vehicles on the road can be transferred, since each company has its own rules about keeping the original lessee financially responsible or not, and how much they charge for making it happen. That kind of information is kept updated on the lease-exchange websites, by the way.

The big worry for the original lessee is that most agreements require him or her to maintain some level of financial responsibility for the car, but again that depends upon the individual contract. That situation could also be less onerous than for people wanting to get out of a lease altogether; that can mean paying the company a significant amount of money as a penalty for them taking the car back.

At the moment the lease-exchange business is being driven largely by young people who grew up with the idea of leasing vehicles, but that should change as more people see the potential.

The bigger players in the U.S. game are LeaseTrader.com and Swapalease.com, while LeaseBusters.com heads the pack in Canada. They all charge the original lessee a fee to list a vehicle, the prospective lessee a fee to search for a suitable vehicle, and another fee to facilitate any deals that actually happen.

Thanks to the web and other methods of person-to-person communications, it's also possible to cut out the middle-man and deal directly. The key is knowing that it's possible for a second person to assume a lease.

This situation also brings up a couple of points when the time comes to lease a new vehicle from a car company.

1) Ask how the company's position about someone else perhaps taking over your lease, since you might be in the position of wanting out of a lease yourself, when the transfer to the Paris office comes through, for example.

2) Think about not making a down payment on a new car when you lease it, or at least go with a smaller amount, so you lose less if you want to get out of the lease on your vehicle.

Not for everyone and great care is required, but another fine line of opportunity.


## Prices Rise To Reflect Fuel Economy

The universal law of supply and demand is much in evidence in new and used car prices, various studies show. Dealers with hybrids are less likely to deal, it seems, and the prices for small, fuel-efficient cars (new and used) are rising along with the number of customers interested in them.

# Motorbikes Can Lower Gas And Time Costs, But Raise The Risk To Your Safety

As anyone who's been to Europe can attest, a two-wheeled vehicle with a motor is a popular and proficient way of getting around the busy city streets.

Whether you call them scooters, motorcycles, mo-peds or whatever, their narrow frames and nimble natures let them weave easily and quickly through the congested streets, and for a lot less money than a car.

While the circumstances aren't exactly the same in North America, it's not impossible to construct a situation in which a motorcycle is a superior choice to a car for modern transportation, or at least a regular alternative.

The advantages to riding a motorbike in the city so that it gets around faster than a car often require a flagrant disregard for various rules of the road, and there's no denying that the risk of injury is much greater than it is in any car if you're in any kind of crash. But those issues are often seen as being part of the appeal.

On top of all their potential utility, motorcycles can also deliver one of the most exhilarating transportation experiences in the world, in the city as well as the country.

Whatever your motivations for thinking about some two-wheeled transport, making the move has been made much easier for women by a motorcycle industry looking to expand its buyer base.

Most importantly, they are creating products that are designed to fit the female form, which usually means the seats are narrower and closer to the ground. Some of them are also having dealership events designed to appeal to women, and riding programs to show off their products.

Good places to start include the American Motorcyclist Association and the Motorcycle Industry Council.

# Minivan Still The Best Choice For Buyers Looking For A Family Hauler

The best part about the growing disinterest in minivans is that it provides the smart consumer with a better chance to get a bargain on the best family hauling vehicle in history.

This is assuming, of course, that you are not (as the Wall Street Journal reported) someone's who's "stuck in a rut of having a family". That general sentiment, by the way, explains why many auto writers refer to the "stigma" of the minivan, as growing numbers of people find them un-cool.

Can't help you if that's the way you feel, but if you're looking for the best way to handle a busy family (and that could include aging parents as much as growing children), this desire on the part of many other buyers to eschew the minivan is good news for you.

After all, no matter how you fool with the passenger box on top of the basic footprint (width and length) of the standard North American vehicle, there's no way you can beat the minivan when it comes to transporting a group of four or more people in comfort, convenience and safety.

The most obvious benefit here is of course the young family, but lots of people have come to value the minivan's ability to transport their parents as well. The seat heights and wide door openings provide the easiest entry of all, and it's easy to convert a minivan to carry a wheelchair

Whoever's going to use it, a minivan's sliding doors, the height from floor to roof, the ability for the front seat passenger to get into the back while the vehicle's moving, seats for six with cargo space to boot, the size and weight to protect everyone better in a crash -- they all just deliver the best user-friendly package on wheels.

Inside of these shapes the car companies have been pouring an increasing level of amenities, mostly aimed at amusing children on the road or catching the interest of gadget-happy adults.

The only bad part of the market is that, with GM out of the minivan market in 2008, there will be no new minivans with OnStar to provide automatic crash notification and a direct connection to emergency assistance (among other things).

But the new Chrysler Town & Country and Dodge Grand Caravan have pretty much everything else the average family could use, except perhaps a small refrigerator for storing food, drinks and medication, and a small kids' toilet for bathroom emergencies.

The best thing about the new models from Chrysler is the optional seating system called Swivel 'n Go that allows the two captains chairs in the middle to spin around to face the back, which creates a table setting the family can sit around. They are even stain and odor resistant, which is not without value in a minivan. It also provides an additional level of safety for the people facing rear, since there'd be less strain on them in a crash.

But there are also several entertainment packages, including for the first time live TV delivered to a pair of rear-seat monitors that also play movies and games. They even come with wireless earphones so the kids can catch a flick while the parents listen to something over the stereo up front.

Minivans from Honda and Toyota usually get the kudos from auto writers comparing vehicles in this segment, but those folks generally display their poor grasp of reality by babbling on about the handling of those models if you push them hard in the corners. What parent with three ice cream-eating kids and a dozing grandmother in the back hasn't wanted to do that?

But lots of people fall for those recommendations and pay too much for the Odyssey and Sienna models, which leaves the Grand Caravan for smarter buyers.

# Natural Gas Cars Can Help You Save Oil
# And End Those Visits To A Gas Station

In many circumstances, using a car that runs on natural gas and/or gasoline could bring you some serious benefits.

Apart from the benefits to the environment and the potential cost savings for you, such a vehicle will get you into those wonderful HOV/carpool lanes by yourself while freeing you from going to a gas station ever again.

Also, unlike other alternative fuel vehicles, natural gas is available now and can be added to many existing models, so you won't have to buy a new car. There is even one new car -- the Honda GX -- on the market that runs on natural gas.

The big problem with natural gas cars is that it's extremely hard to find places that sell natural gas to the public, but that won't mean so much if you get the home refueling outfit (of course it's called Phill). This product from FuelMaker Corp. of Toronto comes with the Honda (the total cost for car and refueling system is around $25,000) and needs a natural gas feed to the house, which is not hard to get in most places.

It takes about 10 seconds to attach Phill to a natural gas car, and in a few hours it fills the vehicle's storage tanks with compressed natural gas. In the Civic's case, that's good enough for maybe 250 miles driving before it has to be filled up again, which could present a problem if you want to go farther and it's your only car. But if you're looking for a regular commuter car and you have another car in the family fleet, it won't matter.

With other cars that run on regular gasoline, adding a natural gas system allows you to run on gasoline or gas. So if you go outside the natural gas fuel range (which will vary by model but usually will always exceed 200 miles) you can always switch to gasoline and keep on motoring. This is more complicated, as you can imagine, and not cheap, but it may present an appealing option to some people.

The cost issue varies depending upon where you live, since some governments offer rebates and natural gas prices vary. There are even some places (LA, for instance) that waive parking meter costs for alternative fuel cars.

But you must also consider the time you might save if you're using the HOV/carpool lanes, as well as the time you save not filling up at service stations. If you live in a big city this could add up to a lot of time. With Phill, you hook up when you get home and the next morning you have a car with a full tank.

There are many questions and issues with going with natural gas, but for lots of people it could be a solution they didn't know was available.

The natural gas option's been around since the early 1990s but has fallen out of fashion in recent times with the advent of hybrids, fuel cells, ethanol and all that noise. But the basic idea of natural gas vehicles is still sound, especially if you don't like going to service stations while helping the planet.

## Shopping For Insurance Pays Off

You have almost certainly heard or read the admonishment to shop around for new automotive insurance coverage and thought it was probably good advice.

But if you haven't actually run a request for different insurance quotes using your own specific information (age, address, driving record, type of vehicle, etc) on one of several web services designed for this, then you can't imagine what a sticker shock moment is likely awaiting you.

Almost certainly you'll get a range of quotes from firms actually willing to take your business that will surprise you, and among them will probably be a couple that are a great deal less expensive than what you're paying now.

A few minutes doing this could save you serious money.

# Longer Car Loans Could Be
# Smart Money Move For Some

If you're planning to buy a car and use it for more than three years, it could make sense to finance it over the same period of time. It might even let you live a more fulfilling life now.

Finance firms servicing the auto business are now quite happy to stretch loan payment programs to six years or even longer, but usually only to people with excellent credit.

To be sure there's some extra interest charges to be borne by the car buyer in such cases, but smart management of the money you're not paying out every month could easily offset that added cost and actually save you cash in the long run.

It's the same principle that makes leasing so attractive to many buyers who could afford the higher payments of regular loans: you take the money that you're not giving to a finance company every month for the car loan/lease and invest it in something else.

So, if you could afford, say, $600 a month for a traditional 36-month car loan and stretch the financing to 72 month, your monthly payments might be $325. That would for sure cost you a couple of thousand more in interest, but you'd also be paying out $9,900 less over the first three years. With that kind of capital to play with you could probably recover the extra interest charge quite easily, through a smart investment or some tax deduction program. Depending upon your situation, there's also the chance that your income will increase in the duration of your extended loan so the payments will become less onerous as time passes.

Or you could use that cash to pay for something else, like a nice holiday every year, or a better apartment, or something for your kids, or whatever works for you. And it is always possible to refinance in the future if your situation changes.

Every case is of course different, but it could make sense for you to choose a longer loan. You need to do the math using the numbers that pertain to your personal situation and you need to be willing to drive the same car for a lot longer than might suit you. You need to make those decisions for yourself.

What makes this all more possible for buyers today is the astonishing quality and durability of modern cars, and the extended limited-warranty programs being offered by such companies as General Motors and Chrysler. There's still risk in owning and paying for a car that's out of its full-warranty coverage, but a buyer's chances of not having to pay a fortune for service and repairs have improved dramatically.

## Flying Car About To Land -- Again

The dream of a thousand scientists in garages everywhere and about a billion people stuck in traffic is still being worked on. Yes, there are folks out there working to create the flying car, once and forever putting roads and congestion behind us, offering us instead our own way through the blue.

Attention on this technology is today focussed on a small operation in Maine, where the visionaries at Terrafugia are working on the Transition, a vehicle that will fly as well as travel on regular roads.

For this to work the company has to overcome considerable difficulties, not the least of which involves meeting the safety requirements of a car as well as an airplane.

The primary goal involves wings that stay firmly in place while flying or tucked against the body on the road.

Transition would be more of special event vehicle (fly somewhere and back for the day) than a daily commuter, but that would have strong appeal for a very large market.

The hope is to have it on the market by the end of the decade, for something above $150,000.

# Resale Values On Used Cars
## More Faith Than Science

For their own selfish marketing reasons, the car companies who do well on surveys that "predict" the resale value of various vehicles try to make the process sound scientific and irrefutable, or at least logical.

In truth, little about residual (or resale) values is any of those things.

What happens is that the people who admire say, Jaguar, decide by osmosis or herd-think or some kind of informal consensus that they are willing to pay a certain amount for a specific Jaguar model in such-and-such condition.

The same thing happens all over the country with all the hundreds of models sold here. The people who are in the business of selling information about residual values gather that information and pass it on to dealers and prospective buyers.

What factors these groups of people use to come up with the amount they're willing to pay for second-hand cars varies by model and/or brand.

Quality, style, cachet and fuel economy would probably be big factors, but those things are more than ever in the eye of the beholder and the psyche of the buyer.

This is particularly true about long-term quality, the reality of which has completely changed in recent years. Basically, these days everyone builds cars with excellent quality scores that are essentially on the same plateau, which should reduce the role that quality plays in resale values, but isn't yet.

Honda and Toyota fans, for example, pay dearly for greater quality scores than actually exist.

With help from the car companies whose fans give them good resale grades, this information tends to transform into the notion that the residual numbers actually represent an unbiased and methodical measure of each vehicle. This is absolutely not what predicted resale values are.

In truth, the resale value of all second-hand cars are where they are because enough people say they're willing to pay that much for them. There's very little science in that.

So you could buy a second-hand car with a lower predicted resale value and get a much better bargain -- and a better vehicle -- than if you bought one with a higher predicted resale value.

## No Car Or Old Car Is Cheapest

In terms of overall transportation costs, the best course might be not to buy a vehicle at all and rely instead on public transit, cabs, rental cars, friends, family, dates, impressionable strangers and whatever else you can find.

That may sound like a step back to your high school days, but it's a truth worth telling and could allow you to wait a while longer for the dream deal on the dream vehicle.

But if you absolutely have to own a car and want to spend the least amount of money (and aren't terribly worried about the environment), a really old and really inexpensive model (a "beater") is the cheapest method.

This is the type of vehicle that you drive until it dies or requires expensive repairs and then you give it to one of those charity recycling places and replace it with another beater.

After all, even it it drinks gasoline by the barrel, a beater will almost certainly cost less than a new model or a less elderly used model.

The downside to all this of course is the inconvenience of asking for rides, waiting for friends, buses and taxis, shopping for replacement cars and so on. But that's the cost of saving money on a car.

Unstylish and unappealing as it may be, this is the economic reality of the car-buying process.

# The Myth Of Residual Value
## In Used Japanese Cars

People have been paying more for used vehicles from Honda, Toyota and, to a lesser extent, some other Japanese brands for a long time now. And for a long time cars and trucks from those brands were worth the extra premium they cost as used vehicles, thanks primarily to the fact that they had greater quality at the time of resale and were therefore likely to cost their new owners less money for service and repair.

But times have changed, and an endless array of quality studies makes it clear that American brands have had the same quality levels as Japanese cars for some time now. Most interestingly, quality levels on three-year-old models (which mostly come from people giving up their leased vehicles at the end of the warranty period) are now about the same. The latest J. D. Power long-term dependability study (of cars sold in 2004) makes this abundantly clear, in fact.

So you probably won't have more trouble with a used Buick, Chevrolet, Ford, Mercury or Pontiac than with a used Honda or Toyota. So why are so many people willing to pay so much more for second-hand Japanese car?

The answer is that, for the most part, the people who buy Hondas and Toyotas don't care or know much about cars and aren't interested in spending the time to find out anything else. For these folks, Japanese nameplates have served them faithfully for many years so why should they change now?

This means they pay what the dealers ask when they're new and what the dealers demand when they're used, no questions asked. Needless to say, the Japanese car companies and their dealers are happy with this arrangement.

Those faithful buyers aren't likely to pay any attention to this reality, of course, but we wanted to put it on the record for everyone with an open mind.

# US/Canada Price Disparity
## Presents Opportunities In Two Countries

If you're an American looking to make a little extra money from selling a car, or a Canadian looking to save a little money on a used (i.e. previously licensed) car, the current pricing disparity between the two countries could help you.

For decades, new vehicles sold in Canada had much higher sticker prices than they did in the US, to allow for the greater value of the American dollar. During that time, lots of Americans found automotive bargains in Canada.

Even though the dollars are now roughly at par, the car companies have not equalized the prices on new Canadian models. So Canadians are being charged thousands more for their new cars, even the ones that are built in Canada.

This means that an American who wants to sell a used car can sell it to a Canadian for more than they would get from another American. This works especially well if the used car is registered by an American but not driven very far, since the American could actually make a little money for buying the new car and selling it to a Canadian, while the Canadian would save thousands of dollars buying a car that is legally "used" from the US.

It may not work for everyone, but if you're an American with a car you want to sell used it might benefit you to sell it to a Canadian. It works better the newer and more expensive the vehicle.

If you're a Canadian looking to save a bunch of money, consult the Register of Imported Vehicles (www.rvi.com) for more details. Do a web search on the subject to find dealers and private citizens in both countries looking to do business. Take a cheap flight to Florida next winter and drive back.

It's not for everyone, but in the right situation it's a sweet deal for both parties.

**Alexander Law & Susan Winlaw** 203

# Vehicle "Siblings" On The Market Can Save You Money

For cost reasons, many car manufacturers like to take the same basic vehicle package (body, engine, transmission and so on) and change some of the smaller features so they can sell two or more versions of it to different customers.

Roughly speaking, it's like taking the same outfit and changing scarves, shoes, belts, purse, hairstyle, nail color, watch and makeup to create different looks for different situations, or to appeal to different people.

In cars, such alterations are done to appeal to a greater range of consumer tastes and/or levels of budget.

So the careful shopper who finds, say, the Buick Enclave crossover vehicle eminently suitable but a little pricey can get pretty much the same vehicle in the GMC Acadia and the Saturn Outlook, with a Chevrolet Traverse version to follow, for less money.

Despite the similarities of those four vehicles, GM has done a masterful job of altering the accessories in terms of style, price, and availability so that you can't completely reproduce a Buick for a Chevrolet price.

It must be noted that the same pricing/features game is played by every company (and that includes most full-line manufacturers, including Chrysler, Ford, Honda, Nissan and Toyota) that produces "sibling" models in order to appeal to more consumers and make more money. Welcome to the free market.

High-profile auto siblings include the Ford Fusion, Mercury Milan and Lincoln MKZ, the Dodge Caliber, Jeep Compass and Jeep Patriot, and the Toyota Camry, Toyota Avalon and Lexus ES 350.

Some of those examples stretch the differences between the siblings more than others, but the sibling rule still applies.

Sometimes, different companies can sell twin versions of the same basic model.

For example, VW is now selling a minivan called the Touran that is a thinly-disguised version of the hugely popular Dodge Grand Caravan, and Pontiac and Toyota have been selling, respectively, Vibe and Matrix mini-wagons from the same package for a few years.

Indeed, there is no better example than the Pontiac Vibe and the Toyota Matrix to show you how it's possible to get a better deal on a vehicle package that appeals to you..

Under the sheet metal they're both essentially the same vehicle made by the same people in the same plant, but Pontiac offers more car for the money (including OnStar, roadside assistance, and a bigger dealer network).

Yet uniformed buyers have chosen to buy Matrix more than Vibe, often for more money.

There aren't endless examples of sibling models around, but there are enough so that it would be a smart thing for you to do some web-browsing on a model you're interested in with "sibling", "twin" or "clone" in the search field.

## TV Myths About Cars: Getting Airborne

Endless TV shows and movies do it, but perhaps no show institutionalized the notion of getting a car airborne and then driving away in it like the Dukes of Hazzard did during its six-year run, or does in endless reruns.

In truth, if you get a regular vehicle up in the air more than a couple of inches (yes, it's possible, if you really want to do it) and it crashes into the ground, it's likely not going to work that well afterwards, if at all.

It's certainly not going to let you escape Deputy Hogg the way The General Lee helped Bo and Luke.

Remember that the next time you're running moonshine for Uncle Jesse.

# Prices For Import Cars, Parts
# And Servicing Are Going Up

The cost of buying new import cars and servicing them and existing models should be going up for the next few years, as the Japanese and (particularly) the European firms struggle to make money from the declining US dollar.

Car companies in Europe have largely avoided the need to raise vehicle prices in the U.S. to cover the shift in the exchange rates between their currencies and the dollar, but their ability to do that is about to end.

This could mean a significant increase in sticker prices so the German firms can make some money on new car sales, and it's almost certainly going to mean increases in their prices for replacement parts and out-of-warranty servicing. A lot of the profitability of a car dealer is related to service work, where price increases are not broadcast like MSRPs are and are rarely negotiable.

So, if the Europeans manage to keep their sticker prices from going up too quickly, you can probably count on paying more for service down the road.

As it happens, the prices of cars from Europe have been going up at a brisk pace for a couple of years now, well in excess of what we've seen from the domestic or Asian companies. Prices for the best-selling European model -- the BMW 3-Series -- have gone up about 20 percent in the last five years, and worse may be in store for buyers now that the long-term contracts guaranteeing currency exchange rates ("hedging" is the financial term for that) taken out by the European firms are about to end.

Unless the exchange rate between the Euro and the dollar shifts significantly in the next year or so, anyone importing an Audi, BMW, Mercedes, Smart or Volkswagen can expect to pay more in every way those companies can imagine.

# New Reality Not Getting Through To Toyota Camry And Honda Accord Fans

Over about three decades, the Honda Accord and the Toyota Camry have earned near-mythic status for value and dependability with a major segment of the car-buying public -- the people who don't really know much about cars and don't want to.

For these folks, a car is essentially an appliance and the less time they have to spend buying and maintaining one, the better. So those two Japanese sedans have become the easiest decisions on the market for folks with no real interest in cars and no time to shop for one.

For people who know and appreciate cars, Camry and Accord also hold a special place.

Auto journalists, for example, regularly recommend them to relatives, friends and readers looking to avoid the rigors of finding a car, but wouldn't dream of buying one themselves. Auto manufacturers, on the other hand, curse Camry and Accord for holding on to a huge share of the mid-size market despite their best efforts.

All of that car company frustration has been great for car shoppers, however, since there are now several other mid-size sedans that are as good or better than the Japanese models -- the new Chevrolet Malibu, for example.

But the other manufacturers haven't had much success selling those great new models because so many of the buyers in that segment have closed their minds around Accord and Camry. So they're likely paying more than they have to for a vehicle that's no longer the best buy. One recent study suggests the extra cost for the brands is about $3,000.

There's little chance these comments or anything else will ever get the Camry-Accord acolytes to open their minds, but at least they won't be able to say that no one told them.

# Check A Car And Its
# Insurance Rate Before You Buy

There's never any way of knowing for sure how an insurance company determines what premium it will charge you, but one of the big factors is the type of vehicle you buy.

Before you buy, then, check with an insurance agent to see how a specific vehicle will affect your insurance costs, or take the time to try a set of applications on one of those websites that gather competing quotes for you using the different models you have in mind. They will give you precise quotes from dozens of companies for any vehicle and personal situation (age, address, driving record, and so on) you give them. Leave the personal details the same but try them out on different cars to see what kind of a difference it makes.

Here are some general things worth knowing.

In terms of size, the companies seem to favor the Momma Bear position, which makes mid-size vehicles just right. Really big vehicles like SUVs tend to do more damage to the other vehicles in the crash, which means the insurance company has to pay out more if you're at fault. On the other hand, if you're in a really small car the chances are that it will sustain giant damages, which will cost your insurance company more. Either way, your premium will be higher.

Luxury cars cost more to replace if they're wrecked or stolen and that means you'll pay more to insure them.

Sports cars are usually more dangerous because they're small and low, so that drives up the insurance cost, but history suggests that they are bought to be driven hard and that usually results in tickets and/or crashes, so they'll cost you more to insure as well. The same thing applies to regular cars with extremely powerful engines.

High-tech accessories seem to make the insurance companies nervous as well, since they drive up the price and add distractions and can be the subject of greater theft.

If your vehicle's a favorite target for thieves, that will also make the insurance company unhappy.

But all of those things can be overcome to some extent if you're a mature driver with no tickets or crashes and you live in a spot where car thefts are rare.

So check before you buy.

## Carfax, E-Bay And Care Not Enough

The prime message for people buying used cars is that those reports from Carfax and companies like that are not anywhere near as reliable as you think they are.

The truth is that they only tell you about the wrecks and crashes and other bad things that previous owners report to them. And since reporting a serious crash will greatly reduce the appeal of a vehicle to a future buyer, you can imagine how many people avoid doing that by not reporting it to Carfax.

For an eye-opening view of how things can go wrong when it comes to buying a car on eBay even when you've been smart about things, consult the story on the New York Daily News website of March 10, 2008, involving "Nissan Murano Randy LaFrance Calgary InterCar Brooklyn".

It relates a tale that should give pause to anyone who's thinking of buying a vehicle sight-unseen from a dealer or person a great distance away.

It illuminates a little-known weakness in the Carfax system of reporting a vehicle's history, shows up a possible issue with the eBay warranty and should generally make anyone nervous who relies a lot on systems rather than personal involvement.

It would be smart to consult this story before using eBay or Carfax in the purchase of a used vehicle, or to search out the growing commentary on problems with both of those services.

# Dealing With A Flat Needs
# Time And Attention Before It Happens

By far the easiest way to deal with a flat tire is getting someone else to do it for you while you catch up on your e-mail, so make sure you get an AAA membership if your new car doesn't come with roadside assistance coverage (see Page 95). It's actually a good idea to consider AAA membership even if you do have roadside assistance, since it's likely to be better than whatever service the car company has arranged.

The best bet by far is the OnStar service that can be had with most GM vehicles, since it usually works in areas where cell phones don't connect, and will send help to your precise location, even if you are incapacitated. This can be particularly useful if you regularly travel in rural areas.

There may still come a time, however, when you can't reach help or it will take too long to get there or whatever and you decide to change the flat yourself. This is when you will dearly wish that you took our first piece of advice and did a tire-changing run-through at home when you had the chance.

However the tire-changing drama plays out, remember that changing a flat always comes with a degree of physical risk, ranging from the nail-breaking type all the way up to the chance of death, so act accordingly. If you think we're exaggerating, consider that you might have to lie on a busy road beside the car to put the jack in place, and in anyone's book that's being in harm's way.

A run-through in the safety and convenience of your own driveway will help because, while the general method of changing a flat tire hasn't changed for decades, the specifics have evolved so that they are usually unique to every vehicle and are not always easy to understand or apply. They may also involve the use of tools that have been designed to be compact and light rather than sturdy, simple and ergonomic. It's possible that you won't be able to follow the tire-changing instructions with the tools provided and will want to purchase a few things that make the process easier and safer.

It's much better to have a first look at what you're up against while you're not under pressure, in a dress and heels on your way to somewhere important.

The instructions in your owner's manual will show you where the pre-packaged tool kit lives and where the spare is (it could be under the vehicle rather than in it).

Getting to know your spare tire and its supporting cast of tools before you need them is an especially good idea if you bought a used vehicle, since you only really know if all the bits are there when you actually try to change a tire. Assuming they are all there, it's worthwhile to try to make them work.

But first be sure that all safety suggestions are followed, which probably include putting the hand- or foot-brake on and placing a block of some kind against one of the healthy wheels to stop the vehicle from rolling off the jack. Pay attention to these details.

You might find out that your vehicle has locking hubs, which are an anti-theft device that's supposed to make it impossible to remove the wheel and tires without a key. Without that key, neither you nor anyone else is changing that flat.

You usually have to put the jack in a very precise spot for it to work at all, and that's where the lying on the road part could come in. You may at this moment want to think about using the sweat suit and work gloves from the emergency kit we recommend. (See Page 46.)

You might also at this point give some thought to a way to remind yourself to keep the spare tire inflated so it will be ready if you should ever need it.

Even under ideal situations you are likely going to find that the lug wrench provided by the manufacturer isn't easy to use, mostly because it doesn't provide much leverage when you try to turn it to remove a lug nut. This is why we strongly recommend that you invest in a cross-shaped lug wrench (it usually has three heads for different sized lug nuts as well as a pry bar end) and keep it in your vehicle. It will work in situations where the factory lug wrench will not and will also make a tire change a lot easier for you. In situations involving a lug nut that's been over-tightened with a pneumatic wrench and then been hardened into place by the elements, getting a lug nut off may be impossible without the leverage that a cross-shaped lug wrench provides. If you can't loosen the nut by hand, you can always put your foot on the wrench and use your body weight to turn it.

If you get a flat on the road, here are the general rules that apply:

-Chose a flat spot that's as far from traffic as you can find.

-Apply the emergency brake and maybe the emergency flashers. If you're in a safe spot away from traffic, you may not want to draw attention to the fact that you're not mobile and are out of the car trying to fix it.

-Put a block (a brick, rock, log, a copy of The Da Vinci Code or whatever you can find) against a wheel on the end of the car that's not being jacked up. If the car rolls off the jack, you can be in serious trouble even if you're not injured.

-Do not jack the car up yet.

-Get out the manual, the spare and the tools and put them near the flat. If you've practiced beforehand and bought the right extra equipment, this shouldn't be too daunting.

-If your instruction manual tells you to take some step that we haven't mentioned (it's possible, but unlikely), you should absolutely do what it says, for warranty and legal considerations if nothing else.

-If there's a hubcap over the wheel, remove it and loosen

(turn counter-clockwise) the lug nuts using the tightest-fitting head of the cross-shaped lug wrench. Be sure to do this before you jack the car up, since contact with the ground means you turn the nuts, not the wheel. This is where you will appreciate the cross-headed lug wrench the most. Turn the nuts until they're really loose, but do not take them off.

-Jack the car up until the tire is completely off the ground. If it's really flat it may not be as large as the inflated tire you're putting on, so allow enough space for that.

-You should now be able to take the lug nuts off the bolts that hold the wheel to the car by hand, but the cross-headed wrench works even better since it now turns much easier. Indeed, if the nut's loose you can spin the wrench like a wheel to remove it very quickly.

-Take care to keep all of the lug nuts handy when they're off the bolts.

-As gently as possible so as not to rock the car on the jack, pull the tire off the bolts that the lug nuts were attached to. If you can, slide the tire under the edge of the car so that if it falls off the jack it won't sustain so much damage.

-Put the spare on the bolts and then put the lug nuts back on the bolts, turning clockwise of course. Spin them on with your hand as much as you can, and then use the wrench to turn the nuts back into place until they hit some resistance.

-Once the nuts are all snug on the bolts, tighten them as much as you can.

-Jack the car down until the spare tire is touching the ground enough to stop the wheel from turning, but do not put the full weight of the car on the ground yet. Tighten the nuts as much as possible and remove the flat tire if you put it under the edge of the car.

-Lower the car to the ground and remove the jack. Tighten the nuts again with the lug wrench.

-Gather up all your tools and put them back in the car. Do

not put the flat tire away because the smartest move here is taking it to be repaired by someone you trust. Remember that you no longer have a spare if another tire goes flat and that's a whole new degree of difficulty that you don't want to attempt.

Bear in mind that many spares are not designed to deliver the kind of handling and grip of a regular tire and may even be restricted to 50 MPH or less. They are also temporary at best.

## Amphibious Car Coming To Market Soon

Though they've always had a strong sense of the gimmick or gadget about them, vehicles that are boats as well as cars would probably have some legitimate market appeal.

Now a firm in Michigan hopes to find out with the Aquada, which is meant to be a sportscar and a speed boat.

The plan is for Gibbs Technologies to sell that model and a personal watercraft that turns into an all-terrain vehicle called the Quadski in the U.S. by 2009.

The amphibious Aquada has already crossed the English Channel during testing and won't be cheap (they're shooting for $85,000) when it shows up, but it will meet all of the various regulations for road and waterway.

The Quadski would be sold for about $15,000.

## Calling 511 May Get You Traffic Info

Some states provide information on detours, road closures, accidents, highway conditions, border crossing times (to Canada and Mexico) and so on at 511 on your phone, or even online.

This is a developing system so you might be out of luck in many states, but it should be worth watching as the systems develop and expand.

# Get An Extra Set Of Keys
# Made Now To Avoid Suffering Later

Having car keys replaced has always been something of an inconvenience, but it's much, much worse now.

Replacing today's more sophisticated keys can cost hundreds of dollars and make you go days without your car. If you don't have another car to use or lose your key when you're away from home, you might also have to pay for towing, hotel rooms, rental cars and a bunch more.

In general, it wouldn't be hard for a key replacement to cost you $1,000 without much effort, though it could easily go higher and that doesn't count the inconvenience.

The situation is complicated and maddening and unlikely to be fixed anytime soon (though California is making something of an effort), and the primary villain of the piece appears to be the car companies. They say they're careful about giving out the secret codes needed to replace keys and other people say they're taking advantage of the situation to charge huge prices for replacement keys.

But rather than spending your time trying to figure out what's going on and who to be upset with, you might want to give some thought to having an extra key made under controlled circumstances and thinking out a way to carry it with you all the time as an emergency backup.

But even then, it's best NOT to lose your car keys.

## A Key Decision For You To Make

Group wisdom suggests that it's never a good idea to leave an ignition key in your car, because professional thieves will find it. But there might be a case for leaving a key hidden in a GM car with OnStar, since that service can unlock the vehicle doors remotely. That could be hugely helpful if you lose the other set. How good are you at hiding things?

**Alexander Law & Susan Winlaw  215**

# Even A Little Fender-Bender Crash
# In Today's Vehicles Will Cost You Big

If you're one of those folks who tend to get involved in low-speed (3 to 6 mph) impacts with other vehicles in stop-and-go traffic or walls in mall parking lots or pretty much anything solid anywhere, modern cars could be a repair bill and/or insurance premium nightmare waiting to happen.

Bumpers are supposed to keep low-speed damage from spreading to headlights, hoods and other expensive parts, but style and packaging tend to dictate the shape of cars today, with little apparent thought given to the cost of repair.

A recent test of 17 mid-size cars (Honda Accord, Ford Fusion, Nissan Maxima, Subaru Legacy, Toyota Camry and so on) by the Insurance Institute of Highway Safety (IIHS) found that modern bumpers will probably not keep you from running up a huge tab if you make contact with something solid at very low speeds.

Only three cars kept the damage costs below $1,500 in four bumper tests, while other cars ran up more than $4,500 damage in just one of the four tests, and two cars racked up more than $9,000 in total damage.

Each vehicle was tested in four crashes, so there were 68 results overall to measure. Only two of them resulted in no damage to those expensive body parts.

It's worth pointing out here that these results are bad enough if you bend your own car for several thousand dollars worth of damage against a retaining wall that won't need repairs, but if you hit a vehicle as easy to bend as your vehicle the total costs would go up dramatically.

Consider that if you ran the whole front of a VW Passat into the front end of another VW Passat at 6 mph the damages could come close to $10,000. (IIHS reported $4,594 in damages to the front of the Passat it tested, so twice that is

$9,188, and there are likely to be taxes on top of that.) Compare that to two Saturn Auras in the same situation, where the cost would be $00.00, plus applicable taxes for a total of $00.00. Yes, that's right, a difference of $10,000.

This example isn't meant to draw special attention to the Saturn Aura (though only a fool would ignore it), since every car will behave differently in every crash.

The most important point to take from all this is that extra caution should be applied at low speeds that previously didn't require much caution at all.

In case you're thinking this applies only to mid-size cars, you're out of luck. This particular set of tests pretty much represents the reality of any size of vehicle on the market today, so you can't shrug this off if you drive something other than a mid-size car.

Whatever you drive, more caution in low-speed situations is clearly called for, or it could cost you big time.

## Men Spend More On Cars Than Gifts

British men "spend more time buffing their bonnets than pampering their partners," a recent survey in Great Britain reported.

According to this survey, one in three men spend about $40,000 over their lifetime on extras for their cars, including such things as alloy wheels, the "spoilers" that extend the car's bumpers, and upscale wing (side view) mirrors.

On top of that, one in five of those surveyed spent more than two hours every fortnight (two weeks) scrubbing, rinsing and polishing their cars.

Meanwhile, one in 10 British "blokes" say they've never shown the same attention to their partners and about a third of them claim not to have bought their partner a present for over a month.

How do you think North American men would compare?

# Car Thefts Decrease But
# Likely Will Never End

The good news about car thefts is that they have actually been decreasing across North America for some years. At the same time, modern anti-theft devices in new cars have caused most thieves to switch to older vehicles, to tear them apart so they can have the various components (body panels, airbags, etc) to resell. So, if you're getting a new car your chances of getting ripped off are much, much lower than they once were.

Okay, now here's the less appealing side, best illustrated by a story imparted to us 20 years ago by an executive at a firm that sells tracking devices for stolen vehicles. It's just as germane now as it was then, despite all the really useful advances in anti-theft technology.

A Florida man owned a classic car of which he was exceptionally fond. To prevent anyone from stealing it during the night, he would park the car so he could chain one end to one palm tree and the other end to another palm tree.

One morning he woke up and looked out the window to make sure his baby was okay, and it was. It was still there and chained to the palm trees, but something had changed. The car had been turned around and was facing the opposite direction.

The man rushed out to inspect his beloved car. It was undamaged and the chains were securely locked, but there was a note on the windshield that said: "When we want it, we'll come and get it."

Sadly, that's pretty much still the truth today. If some professional car thief wants your car because it will earn him a small fortune in Asia, Russia, South America or 20 miles from where you live, then he will get it. He'll send a tow truck for it or a crane to lift it up and put it on a truck, or whatever it takes.

That said, there are many things that you can do to make it harder for thieves of any kind to steal your car, which increases their exposure and perhaps forces them to rethink their risk and look for another vehicle.

The web is full sites offering tips on this subject, but one of the best can be found at www.watchyourcar.org and is the work of the Pennsylvania Auto Theft Prevention Authority.

## Your Kids Are At Risk In Your Car

Pretty much every adult understands that children need to use specific kinds of car safety seats through various stages of their lives, but it also looks like a great many of them don't know how to do that. As a result, the young passengers in our cars are being put at risk unnecessarily.

According to the National Highway Traffic Safety Administration (NHTSA), the vast majority (over 85 percent) of all child restraints are used incorrectly, including rear-facing infant seats, forward-facing seats for toddlers, and safety belts for older kids.

Check www.nhtsa.dot.gov for more info on this, as it includes great detail on all child restraint issues and a list of sites across the country where you can get installation help.

## Taking Someone For Help After A Crash

The rules of first aid after a car crash generally involve calling for help and doing your best to stop any bleeding, and to not move the person in case you worsen any other injury.

This works if you're close to good medical care and the ambulance isn't far away. But if you're a long way from help and the bleeding or breathing is bad, you might want to consider putting the victim in your car and heading for help.

It might be risky, but it might also be worth thinking about in certain situations. You may have to take a chance.

# It Takes Time And Effort, But You Can Bring Auto Insurance Rates Down

The quick and easy step to paying smaller premiums for car insurance is to look around for a new insurance company right now, not when your policy comes up for renewal.

To maintain the lowest rates possible as time passes, you must then pay regular attention to how changes in your life can reduce your auto insurance premiums.

Before we go into details on these points, don't forget that it may not be smart to have the absolute lowest insurance rates possible.

You may not want to have the minimum coverage to deal with crashes with uninsured or hit-and-run drivers, for example, or the highest collision deductible, or any number of things.

You need to look at your own personal situation within the laws of your state and strike a balance between what you can afford and what you're willing to risk. You could save a couple of hundred dollars a year on insurance and end up paying out thousands and thousands if you get a bad break.

But no matter what, go to at least a couple of those websites that allow you to apply to a bunch of insurance companies and prepare to be amazed. They don't all supply quotes from the same firms, but almost certainly you will find a company offering lower rate than what you're currently paying.

The range of quotes you get from the various insurance firms will surprise you. In certain circumstances it may even amaze you; it's not impossible that the quotes you get may differ by thousands or many thousands of dollars a year.

If you don't want to switch your insurance company for some reason, show your agent the quote you got from the other firm and see if your old firm will match it or offer a discount or something.

To get virtually every insurance company's best rate, there are a bunch of things you can do.

-Avoid crashes and moving violations of all kinds, since they are the biggest concerns for insurers everywhere. This is the prime directive for lowering your insurance premium, or for keeping your premiums from rising.

-Keep your credit record clean, since many insurance companies consider the behavior that results in a poor credit record to be indicative of the kind of behavior that results in crashes. This means not paying bills late, avoiding loans if possible, and keeping credit card debt low. There is some political resistance growing to this, but for now it's perfectly legal.

-If you're going to buy a new vehicle, consider the insurance risks associated with each type of vehicle. This is an extremely complex subject, so talk to an insurance agent about the relative rates on specific vehicles you are considering.

-If you're going to buy a new vehicle, get the insurance coverage lined up so you're not coerced into using the stuff lined up by the dealer, which is usually more expensive.

-Agree to higher deductibles where they're available. This means you'll pay more out-of-pocket expenses before your insurance takes over if you do have a crash, but it will also lower your rates by about 15 percent or more. No crashes and you win, which is another incentive to avoid the driving behavior that generates tickets. On top of that, it's sometimes smarter to pay for some insured repairs out of your own pocket than it is to tell your insurance company that you had a crash. Bear in mind, however, that you're probably obligated to report all crashes to your insurer, so doing this raises the specter of having your coverage nullified. On the other hand, having a crash and a couple of tickets can also result in you losing your coverage.

-Insurance companies usually reward consumers who buy

different kinds of coverage from them, so it may make sense to do a deal for some house and life insurance as well.

-When you've run out of suggestions for saving on your insurance rate, don't forget to ask the agent if there are any more deductions available. They may have forgotten to mention something, or aren't supposed to talk about it until you ask, or whatever. So if you flat-out ask them about further discounts, they will most likely tell you. It can't hurt.

-When it comes to choosing a place to live, you might want to add potential insurance premiums to the list of variables. The difference in costs between locations can be significant enough that picking one house over another for insurance reasons might allow you to buy a more expensive place. It's certainly worth a look. This situation could be changing soon in some places (notably California) as local governments try to change this. A different location might also reduce the chance that you'll encounter uninsured drivers, which is also a good thing.

-If you have good health coverage, you might be able to leave medical coverage off of your car insurance. Great care is needed on this point, for obvious reasons, but it's worth considering since it can save you a lot of money.

-If you're buying a vehicle, consider an older model with a low risk rate, since you'll get a good basic rate and you can skip the deductible and write it off after a crash. This is all part of the scenario that can make really old vehicles (sometimes called "beaters") the most economical type of purchase.

-If your car is old, it may make sense to drop the coverage that would help you pay to have it fixed if it's in a crash or replace if it's stolen -- i.e. the collision and comprehensive coverage. Find out what you're paying for that stuff and then have a look at its likely resale value (www.kbb.com)

-Do anything you can to reduce the distance you drive, such as car-pooling or using public transit or a bicycle or whatever, and be sure to alert your insurance company to the reduced distance you cover. (See story about insurance plans that charge for actual mileage on Page 224.)

-Consider taking driving courses (usually they're called "defensive" driving courses) that your insurer thinks will reduce the risk of insuring you.

-Look around for a group to join that may earn you lower rates, such as a professional or alumni association, community clubs, or anybody you can find. You might even get a price break if you get another university degree.

-Adding a theft deterrent system or a GPS tracking device may earn you a lower rate, so check with your agent.

-Ask your agent for a list of things like the ones listed above that might reduce your rates. They'll tell you if asked but aren't prone to offering you suggestions about ways you can pay them less money.

-Work at home if you can, since people who don't commute someplace on a regular basis pay a lot less. This also works if you retire.

-If your partner and you both have vehicles, it could be smart to agree on using one vehicle for commuting or other regular travel and register the other for occasional use. This of course requires that you and your partner are comfortable with splitting a single insurance policy, which can save money in many ways.

-If you have several drivers on your policy, it might be possible to assign certain drivers to certain cars. For example, it costs less to insure a teenage boy to drive an elderly minivan than almost anything else on wheels.

-Encourage your children to get better grades, since that can earn you a discount.

-Start a career as a professional, since some insurance companies charge lawyers and the like about half of what they charge a waitress. Several governments are investigating.

**Alexander Law & Susan Winlaw   223**

# Insurance Firms Now Offering You A Chance To Pay Less For Driving Less

If you drive less than average and are willing to allow technology to track your actual miles, there are companies that will charge you less for car insurance. And you don't have to drive much under the average distance to qualify.

Key to the plans from GMAC Insurance and Progressive Corp. is the notion that people who drive less are, mathematically and maybe culturally, less likely to get into a crash. That means an insurance firm can charge you less money a year but still make a profit from your premiums.

In the case of GMAC Insurance, that discount can range from 15 to 54 percent and is widely available across the U.S., while Progressive is rolling out a program that could also offer significant savings. If this initiative works, you can expect other firms to get onboard quickly. After all, taking money from clients and paying none out in claims is the dream of every insurance firm.

The technology that makes this work better than previous self-reporting systems actually measures the distance you travel and reports back to the insurance company on a regular basis. Previously, the customers reported the distance they drove, and the insurance firms found them to be "unreliable" in reporting distances acurately.

GMAC uses the OnStar safety-security-guidance system that's been included in virtually all of the new models sold through the various GM brands for years. OnStar records the distance the customer drives and reports it to GMAC.

More work is involved in the TripSense plan, since consumers have to get a small measuring device installed into their car's onboard diagnostic port, download it to their home computer, and send it to Progressive at prescribed intervals.

It could easily be worth the trouble involved.

# Getting Fair Car Service
# May Be Impossible In Free Market

When it comes to finding a good auto repair service, the general attitude of anyone offering advice on cars is that you ask everyone you know for a trusted name, call the BBB, look for ASE- and AAA-approved shops, search the web for any evidence of wrong-doing, consult the stars or the tarot cards, demand the old parts you paid to have replaced, consult your local government's consumer department, pray for guidance, and keep your fingers crossed throughout.

All of that is excellent advice. But if you follow the history of the auto repair industry closely, it's hard to get around the feeling that it may be difficult to impossible to find fair and honest service for your car.

Every time a TV station does one of those hidden camera investigative reports, or a consumer group runs a program to check the ability of local mechanics, or a government agency looks into reports of illegal behavior, the results are depressing.

There are knowledgeable people in various levels of government, legal affairs and the auto business who think reliable or ethical auto service may be an impossible goal on a wide-spread level.

There will always be fair and ethical service providers, it seems, but the providers that aren't those things will survive in the current system.

Which makes it impossible to offer advice except to repeat the rules that are suggested at the top of the story.

The other answer is to avoid paying for service work altogether, which can be done in two ways: 1) Buy the cheapest car you can find, scrap it when it stops working or needs service, and do that again and again. 2) Lease a new car and its warranty and go to a new one when the warranty is up.

**Alexander Law & Susan Winlaw** 225

# Too Many Oil Changes Can Be Bad
# For Our Air And Your Finances

As well as being the most famous Old Husbands' Tale in the world, ''Change your oil regularly'' is also the one with the least relevance to anyone who drives a vehicle that was bought new in this century.

Not only is there probably little or no maintenance value to be found in changing the oil in a new or newish vehicle every 3,000 miles or every three or four months, it also wastes the world's oil resources and puts a greater strain on the environment. And if that's not enough reason to abandon that particular Old Husbands' Tale, it causes North American consumers to waste billions of dollars on unnecessary service work.

Simply change the oil in your vehicle only as often as its owner's manual and/or warranty agreement requires. Your car may even advise you with a message on the dashboard when it's time to change your oil. No company lists any distance less than 5,000 miles, so anything more frequent than that is almost certainly a waste of money, oil and time.

The most recent study of oil and engine wear found that the average driver only needs to change the oil in her car every 8,000 to 10,000 miles.

The issue is so big, one study estimates, that the U.S. uses as much as 1.5 billion more liters of oil a year than it needs to, at a cost in excess of US$1.5 billion, and that doesn't include the cost of the labor.

If you're an obsessive-compulsive type who's afraid that your car's engine will run out of oil, causing it to blow up and leave her stranded in a bad part of town, then keep a wary eye on the car's dashboard for any alerts related to oil. On that point, red lights of any kind should probably earn your immediate attention.

If you're really worried, learn to check the oil level, but

only when the car has been sitting for several hours and the oil has had time to settle in the oil pan. Every car has a long shaft of thin metal called a "dip-stick" that reaches into the bowels of the engine to see how much oil's in there. It should be obvious by the round metal ring amongst the other engine parts, but check your owner's manual for a specific location and guidance on what to do and what to look for. It's an extremely low-tech process, with a little nail-damaging risk.

But as long as you stick to the oil change schedule required by the manufacturer you can ignore the dip-stick and drive with maximum confidence.

Some new cars, including almost all models from General Motors, are designed to measure the wear and tear on the engine oil on an ongoing basis and advise the driver on the need for service.

If you're thinking this might be some kind of car company trick to make you buy more service work or something, consider that the warranty makes the company responsible for repairs to the engine if the owner follows such maintenance rules as how often to change the oil.

As bad as the creation of extra oil for unnecessary oil changes is for the environment, the disposal of the used oil is where the real danger lies. In commercial operations the old oil is recycled into another useful life, but many do-it-yourselfers simply dump the oil wherever they can and that's a real environmental problem.

Used engine oil can be reprocessed and used in furnaces for heat, or in power plants to generate electricity for homes, schools and businesses, and it only takes about eight litres of recycled oil to run the average household for 24 hours.

The correct range for an oil change varies by vehicle and driving patterns, experts say, but it can run from 2,000 miles to well over 15,000 miles.

Most of the firms selling vehicles cars in North America

ally recommend changing the oil for automobiles and light trucks burning gasoline once a year or every 7,500 miles, whichever occurs first, though for diesel engines and turbocharged gasoline engines the recommendation is typically a more accelerated 3,000 miles or six months.

It's interesting to note that the companies who sell the same vehicles in Europe as they do in North America often suggest fewer oil changes to their European customers. Maybe the Europeans aren't as gullible as we are about this kind of thing.

For sure the companies do this to ensure their products' health, but it is widely understood that there's also some desire to keep the customers coming back to the dealerships, where sometimes they are shown the need for other service work.

Whatever the recommended distance between oil changes, it always involves driving done ''under normal or ideal conditions,'' and that can be a problem.

What many perceive to be ''normal'' driving is actually "severe service" driving from the standpoint of the oil, since examples of severe service driving include frequent short trips (especially during cold weather), stop-and-go driving, driving in dusty conditions (gravel roads), and high-temperature conditions.

Under such conditions, the general recommendation found in owners' manuals is to change the oil every 3,000 miles or six months.

GM has an idea of how to deal with this and has created the General Motors Oil Life System (GMOLS), which keeps track of each vehicle's unique driving patterns and gives specific advice to the driver on when to change the oil.

GM says this system can double or even triple the time between oil changes when compared to the common 3,000-mile recommendation simply by evaluating driving conditions.

Honda added a similar system to its cars, and Chrysler is following suit with its 2008 models.

However often you change your vehicle's oil, you must be careful to use the right grade of oil, since today's sophisticated engines produce more power than ever before and need to be looked after. This data should be in the owner's manual.

Put in the correct oil when it's needed, then, but not before.

## Saturn Is Best Dealership For Most

Saturn gained its early success by providing the kind of buying experience that many people dream of -- no-haggle deals with a money-back guarantee in an environment that put respect for the customer above all else.

This worked amazingly well for the division of General Motors, even though for the first 15 years of its existence it had only second- and third-rate products to sell.

About five years ago Saturn's product lineup began to change with the introduction of the Sky roadster. Now the brand is the primary outlet for vehicles originally designed to be sold in Europe, and these products are better than anything the brand has ever seen.

Saturn of late has played up the improved status of its vehicles in its advertising and it's hard to blame them. But that tends to make Saturn look like just another car brand trumpeting product over process.

But the process at Saturn (i.e. what it's like for a person to buy and service a car) has not changed that much, even though it has much better product to sell.

On the annual J. D. Power survey of sales and service satisfaction, Saturn always challenges for the top spot and is only outranked by the luxury brands (BMW, Cadillac, Lexus, Lincoln) that spend money to please their clients.

Saturn still relies on respect, which has no extra cost.

# Shopping To Upgrade And
# Improve A Car You Already Own

To a degree that might surprise you, it is possible to do a lot to your car that will make it more closely suit your tastes and needs.

You can of course spend a fortune getting a vehicle customized to reach excessive levels of appearance and performance, but there is also a large variety of things that can be altered or added that will make your vehicle safer, more comfortable and more convenient, for modest amounts of money.

The best place to start is www.enjoythedrive.com, a consumer-oriented website run by the group (SEMA, for Specialty Equipment Manufacturers Association) that represents many of those auto-related businesses that line the suburban roads of every city on the continent.

The site's aim is to show you how to "customize your vehicle for the way you live". It offers you the chance to search by type of vehicle (SUV, minivan, family car and so on), how you use it (family shuttle, daily commute, etc), or by area of concern (safety, security, convenience, etc).

In general, the site is quite appealing to look at and read, and easy to navigate, at least at first. The home page offers you a chance to browse by the type of vehicle you drive (minivan, sports car, luxury car, etc), the general nature of how you use it (family shuttle, daily commute, etc), or what feature you'd like to improve (security, safety, working on the road, etc).

Any one of these areas can lead you to stories that describe in general terms some items that can upgrade some aspect of your vehicle. Some of the things might surprise you. Who knew, for example, that you could get a gun safe for the car?

Of course, once you knew that a gun safe or whatever it is existed, you can continue to keep searching the web on your own for whatever makes your car better.

# Reduce Water And Chemical Use
# When Cleaning Your Car

Though it seems unlikely, it is now apparently possible to wash your car without using any water and maybe no chemicals that hurt the environment or affect allergies.

Several companies now offer products over the internet that perform this task and early reports are encouraging.

The process probably takes longer than using a commercial wash or even a garden hose setup at home, and it costs about $3 to $5 a vehicle.

As a bonus, the waterless systems do not send soapy water into the storm drains, which end up adding pollution to local rivers, lakes and oceans.

The problem of polluted (by the chemicals in soap and other cleaning agents, and the dirt from the cars) water from street-side car washes is becoming an environmental issue in many communities, where outright bans are being considered to reduce the amount of untreated water running into water sources.

The fact that these bans would include those popular weekend fund-raising car washes would be included in these bans might suggest how serious the problem is.

Some of the companies offering the product include Eco Touch of New Hampshire, Freedom Waterless Car Wash, Green Earth Waterless Car Wash, and No-Wet Waterless Concepts in New Jersey. Undoubtedly others exist and/or will follow; search "waterless car wash" to see your choices.

There may even be a chance that someone will come to your house or business and waterless wash your vehicle.

## Avoid Sex In The Car

The best case for avoiding sexual acts in the car is in the book and movie versions of The World According To Garp.

# Your Behavior After A Crash Can Have Greater Consequences Than You Imagine

What we're going to propose here may seem strange, or insensitive, or callous, but it's really just smart, since a car crash can be the opening act in a legal and financial nightmare for you and your family.

Indeed, a car crash is the primary reason most people get involved in the criminal justice system and the serious risks that entails. If you're successfully sued by a participant in an auto crash it can dramatically affect your life financially and emotionally.

Sure, a car crash isn't usually any of those things if no one's hurt, but treating it like it could turn ugly is -- unfortunately -- the best attitude.

So, if you are involved in a vehicular collision, the most important things to remember are things that you should NOT do.

Do not leave the scene until the police say it's okay, since the authorities might tend to view it as a hit-and-run incident, and that's a very bad thing.

Do not apologize or say anything that could remotely be considered an expression of guilt or an admission of fault. This would include the "I'm sorry, I'm sorry, I'm so sorry" that most people genuinely feel when they've hurt another person, even accidentally, or "I didn't see you coming" or anything else.

Do not treat lightly the need to get as much information as possible about the crash scene, the damage to the vehicles involved and the particulars of any witnesses. This is why you should use your cell phone or a digital camera to take as many pictures as possible. If you can record conversations from the site of the crash on your cell phone or digital camera (most of them take low-quality video) or on your lawyer's answering machine or whatever, that also might be smart.

Do not be rude, boorish or pushy in the performance of those important chores, since you do not want to alienate any witnesses or emergency workers who might later take part in legal proceedings.

Do not ask occupants of the other car if they're hurt, since it might give them ideas. This is especially wise if there are witnesses around to take note of their injuries. Telling the witnesses and the police that you have been hurt (assuming your really have) is also not a bad idea, since it looks suspicious to complain about some ailment later that you didn't mention at the time.

Do not think that writing down the other driver's name, address and phone number is enough, since they might be lying because it suits their own interests. Ask to see their paperwork, including their driver's license.

Write everything down, including the number on the driver's license, the number on the license plate, even the car's VIN number from the plaque along the bottom of the windshield.

Do this with the witnesses, too, and take pictures of them and the occupants of the other car.  Indeed, it's smart to get the license plate numbers of any vehicles that stop at the scene, even if they arrive after the crash.

If there's a way to get fingerprints and DNA (like giving them a container of water and then holding onto it) that would also be good, and that's not a joke.

Just as importantly, get all the details from the other driver's insurance card -- number, address, phone, and so on.

Get every license plate number on paper and on film. If you ever have to take legal action against them or defend yourself from their legal action, this could be important.

To be sure, this is all very depressing and probably won't be necessary, but there are no guarantees.

# Lemon Laws There To Help
# Owners Who Get A Bad Car

Though owning a car with recurring problems will still mean a lot of aggravation for the owner, things have vastly improved over the years with regard to dealing with a "lemon".

In the first place, new vehicle quality has gone up at every car manufacturer (see Page 156), so the chances of getting a lemon are reduced.

Secondly, every state now has a "Lemon Law," though they vary widely in the way they work. You can check your own state's regulations at http://autopedia.com/html/HotLinks_Lemon2.html.

Thirdly, we're in the middle of the greatest buyers' markets of all time (see Page 4), so the car companies are extra anxious to keep you happy and avoid messy struggles over vehicle quality.

As a result, if you keep extremely thorough records, practice patience and persistence, stay calm and polite and follow the process, you're likely to get some kind of satisfaction in due course. Quite often the car company will step in to resolve the problem before the consumer has to call a lawyer or file a lemon law claim, since that usually means the kind of negative publicity they hate.

The manufacturer and dealer associations have both gone on record as saying they want to do whatever they can to prevent such situations from going to the lemon law level.

However, the dealers and car companies will almost certainly let you bear the brunt of the problem if you don't press your own case in a thorough and relentless manner. When they're helpful to the consumer it's almost always out of a sense of enlightened self-interest, not guilt or the milk of human kindness. They're perfectly willing to let you pay for their mistakes, in other words, if you don't assert your rights.

One of the keys to getting satisfaction is keeping comprehensive records of every part of the problem, the odometer reading at which it occurred, and your efforts to solve it. Keep copies of all bills and any other paperwork, records (time and duration) of all phone calls, the names and numbers of all contacts and anything else you can think of. Take photos of the problem, if possible, or a video if your car has a noise or vibration issue. You may never have to use this data, but calm, polite customers with extensive records and a determined attitude are usually the last kind of owners the car companies want trouble with. It also helps if you have some kind of leverage that might hurt their future sales.

Go through channels at the dealership first (service adviser, service manager, general manager, dealer) and then take it to the manufacturer, which has a clearly defined process.

Check in the "vehicles and equipment" section at www.nhtsa.gov to see if your problem is common in your model. There are also many lively blog communities devoted to specific models in those auto-related websites so you might be able to get some information, help or emotional support there.

If you do go the lemon law route, it never means more than four attempts by the car company to solve the problems in 24,000 miles or 24 months and the vehicle being out of service for more than 30 days, but some states require fewer attempts, especially if it's a safety-related item.

Assuming you win, the lemon laws generally result in you getting a new vehicle or your money back, usually with some allowance for the mileage you put on. Your legal costs may be also be covered by the car company if your lawyer files under the Federal Magnuson-Moss Warranty Act.

There's a short list of lawyers at autosafety.org.

# Online Auto Insurance Use
# Grows As Services Improve

Thanks to the positive experiences of others and company efforts to improve their online offerings, people are becoming more comfortable with the concept of buying auto insurance online and then using the web to maintain their policies.

According to a recent study, consumers submitted 32 million requests for online quotes in 2007 and 2 million of them purchased policies online. Both are records, and big increases from 2006.

In a separate study by The Consumer Respect Group for the first-quarter of 2008, respondents gave improving grades to insurance companies that had significantly improved their online services. Their average score was 5.5 out of 10, which brings them to a level found in other businesses.

The companies that did better than average with their online sites were:

-Progressive Casualty, 7.5
-Geico, 6.9
-Liberty Mutual, 6.5
-Nationwide, 6.4
-MetLife Auto & Home, 6.3
-AIG Direct, 6.1
-Cincinnati Insurance, 6.0
-Erie Insurance, 6.0
-Allstate Insurance, 5.9
-Farmer's Insurance, 5.9
-Esurance, 5.5

These scores are not likely to fall as more people move to online insurance, but it is seems likely that the other companies offering online-buying will be improving their services.

Many of them have been making their sites more useful to consumers; a year ago only five percent of the sites allowed people to actually complete a policy sale and print out the paperwork, but in the most recent study 23 percent did. Other improvements included better inter-active chats, direct phone connections, more helpful e-mail responses, and so on.

The primary charm of online insurance is that it's usually the quickest and easiest way to gather a wide-ranging collection of quotes for your auto insurance business, which almost always ends up with you paying less for your car insurance.

But the ability to go online and manage your auto insurance account is also appealing to a lot of consumers, who prefer that to dealing with a digital phone system or even a real person. Just as importantly, perhaps, the insurance companies also like it, since it allows them to save money on their overheads which, the theory goes, allows them to reduce the premiums they charge their clients.

There's already been talk in the auto insurance industry about people who buy and manage their policies online getting a lower premium than the folks who use the traditional methods of using an agent or the company who left a flyer on the doorstep yesterday.

## A Record Insurance Premium?

If you think your insurance rate's too high, consider the family in Edmonton, Alberta, who saw their annual premium go from about $15,000 a year to $104,566.33 -- yes, that's $104,566.33 -- a year.

The primary cause was the driving record of the 19-year-old son, who managed to get 10 speeding tickets between being in two fender-benders and a crash that totaled his car.

Before that, there had been a pair of license suspensions.

The family went looking for another insurance firm and found one, which only wanted $50,000 a year.

# GPS Navigation Can Save
# Gas, Time and Maybe Even You

If you ever travel anywhere outside of those places that you know like the back of your hand, for the sake of safety, time and the environment you should consider getting a GPS navigation device.

With a global positioning system (which can be had for about $100 and works anywhere), you always know where you are and how to get where you're going anywhere in the U.S. and Canada. That means you never have to drive around in a strange place looking for something, wasting time and gas and perhaps putting yourself in harm's way. You also never have to get out of the car to ask for directions, and a GPS system will provide you with directions and details (address and phone number) to the nearest services (gas, hospitals, ATMs, washrooms, etc) and millions of other useful sites.

With voice directions, you are free to pay attention to where you're headed and what's going on around you.

Electronic navigation devices also work from almost anywhere, since they don't need a phone signal to connect with the satellites that provide them with their exact location.

One of the least expensive GPS navigation systems is a package from DeLorme that includes Street Atlas software that loads into your laptop and a GPS device that attaches to it. The system tells you precisely where you are and will show or tell you how to get somewhere else. If you're already carrying a laptop and don't want to add bulk or weight, this makes the most sense. You can also transfer maps to a PDA for improved portability.

On some new vehicles you can get a nav system with the car, but it costs a lot of money and has no portability.

For less money than a fixed system you can buy one of the stand-alone GPS navigation systems, which come with smaller screens and are usually portable. New variations on this theme are being unveiled on a regular basis, sometimes with traffic information as an optional feature.

If you have a GM vehicle, you can get excellent navigation help from the OnStar system that's probably part of the vehicle already. The service costs a decent amount a year but includes many other excellent safety and security features.

If you ever travel someplace that you don't know well, a laptop-based GPS system is an excellent investment in keeping you safe and saving you time and money.

## Green Cars Are Hot, Baby

While it's still not entirely easy being green, it is at least apparently hot.

Nine of 10 women responding to a recent survey said they would rather talk to the guy with the latest "green" vehicle than the guy with the hottest sportscar, which suggests that hybrid cars have completed the unlikely transformation from "geek mobile" to "chick magnet" in a decade.

This is the most interesting finding of a survey taken to promote the Challenge X program, which is a continental collegiate engineering competition sponsored by the U.S. Department of Energy and General Motors.

But the survey also shows that 80 percent of American car buyers would find someone with the latest fuel-efficient car more interesting to talk to at a party than someone with the latest model sports car.

Forty-five percent of people between 18 and 43 years say it's a fashion faux-pas nowadays to have a car that is not green or environmentally friendly.

More than seven in 10 car buyers say if there were a reality TV show like "Project Runway" that was about designing the best-looking fuel-efficient and emissions-free car rather than designing clothes, they'd definitely watch. Attention, NBC.

# Treat IIHS "Top Safety Picks"
# With Caution When Picking A Car

If surviving a crash were the only safety feature that counted, the annual list of Top Safety Picks from the Insurance Institute for Highway Safety (IIHS) would still be suspect. But since complete safety involves a lot more than a vehicle's crash-worthiness, the annual selections from the firm that's owned and operated by various insurance companies really needs to be treated with lashings of salt.

In the first place, these tests are done in a laboratory using repeatable, but narrow, crash circumstances involving speed, angle of impact, weight and shape of object struck, weight and shape of occupants, and so on.

This makes it easier to compare results of the different vehicles on bodies of a specific size, but it does little to predict the results of the different vehicles in a real world crash with people of different sizes and ages in them going different speeds and all the other variables.

Plain and simple, it is impossible to measure the true crash-worthiness of a vehicle in a laboratory, either the one run by the insurance companies or the one run by the federal government.

On top of that, the results from the IIHS are not always current, since vehicles are revised or upgraded faster than they can be crashed and measured.

Most importantly, the IIHS evaluation process includes only some of the safety equipment now available on the market, including side and front airbags, stability control and the ability of the seats to keep the passengers from whiplash injuries in a rear-end collision.

The big fault with the IIHS program is that it acts as if the danger to a vehicle occupant is over as soon as the crash is complete. In these tests, damage to the dummies is measured and the test ends.

In the real world, the danger from a crash does not end with the crash itself. In many cases, the crash sets the clock racing on getting the occupant to the hospital, and the IIHS has not taken that into consideration at all.

The chances of surviving many crashes includes the amount of time it takes for an injured person to get help after the crash, and on that front a crash-notification system (which essentially means GM's OnStar system) is the only one that works with or without the occupant's involvement and in places cell phones won't operate.

That, too, is ignored by the IIHS and pretty much everyone else who uses crash test ratings as "safety" ratings.

The IIHS results should be considered by anyone interested in safety, but not considered the ultimate word in finding a vehicle that will protect you and your family.

Information about the Top Safety Picks and the IIHS test process can be found at www.iihs.org.

## Koreans To Use Microsoft Infotainment

Microsoft will be supplying infotainment systems to some or all of the Korean cars for North America from Hyundai and Kia by 2010, though details on cost, availability and functionality are sketchy.

It's likely that various levels of performance will be developed so it can offer limited skills in, say, a Kia Spectra for one price and be more sophisticated in a Hyundai Genesis for more money.

This will be the second use of Microsoft's automotive platform, and it should be different from the first application called Sync that's already being sold in some cars from Ford. The computer firm has made it plain that it will continue to shop the technology around to other car companies, which probably means more applications early in the next decade.

# No Need To Worry About "Handling" When Deciding On A New Car

Wasting your money is an unfortunate side-effect of most of the Old Husbands' Tales about cars making the rounds, but the most expensive one by far involves the claim that it's worth spending more to get a vehicle that "handles" better.

This can mean you have to spend more for a version of the car that features upgraded equipment, racier tires and wheels, and fancy badges.

It may also mean that you're pressured into getting a car that you don't really like but costs a lot more money because a bunch of male auto writers have convinced some other men it has greater ability in "aggressive" driving or is more "fun-to-drive".

While there's no denying that some people enjoy the way different cars feel on the road, there's virtually no case to be made for the idea that you have to spend more money for one to bring it up to acceptable handling levels.

Today's new cars are so well-engineered that they can quite safely travel at 125 percent of the legal limits without any fuss or danger whatsoever. That means you should be able to take a curve marked for 60 mph at 75 mph in virtually every new vehicle on the market and not have to worry about it, no matter who made it or how much it cost. And those are the everyday commuter cars or family haulers; the sportier models can go even faster without concern.

But why would you want to go faster than 25 percent above the legal speed limit? On top of being illegal and more dangerous (more speed means the driver has less time to react and the car needs more distance to stop), going hugely faster than the legal limit is also more uncomfortable for everyone in the car except the driver.

Beyond that, the engineering features that do make a car

capable of greater speeds in a corner also make it less forgiving of bumps, cracks and potholes, so the ride will be less smooth.

Not all engineering upgrades are bad, especially if you live somewhere where the weather can create bad road surfaces. It might be worth buying all-wheel-drive, for example, if it's available on the model you want and you drive in snow a lot.

And if the only way to get stability control involves an upgraded suspension package or anything else it's absolutely worth considering if you ever encounter snow or really wet roads when you drive.

Stability control is not a classic "handling" feature, by the way, it's a safety feature that can do something you can't (activate one brake at a time to stop a skid) if you've been driving the car too hard for the prevailing conditions.

So if you find a car you like to drive, don't feel you have to spend any extra money to make it safe enough to drive.

## Hiring People To Do Car Chores

Though it may not be a widespread industry yet, there are people around who will do auto-related chores on your behalf for a fee.

For example, there are people who will fill out various forms and take them to the DMV, and other people who will ferry your car in for service.

There aren't many of them but they are out there, and you might be able to find someone trustworthy on the web or a grocery store bulletin board or through your friends. If not, there may be someone willing to do this stuff for you who hadn't thought of it before.

If you're really ambitious, you might even turn the idea into a national web-based business and never have to visit the DMV or the dealer's service center again.

# A Vehicle's Range Is Often
# An Overlooked Value

A vehicle's range may play some small part in some smart consumers' thinking, but it's unlikely many people consider the notion of an engine's run time.

We think both items should be included in the buying process if you're determined to consider a vehicle's safety features in the broadest sense.

But before we get to the safety value of a gasoline tank, let us consider the part it plays in determining a vehicle's range (the distance it will travel on a tank of fuel) and how many stops you have to make at gas stations to fill up.

The lower the vehicle range, the more stops you'll have to make for fuel, and the difference in range between comparable vehicles can be remarkable.

Compare the Mini to the Honda Civic coupe, for example, and you end up making a lot more visits to the gas station with the Mini.

Having a lower range can also mean you perhaps can't get someplace as quickly as you have to in an emergency, or you might be forced to stop where you don't want to or face running out of fuel. Lower range just forces you into making the gas stop decision more often.

So you might want to check with one of those data-centric websites (such as Edmunds.com) where they have helpfully done the range calculation for you. It's not hard to do yourself. Just take a vehicle's projected fuel economy number (city or highway, to match your driving style) and multiply it by the number of gallons the tank will hold.

Remember also that the bigger the gas tank the more hours of heat, light and power you'll get if you're in one of those monster traffic jams that keep people stranded in their vehicles for hours.

# More Wrecks Hidden In
# Used Car Market Than Ever

Millions of severely damaged cars are showing up on the used car market, which increases the likelihood that some buyer might pay a higher price than she should and get stuck with more problems than she'd expect.

This grim news comes from the company whose job it is to track the histories of used cars (though it freely admits it doesn't always succeed in doing a complete job of that) -- Carfax.

According to Carfax, about five million cars are deemed to be salvage after severe crashes, more than half of which are resold, "many by sellers who intentionally hide their damaged past from unknowing consumers."

Even though they don't always know if a car's been severely damaged unless the seller (the one who's trying to keep it a secret) or some agency tells them, Carfax is still anxious that you spend money on their service first.

If they send you a report that neglects to tell you the car was wrecked, you MIGHT be entitled to a refund from them. Check the small print on their website first.

The best move of course is to buy from a dealer you know (who is going to be there after the sale) and to look closely at the car yourself, or get someone to do it for you.

In most cases, it's easy for an experienced individual to spot a severely wrecked car, often without a test drive. Buying cars online and sight-unseen from someone in-town or across-country can be a very risky thing to do, and online insurance programs and other consumer protection aids may not be enough.

As Carfax dryly notes, "the used car market is a target-rich environment for scam artists." Meaning they're out to take your money if you give them half a chance.

# In-Car Connectivity: Boon
# And Bane For Drivers Everywhere

There are two very powerful but opposing societal forces swirling around the private car right now, and no clear method of accommodating the pair of them available at the moment.

On the one hand there's the proliferation of devices that allow you to enjoy music, videos, e-mail, voicemail, instant messages, spreadsheets and all kinds of things in your car.

On the other hand there's the growing concern about the risks associated with the distractions that come with enjoying music, videos, e-mail and so on in your car.

Distracted drivers have always played a major role in the amount of death and destruction that happens on our highways every year, and now a lot of lawmakers are worried that it's going to get worse with all these new portable devices. So new proposals to ban various devices turn up on a regular basis and we can expect this political effort to continue.

So there are big companies trying to come up with a solution that will deliver all that information and entertainment to the driver in a safe way. Previous efforts have not been successful, with Microsoft's fruitless attempts with AutoPC at the top of the list.

The biggest problem with previous systems was the sorry state of the voice recognition that was necessary for drivers to open files and change stations and what have you without taking their eyes off the road or their hands off the wheel. That seems to be less of an issue now than ever before, which is the best solution, but technology is now coming out that lets the driver hook up the gadget du jour and control it through the knobs and switches of the car's built-in sound system.

So it is that Ford's now selling a Sync system with many of its vehicles that allows drivers to plug their devices into a USB port or connect through Bluetooth wireless technology and use them through the car's own audio system controls, and a voice recognition system.

This system has been extremely well received and Ford is working hard to improve its services and expand its availability, and undoubtedly the others car companies will as well if they think they must to stay competitive.

But if society is to find a common ground for more gadgets and fewer distractions, Sync or something like it will have to work very well and be available at a more accessible price on many more cars.

## Beware Auto Warranty Sales By Phone

First off, buying an extended warranty on your car is almost certainly not a good idea at any time, either from the dealer at the point-of-purchase or later on when the original coverage is coming to an end.

Studies show that you will almost certainly end up paying more for warranty coverage than you will for whatever auto repairs the extended policy covers.

But if you're one of those folks who feel better with some kind of warranty coverage beyond what the car companies offer, you should commit a search of your own to find out which companies offer the best deals. The web was created for just such chores.

Most important of all, just say no if someone calls you up and tries to coerce or scare you into buying a policy over the phone. Do not give them your credit card number under any circumstances since it may be impossible to get the charge cancelled in the future.

## Big Drop For In-Car GPS Prices

Suzuki will sell a small car that has maps, traffic, weather, e-mail and other benefits for about $16,500 this year.

# Get Your Message Out To Other Drivers
## As You Roll Along The Road

For many people the great joy of a car is that it's the one place in the world where they can be alone.

But there are many other people who can't imagine not being in contact with other people, even in the car, and it's those folks that a bunch of companies are trying to reach. For the most part this means delivering messages that have traditionally been handled with a facial or finger expression, but more sophisticated messages are also on offer.

There are several devices that allow someone to send pre-fab bulletins covering most of the sentiments that pass between two drivers, such as "Thanks" or "Idiot," or even short personalized greetings created by the driver. These devices usually stick to the window, but there are also some that frame the car's license plate. Any decent after-market store will sell them, or you can dig them up on the web.

The more advanced efforts are trying to create a cell phone bridge between people in two different vehicles. If you register your cell phone number with SameLane (at www.samelane.com), for example, you get a sticker that attaches to your car and then anyone who sees it can call SameLane and be connected to your cell phone, for $1.99 a minute. They do not get your number and you do not get theirs. If you want to talk longer or again, you can then exchange phone numbers. If all you want to do is offer up a critique of that person's driving ability, you can do that as well.

Undoubtedly other such systems, or something else, will soon be with us. It's a priority of the industry's to develop a technology that will allow vehicles to talk to each other for safety reasons ("Excuse me, Chevrolet Malibu, but I'm over here on your right blind spot") but that probably means someone will also figure out how the drivers can talk as well.

# New Evidence On Whether
# Men Or Women Are Better Drivers

There was a flap when a major newspaper ran a story quoting a famous 1998 study that showed that women were worse drivers than men even though they drove a lot less.

The facts for that study came from crash statistics for 1990, which means that data is now about 20 years old, at which time societal norms had men doing the lion's share of the driving. The big difference between the sexes then was that men had a lot more driving experience than women did, and it's hard to overestimate the importance of real-world experience in pushing the crash and death rates down.

For evidence of which sex is more likely to get into a crash, consult your auto insurance bill, where women generally pay less than men. Given the slavish devotion shown to actuarial tables by the insurance companies, this provides irrefutable proof that women tend to get into fewer crashes than men.

The gap in crash rates is most pronounced in young people, where men are notoriously more likely to get into trouble. But apparently that gap is closing, as more women exhibit the kind of reckless behavior -- speeding, drinking, no seatbelts -- that has traditionally gotten men into trouble.

## Best Car Cleaning Tip Ever

There are about 2,226,003 places on the web to give you advice on how to clean your car, inside and out, but our favorite-ever advice includes the sentence "Love happens, and sometimes it happens in cars" and goes on to include advice on how to get lipstick out of your car's upholstery.

It could come in handy, if you're lucky.

Mag Ruffman's car cleaning tips can be found in the Renovations section of www.Homeandgarden.canoe.ca.

# Devices Will Let You Be A
# Disc Jockey With Your Car Horn

If you've ever wished that your car horn could play things like Fiddler on the Roof or New York, New York or the Macarena or Dixie or The Stars and Stripes or pretty much anything else instead of that standard bleat, the wonderful world of aftermarket accessories is waiting out there to help you.

Search "car horn downloadable tones" and be prepared to be amazed at the variety of sounds and songs awaiting you. You can spend a little or a lot to get the equipment needed to make your DJ dream happen, but be careful of spinning some original sounds near the police.

The horn is a required part of a car's safety setup in most jurisdictions, after all, and you'll need to keep the original tone to satisfy the regulations.

## Be Polite And Then Fight Speeding Ticket

The primary rules are to say "No" if an officer asks you if you know why he pulled you over (another answer can be seen as an admission of guilt) and to stay polite at all times.

If you upset the officer, he or she can make a note on the ticket that will remind him and others that you were rude and not to give you a deal.

After that, consider fighting the ticket (even if you have to hire someone) because having a conviction for speeding on your record can cost you big time on your insurance.

## Help With Parking Is Available

When it comes to providing a better view of what's around you in a tight parking or backing-up situation, nothing comes close to the multi-camera Around View Monitor on the upscale Infiniti EX 35 wagon/CUV/SUV.

# Push-Button Starting
## May Not Go Over With Consumers

In response to very little demand that we know of, the auto industry is trying to replace the key-crank start with the push-button start.

The push-button system requires a "smart" key with a transponder that you take to the car with you, which sends a signal to the anti-theft system when it's close enough that allows the engine to start when you push the button. It does not have to be inserted in anything. The button you push would be on the flat part of the dash or the console or wherever, rather than on the steering wheel column.

Any demand for this technology would probably come from people with arthritis or some other ailment, and perhaps women with extremely fragile nails.

Beyond that it's hard to see any value to this unless you leave the car key in the wallet or handbag you always carry, which would make it harder to lose the key by itself. If you did lose the key, however, replacing it would likely be irritating and more expensive than replacing a regular key.

The car companies really like this technology because it allows them to move the start switch away from the steering wheel, which is good for technical and aesthetic reasons. They're always looking for ways to separate themselves from the other brands, you see, and something smart on what is sometimes called the "beachfront property" near the driver is the prime place to do it.

Nearly 50 upscale models have the "smart" key as an option now, but it will likely be working its way into more reasonably-priced models soon, probably as an option.

Not much you can do about it except decline to spend extra money for the answer to a question not many people were asking.

**Alexander Law & Susan Winlaw**

# ASE Insignia May Mean You
# Get Better Auto Service

Word-of-mouth is still widely regarded as the best method of finding a good place to get your car serviced, even by California's Department of Consumer Affairs Bureau of Automotive Repair.

But that agency and many others like it are also glad to suggest a non-profit operation whose job it is to test and certify individual auto technicians (not repair shops in general, it must be noted) -- the National Institute for Automotive Service Excellence, or simply the ASE.

Going to a shop that promotes the ASE's work and employs technicians who wear a blue ASE patch on their shirts or coveralls may not be the answer to all of your automotive service problems, but it should give you a better chance for satisfaction.

Look most particularly for a repair business that has the ASE's "Blue Seal of Excellence," since it means that at least three-quarters of the technicians have ASE accreditation.

ASE tests service people in all major areas of repair and service and currently has nearly 400,000 certified technicians, who can be found at every type of service facility, in dealerships, gas stations, corner garages, franchised service centers and parts stores.

If the repair establishment doesn't have enough ASE technicians to rate the Blue Seal of Excellence, it can display a blue and white ASE sign if it has one certified technician.

Looking for a service facility with ASE approval's a good place to start, but the Virginia-based association also has other tips on getting ready for an auto repair incident.

-The smart move is to search for a service center before you need it, the ASE and a bunch of other agencies suggest, since a decision made under the stress of a malfunctioning car is more likely to come to grief.

-The best service facility may not be close to your home or office, so be prepared to set up a ride in advance. Convenience may have to suffer in return for quality, in other words.

-Read your owner's manual so you know what your vehicle's about, and be sure to get the work done that's required by your warranty agreement. Following the other suggested service stuff could also reduce the chance of trouble.

-Ask friends and co-workers for recommendations, and look at your local web sites for online tips. It actually wouldn't hurt to do that before you buy any type of car.

-Check you local consumer organization(s) about the reputation of a particular repair shop, specifically with regard to complaints and the rate of their resolution.

-When you find a repair shop that looks promising, start off with a minor job if you can. If you like the results, trust them with more complicated repairs later.

-Before you go into the facility, check for vehicles in the parking lot of equal value and condition to your own, since their presence suggests that other owners trust the facility.

-Keep an eye out for vehicles like yours and then ask the shop about what kinds of cars they usually service, since technology differs from car-to-car and it helps if they have some familiarity with your model.

-Inside the facility, look to see if it's neat and well-organized, and check out the equipment in the service bays to see if it looks modern. You could also ask any obsessive-compulsives you know where they get their car serviced.

-Places that are well run should have a courteous, helpful staff, with service writers who are willing to answer all of your questions. If you don't like the way they treat you on your fact-finding visit, it's unlikely they're going to treat you better when you're a customer.

- Look for "signs of professionalism" in the customer service area, including civic and community service awards, membership in the Better Business Bureau, AAA-Approved Auto Repair status, or customer service awards.

-Ask for the names of a few customers and call them for their thoughts on the place.

-The business' policies with regard to labor rates, guarantees, methods of payment and so on should be posted and/or explained to your satisfaction.

-Especially if you need major work, ask if the shop usually does your type of repair or your model of car.

-When you need some work done on your car, describe the symptoms but don't suggest a course of treatment. They may do the work you mention if your car didn't need it and then claim that you asked them to do it.

-If the service experience isn't good, moving to another shop may not be the answer. Discuss the problem with the service manager or owner and give them a chance to resolve the problem. The theory here is that reputable shops will be glad to listen and perhaps make an effort to keep your business and stop you from dissing them with other clients.

-No matter what happens, keep good records (including the date and times of all phone calls), the paperwork and even the parts that were replaced.

-Rewarding good service with repeat business could also be good for you and the shop owner.

-Keep an eye on the shop even when you're not using it, since things can change quickly in business and the auto service industry is no exception.

-If things do go wrong, don't be afraid to forward information about your problems to various elected officials and even the bureaucrats. Sometimes the only things that can help consumers are changes in legislation.

The ultimate solution is to buy cheap old cars that you scrap when they break, or a new car with a warranty.

# Aftermarket Device Can Help You Avoid Handling Gas Caps

There are lots of reasons why people don't like stopping for gas at the service station, but perhaps the most common is the need to handle the smelly gas cap when they're filling up and having the gas fume reminder on their hand for hours.

Well, for a modest investment (maybe $25) you can buy a gas cap that you will never have to touch again after you install it, and if you're not good about tightening the car's original cap every time you stop for fuel, the new cap may even pay for itself.

The part in question is the InStant Fill (trademark registered) fuel cap from Stant Manufacturing, which replaces the car's original gas cap.

It locks into place so gas can't evaporate (that's the money-saving part) and has a special hole in the middle that allows you to insert the gas nozzle directly. When you've pumped the gas, you remove the nozzle, the cap seals automatically, you flip the little trapdoor closed and away you go.

It doesn't work so well with those hooded nozzles that California gas stations use to trap fumes and it may not fit older vehicles, but the InStant Fill gas cap can help you deal with one of the more unpleasant aspects of running a vehicle.

It would also be extremely useful for anyone who has problems gripping things because of arthritis or some other infirmity, and of course it reduces the chances of breaking a nail.

Finally, the InStant Fill cap will actually be a little quicker than the traditional cap, which brings a hint of Nascar to the proceedings if that appeals to you. And since you don't remove it there's no chance you can leave it behind.

The car companies are finally getting wise to this problem, by the way, and it may mean similar products may become a part of new cars, though probably not anytime soon.

**Alexander Law & Susan Winlaw**

## Joni Mitchell Never Sang About This Part Of Paris

The appeal of Paris was probably never given more vivid life than it was by Joni Mitchell, and the idea of wandering down the Champs-Élysées has played a huge role in the dreams of millions of us ever since.

Those who haven't actually taken that great 1.5-mile stroll from the Arc de Triomphe to the Place de la Concorde will find it hard to believe that a lot of the charm of the tree-lined street comes from its new car dealerships as much as its cafes and cabarets, but it's true. They are fashionable and quite often serve as places for after-hours dancing and relaxing as well as car-buying during the day.

Citroen has just opened the first new building on the street in 30 years in the middle of the Champs and it's meant to be as much a tourist attraction as, for example, Fouquet's Restaurant near the Arc itself.

Who goes to San Francisco and visits a car dealership?

There's also heavy traffic in stores selling new frames for glasses, but that's best left for another book.

## TV Myths About Cars: Airbags

Airbags on TV for the most part have been played for laughs, pillowy-billowy things that ease their way out of the steering wheel and stay inflated long enough to trap our hapless hero in place so the camera can get a good look at his facial expression.

In real life, an airbag is fired by an explosive device and comes out so quickly it can actually kill you if you're too close to it and then deflate almost as quickly. They're out and down so swiftly, in fact, that many people who survive their deployment don't even notice them during the crash.

# Keep Your Paperwork Safe Forever
# When You Sell Car To Someone Else

If you're not extremely careful with the paperwork when you sell a car to someone else, you could very easily end up responsible for that car's financial and legal charges years and years into the future.

That could mean thousands of dollars, especially if there are lawsuits pending on the car and you're the last owner of record, even if you sold the car a decade ago. That is the hard and ugly reality involved with the transfer of title between you and the new owner. There are all kinds of horror stories available on the web to make the danger clear, but thankfully there is also lots of good advice on what you have to do to keep yourself from potential legal troubles.

Because each state has different requirements for title transfer and different ways of accessing responsibility for future problems it's impossible to outline the procedures here. For the best advice, start with the department of motor vehicles office in your home state, which are all listed on one of the web's best auto-related sites --- www.dmv.org.

If you're going to sell a car to someone else, making sure you understand the right way to transfer its title should be a priority. And when the paperwork is all done and correct, hang on to it forever in case ownership becomes an issue sometime in the future.

In a decade or so this may seem a bit much for a car you haven't seen in for years, but unfortunately it could be just as great an issue then as now.

## Basil Fawlty And The Tree Branch

Lots of people have their favorite film and TV moments featuring a car, but in reality the Gourmet Dinner episode of Fawlty Towers has the best car-involved laugh ever. Really.

**Alexander Law & Susan Winlaw** 257

# Infotainment: From Desoto's Turntable To Ford's Sync And Who Knows Where

For decades there was no need for the auto industry to keep up with advances in infotainment systems because there were none -- the radio looked after both information and entertainment for about half-a-century.

It should also be noted that the auto industry did not offer radios right away, so consumers had to buy them separately and have them installed. Eventually, however, they caught on and in time became virtually universal.

As for alternatives, there was a laughable attempt in the late 1950s by Chrysler to sell Desoto models with turntables in the dash that played special 16-rpm records, which at least added the notion of consumer choice to in-car entertainment.

Then came eight-track and cassette systems, which greatly increased the possibility of customer choice, and finally CDs, which increased the level of sound quality and consumer choice.

Video players were introduced in the late 1990s, but the auto industry was sure that they would be a niche feature at best, limited to high-end buyers of minivans.

About the same time the internet was catching on with the public and the auto companies and lots of outside firms starting working on ways to bring all that promised into the cars.

For the most part the success rate on that has been spotty, due largely to ever-developing technologies that went out of date faster than the auto companies could cope with, and the growing demand to stop infotainment devices from being driver distractions. So the auto companies realized the smartest thing to do was make their sound systems compatible with technologies created by other companies, and that has brought us to attempts to allow the connection of various portable devices.

At the moment, the most comprehensive effort to enable personal infotainment equipment is from Ford -- the Sync system, powered by Microsoft Auto software, which provides voice-activated control of mobile phones and digital music players. It is also of course upgradeable "to support the devices and services of tomorrow."

Sync debuted in Ford Focus lineup of compact sedans, but Ford promises it will turn up in a dozen products bearing a Ford, Lincoln or Mercury badge soon. Those models include the Ford Focus, Fusion, Edge, Freestyle, Explorer, Sport Trac and Taurus, the Mercury Milan, Montego and Mountaineer, and Lincoln MKX and MKZ. Eventually, all Ford, Lincoln and Mercury models will be Sync-ready.

Users can access their mobile phone or digital music player through voice commands or the stereo system's control knobs. This includes access to genre, album, artist and song title, while the names and numbers in a mobile phone's address book are wirelessly and automatically transferred to the vehicle.

Sync can host nearly any digital media player, including the Apple iPod, Microsoft Zune, PlaysForSure players and most USB storage devices, which can also be recharged. Supported formats include MP3, AAC, WMA, WAV and PCM.

Overall, the Sync system should meet most of the demands that people who speak English, French and Spanish would have with such devices, and no doubt the gnomes at Microsoft are working on ways to make them work even better.

Sync retails for less than $400, but bear in mind that literally everything involved in a new car purchase except government-mandated taxes and fees is negotiable during the purchase process.

Sadly, you can't play vinyl records on Sync, but no doubt someone out there's got a Desoto with a built-in turntable that he'll be glad to sell you.

# iPod, GPS, PDAs Et Al
# Put Car Batteries At Risk

Few things are as irritating as a big, expensive car that won't start, and that's particularly true when the cause is a flat battery.

For a while that wasn't a problem in new cars, as battery technology improvements managed to stretch the life of a battery to three, four or even five years. But now that awful grumping sound (as in a grumpy guy grunting) of a battery refusing to turn over is starting to show up in cars that are only two years old, and all of those electronic toys we've started to recharge in the car over the last couple of years (phones, iPods, laptops, GPS devices, etc) are largely at fault.

As well as being irritating and maybe even a risk to your safety and security, a flat battery can also be an added expense ($150 is not unusual) if it's worn down beyond redemption.

The first thing you should do is consult your vehicle's owner's manual to see what the manufacturer has to say and then follow those guidelines. You can also do a lot to put off the need for a battery replacement with a trickle-charger.

This little device costs less than a new battery and will reduce the likelihood of your car letting you down when it's most inconvenient. It plugs into one of your vehicle's re-charging points and keeps the battery topped up, and usually uses solar power to do it. Check the web for more details.

## No Reason For Transmission Flush

Lots of service centers are talking consumers into "transmission flushes" these days, as if there were an epidemic of trouble in all brands. Well, the truth is that it's probably not necessary, since cars almost never need them and the car companies don't recommend them.

# In-Car Power Plugs Can
# Deliver Power To All Those Devices

Though there are a couple of vehicles with built-in two-prong plugs, the vast majority of new vehicles still only come with those circular power points that were initially designed to house cigarette lighters.

This means you have to carry a special power cord to link your laptop to the recharging point, and also a unique cable for your iPod, cell, digital camera, GPS device and so on. It's irritating enough that these plugs never work with any other devices and are often expensive and/or hard to find, so adding to the clutter in your car is a serious annoyance.

Perhaps it makes sense to buy an inverter, which plugs into a car's recharging point at one end and provides you with one or more three-pronged receptacles at the other end.

This means you can charge more than one device at a time and not have to worry about having the wrong cord or even buying such a cord in the first place.

Inverters and such things can be inexpensive ($40), but they usually cost more as the number of plug points grows, so one with three plug points will cost about $100.

The only problem with such devices, of course, is that they encourage people to leave things loose in the car, which turns them into dangerous flying objects in a crash or rollover.

## Insurance Costs Drop With Fraud Rate

A police crackdown in Lawrence, Massachusetts, showed that individual insurance rates would actually go down if the incidence of fraud did. Because they had to pay for fewer fraudulent claims, policy holders there saw their premiums decrease $400, on average, for a total cost reduction of $10 million.

# Honda-Acura Benefits For Customers With Auto Odometers That Cost Them Millions

You may have missed it, but Honda installed odometers in millions of Honda and Acura cars between 2002 and 2006 that incorrectly measured the distance they covered. Apparently, the odometers recorded about 5 percent greater distance than the cars actually covered.

This is a bad thing for those millions of consumers because it meant their warranties ended early so they had to pay for work they should have got for free.

It also meant that some people with mileage penalties on their leasing contracts would have to be more than they should have.

Finally, this problem made it look like your car was getting better fuel economy than it actually was, which might have caused you to buy another Honda or Acura and be faced with the same undue extra costs again.

And how about those friends who bought a Honda or Acura because of your experiences?

Anyway, the company is offering financial incentives to affected owners, but only until June 26, 2008.

Despite these incentives, this situation has been extremely helpful for Honda because most of the people who were charged these unnecessary fees don't know what's happening, or sold the car, or can't be bothered, or whatever.

Honda denies wrong-doing in this matter, saying only that the company's odometer specifications for the vehicles in the settlement were within industry standards.

It is true that industry standards allow for slight variations on mileage, but it is also remarkable that so many millions of Honda models ended up with the variation that helped the company and not the consumer.

To explain why it was willing to offer those incentives to

millions of unsatisfied customers, Honda noted that it had determined "that its internal standard did not match current customer expectations." Also, the effort to fight and win the case would have brought them too much bad PR and ill-will.

The details on the financial paybacks to the Honda and Acura owners are available at www.odosettlementinfo.com or www.hondaodometerclassaction.com.

This is quite a remarkable turn of events for a company that likes to brag about the engineering excellence of its products. It just goes to show that even Honda can make mistakes, even if this one turned out so well for them and so badly for many of its customers.

## Carry Repair Records On The Road

If you have paperwork related to repairs done to your car or changes to your insurance coverage or anything else, it might be a good idea to scan it onto the memory stick you should already have filled with other important personal information and carry with your everywhere you go.

This paranoid's view of the way life works may seem excessive, but you won't think so if you're talking to the service manager of the Atlanta branch of the national auto service chain whose branch near your house fixed the same problem under warranty two months before. He likely won't believe you and will want you to pay to have it fixed again. Proof of that warranty could save you from paying again to have the problem fixed.

If that situation doesn't apply to you, you should maybe let your mind imagine what kind of paperwork you'd be in trouble without (it doesn't have to be auto-related) and scan it onto that memory stick.

This is easier than carrying the originals and smarter, because it's easier to hide the memory stick from thieves and you can replace the information if you lose it.

# The Truth About Oprah And
# All Those Free Pontiacs

If you're like the vast majority of people who know about that famous new car giveaway on the Oprah Winfrey show a few years back, you probably think of it as the greatest example yet of the popular star's generosity.

Well, as wonderful as Oprah Winfrey is and as great a force for good as she can be, we have to point out that she should not be given credit for giving away those Pontiacs on her TV show.

It was General Motors that gave away G-6 sedans to the members of the Oprah show's studio audience in September of 2004, choosing to absorb the cost in exchange for national exposure to help launch the car.

Not only was it GM and not Oprah who paid the $7,866,000 bill for the cars and the state taxes and licensing fees that went with them, but GM may even have paid Oprah for the privilege of using her show to give the cars away.

This is what TV shows mean when they say "promotional consideration paid for by the following companies".

The facts of the new car giveaway did not get in the way of many news reports of the time, and since then the truth has faded even farther into the background.

GM doesn't really care what the media reports and the public thinks about this subject, but it's amazing how quickly and how thoroughly the truth of this situation got lost.

It probably says something serious about the force of myth and the desire of people to believe a version of events that they like, rather than the truth, which doesn't do much harm here but should maybe be considered in other automotive contexts. Such as:

"This little car with a five-star crash rating is just as safe as a large sedan with a five-star crash rating," or

"You absolutely must pay the transportation fee we spring on you after we've agreed on a price," or

"Our cars have the best quality on the market and that's why we charge more for them than other companies, but we still want you to buy this expensive extended warranty."

This is no slam against Oprah, just an effort to keep the record straight on one popular topic and perhaps keep you wary about what you are being told is the truth.

## Asian Car Companies And Sexism

It's more than a little ironic that the car companies of Japan and Korea have earned much of their success by selling millions of vehicles to people they generally disparage -- women.

This truth is self-evident to anyone who's ever seen the way Japanese and Korean car companies behalf toward women in North America and, most particularly, in their home countries. This sexist attitude on the part of Honda, Hyundai, Kia, Subaru, and Toyota is actually worse than the level of sexism that exists in the cultures of those two countries.

On numbers alone, Korea does better than Japan in various examinations of women's political status (women in parliaments, for example). Experience shows, however, that the car companies of both countries are demonstrably sexist in their management and hiring attitudes. This is particularly true in Japan and Korea where female engineers and executives are virtually non-existent, but less so in countries (such as Canada and the U.S.) with more enlightened attitudes, in which the occasional female face turns up. But don't be fooled by that, as Japanese and Korean car companies are run by men who make little effort to hide their sexist attitudes.

Minor exemptions have to go to Mazda and Nissan, which are controlled by Ford and Renault. They're still a long way from the inclusionary natures of General Motors and Ford.

# Governments Look Into "Cost-Recovery" For Services Provided In A Crash

If you need another incentive to drive slowly and carefully enough so that you're never breaking any traffic laws or likely to cause a crash, consider that many governments are considering laws that would charge drivers for the costs incurred in providing various police and emergency services.

That is to say, drivers might have to pay to have a crash investigated by the police, for the ambulance service that provided medical aid, for maintenance work to repair fences and signs knocked down by the car, and so on.

It's all part of various "cost-recovery programs" governments hope will help them deal with decreasing tax revenue.

This movement could be particularly troublesome for people away from home, since some legislative proposals would cover locals (as in those who pay taxes there) but send bills to visitors or their insurance companies.

Something to think about if you're going to be doing any cross-country travelling.

## Real-Time Traffic Info Without The Web

An interesting new navigation system from Microsoft called Streets & Trips 2008 with Connected Services could help you find the best way between places while steering you away from traffic jams and toward the cheapest gas prices -- without an onboard internet connection.

The latest version of the big-selling software works anywhere in the U.S. and Canada as a laptop-operated map, but with the MSN Direct radio receiver and its GPS locater it can also supply current traffic conditions and the locations of the lowest gas prices in the area.

That service is free for a year with the software, but after that you will have to pay a small monthly fee.

# HD Radio Enters In-Car Entertainment
# With Free Service For New Sound Systems

If you're looking for a better stereo sound but aren't interested in paying for satellite radio stations or hooking up portable music players and iPods, or carrying CDs, perhaps HD radio's for you.

It's pretty much what you might guess -- a "high-definition" version of the signal that you already get for free on your radio right now, commercials and all.

More free radio stations (as opposed to the satellite radio service, which has a monthly fee) are adding an HD signal and all you need to hear it is an HD radio.

That new radio should set you back a couple of hundred dollars and can be added to an existing car. In time, the service should also be available in more new cars, though they will likely charge you for it.

HD radio quality's supposed to be almost as good as what you'd get from a CD and perhaps better than what you get from a satellite system, but the quality should drop off as the signal fades when you start to get away from the station's broadcast region.

Only about a tenth of the radio stations are making a HD signal available right now, and the number's only expected to grow about a quarter by 2010.

It is possible, however, that many of those stations will also be putting out more than one signal, which means more choices. How many more choices will depend upon demand.

Another benefit of HD radio stations is that they display the song title and artist, as satellite does, which will put an end to those memory-spelunking sessions trying to figure out who sang the last song.

For a list of the stations broadcasting HD signals, go to www.hdradio.com.

# Getting Rid Of Dealers
# Will Be Bad For Customers

When the previous boss of Toyota (he's now a big cheese at Chrysler) was asked if he wanted to add any more dealerships to give consumers more places to shop and have service done, he said he didn't. He said he preferred to work with the Japanese firm's existing stores so they would improve their service excellence.

Yeah, customer service and product pricing always improve when you reduce the number of competitors in a segment.

Unfortunately for consumers, Toyota's not alone in wanting to keep its dealer count down so consumers have less chance to get competitive prices for vehicles or places to go to have them serviced. The other companies that have a limited number of dealerships now (the foreign firms) are also looking to maintain their low dealer counts, and the companies with lots of dealers (GM and Ford, but particularly Chrysler) are looking for ways to reduce their dealer count. This will apply especially to large urban areas, where car company execs would like to see the dealer count drop by half.

This is definitely a bad thing for consumers, as anyone who has to put up with snotty service at a dealer because there's nowhere else for her to go can tell you. You can of course visit an independent service center instead of a factory store and most of you already do, but there's not much to be done about fewer places to buy vehicles in the first place.

You can try visiting the small existing dealerships that don't advertise so often or offer much in the way of amenities since they might appreciate your business more as they struggle to stay viable. Remember that no matter where you buy a certain brand, all of its dealers are able to service it for you.

Consider also the huge dealer base of the three domestic firms as a plus in their favor when choosing a new model.

# Try Garage Updates
# To Upgrade House Value

Like pretty much every other part of a house today, garages are being upgraded to maximize their utility for the current owner and, of course, their appeal to potential buyers.

The primary function of garage-upgrading firms is to provide storage guidance and containers, but there are also people who will refinish the floor and increase the garage's general appeal through more electrical outlets, workbenches, a sink, increased insulation, better lighting, and so on.

No guarantee that such an upgrade will have the same affect on a house price the way updated kitchens and en-suite master bathrooms do, but it could be the feature of a house that sets it apart in a buyers' market. On top of which, a killer garage has the same appeal for many men that a fabulous and well-equipped kitchen has for many women.

General organizing equipment for a garage can be had for less than $1,000, but if you find a professional garage organizing firm or a general contractor they can probably think of ways to spend many thousands of your hard-earned dollars.

## Falling Asleep While Driving

Along with all those drivers texting, eating, flossing, drinking, smoking, talking and what have you, it turns out that about a third of American drivers have nodded off or fallen asleep while driving. That thought alone should keep a sensible driver awake.

## Driving While Asleep

Today's serious sleeping pills can sometimes cause you to drive while you sleep, so you should start hiding your car keys and put an alarm on your bedroom door. No joke.

# Compact Crossovers From GM And Toyota Are A Solid Choice

If you're looking for a vehicle that strikes a fine balance between utility, fuel economy, safety, style, dependability and reasonable cost, it would be hard to beat the Pontiac Vibe and Toyota Martix.

With one glaring exception (the inclusion of the OnStar system on the Vibe but not the Matrix) these two reasonably priced four-door, five-seat vehicles are essentially the same car, and are indeed built on the same assembly line. They share a similar body structure and many of the key mechanical parts, which are covered by different suits.

This means you can expect essentially the same quality levels from both cars for about the same price.

Matrix and Vibe are essentially station wagon versions of the Toyota Corolla, and that's an excellent thing to be in a society that's moving away from the traditional car shape to a taller, boxier look.

The cars are well built and comfortable, and they will handle 95 percent of any situation that might come along in most peoples lives.

Matrix and Vibe come with enough powertrain variables to let the customer decide on the performance/fuel economy balance, and there's all-wheel-drive available.

Exterior styling is the most visible difference between the two models and that means it's strictly a matter of choice.

There's also the warranty difference, with Pontiac winning that one because it comes with roadside assistance and better coverage on major mechanical parts.

The presence of OnStar on the Vibe puts it way ahead on the safety and security front, since that feature includes crash notification and many other worthwhile functions.

With either car, the smart shopper will be well-served.

## Companies And Dealers Aren't The Monolith Many Consumers Expect

Though you've probably never given it much thought, on some level you probably believe the various car companies and their dealer networks work closely as a team to provide you with the best car-owning experience ever or make your life a living hell while screwing you out of as much money as possible, or maybe even something in between.

In reality, the two major players in the auto industry are in something of a forced marriage, and attempts by either side to alter the conditions of the contract usually involve lawyers, lobbyists, and big money. For the most part, it's not exaggerating to say that the manufacturers usually have better relationships with their unions than they do with their dealers. To a surprising degree, the manufacturers have little control over the actions of their dealers, either individually or in groups.

When they speak publicly about their dealers, car executives usually stick to pointing out that they are "independent business people" and try not to let the gritted teeth show.

The cause of this is too involved and arcane to go into here, and for the most part consumers don't need to worry about this struggle. But it's always good to be aware of the true nature of any business relationship, especially when you're spending so much money on its products.

The one overriding lesson for someone looking to buy or service a car is that your experience with one dealer of a certain brand does not necessarily reflect the kind of experience you'll have with other dealers of the same brand. If it's bad at one place it could be a lot better at several other places, or even worse. Except for GM's Saturn brand (which is a whole other story), the new car dealer network does not always offer the kind of re-assuring sameness and co-operation between stores that you expect from most other mega-brand chains.

# Maybe We Need Airbags
# That Turn Into Parachutes

There's a widespread sense among consumers that if the government or the car companies or somebody would just create enough safety systems then we'd never have to worry when we were in our cars.

And then you hear about the poor man in Houston who died when the car he was backing up went through the wall of a parking garage and fell five stories to the ground below.

There are also stories of people who were killed or hurt when a car crashed into their house while they were eating, sleeping or watching TV.

Parts fly off cars and kill people, or people don't see cars headed their way and get run over, and on and on it goes.

All of these things just show that there is no way to remove all risk from the experience of having cars to ride in.

It just isn't possible to put humans and all their limitations in something that big and powerful and not expect terrible things to happen from time to time.

We should indeed struggle like crazy to make it impossible for people to get hurt in car crashes, but we should also bear in mind that it isn't going to happen anytime soon (if ever) and simply be more careful.

## Microsoft Wants Ads In Your Car

To help pay for advanced network connectivity for cars in the medium-future, Microsoft thinks it would be a good idea to pump commercials onto a monitor on your dashboard. Not just any commercials -- commercials determined by the position of your vehicle at that moment.

This service would also allow you to use MS's Sync device to download video games and movies to your vehicle, or get directions to the nearest ATM or Thai takeout or whatever.

# Make It Impossible To Drive
# Without Seatbelts Being Done Up First

The biggest single cause of death in car crashes is people not wearing their seatbelts, but the simple technological change that could solve the problem to a large degree is not even being considered by the auto industry or society.

Only a fairly simple software rewiring would be needed to create cars that wouldn't start until all of the seatbelts were done up first. And if that idea gives your sense of individual freedom pause, it wouldn't take much extra work to make such a system optional, so parents could turn it on any time their children went out alone in the family car.

Having a system that could keep teens restrained within a car would go a long way toward reducing the appalling death rates of young people in cars, which are in many instances due to the fact that they're not wearing seatbelts in what would otherwise be a survivable crash.

Car companies have tested this system in the past but have backed off in the face of consumer complaints. Apparently, even people who wouldn't consider driving a foot without their seatbelts on resist the idea of seatbelts being done up before the car starts. The problem is that many people like to start their car and go through a little routine of seat-adjusting, mirror-tilting, make-up freshening, cigarette-lighting and what-have-you before doing up their seatbelt and driving away.

To accommodate the demand for a state of start-up grace where you adjust the seat and tune the radio station, the car could be wired so that it couldn't be put in gear until the seatbelts are done up.

There are indeed many fairly simple technical solutions to one of society's most significant safety problems. What's missing is society's desire to have it done.

**Alexander Law & Susan Winlaw   273**

# Legal Liability Mounts Over
# Cell Phone Use In Crashes

When it comes to cell phones, it's not a good idea to use them while you're driving, as they can lead to the kind of distraction that leads to crashes, which can lead to injuries and deaths -- yours included. So it's not only the right thing to do, it's also the smart thing to do.

To the normal list of worries involving a cell phone-involved crash should be added the growing incidence of liability lawsuits.

Cell phone records make it easy to prove exactly what time is was when you were on the phone, and lots of places are holding people responsible for being on the phone at the moment of a crash.

There's also a growing trend toward suing the employer of the person using the cell phone, if the call she was making at the time of the crash was business-related.

This can be good for the employee and bad for the employer, but that can be turned around if the employer takes the right steps ahead of time.

The employee should also be aware of this, since she might be found solely responsible for making a business call if she wasn't supposed to. A legal quagmire that could probably stand to be drained right away.

What those steps might be depends upon the legal situation in your area, but the first step is a renewed determination not to use a cell phone while the car's moving. It's illegal in many places and dangerous in almost all of them.

## New Car Affordability Improving

It only takes 23.9 weeks of median family income to pay for the average new car, the lowest figure in six years.

# There's A Legal Risk Of Not Responding To Recalls For Your Car

About a third of car owners who get recall notices from the auto company simply ignore them. This of course puts them in greater danger of being hurt if the recalled part fails, but it could also put them in greater legal danger as well.

In the first place, it's likely harder to get a financial settlement from a company that offered to fix the part in question before it broke and hurt you.

But there's also the chance that by not responding to a recall notice you will be moving into the product liability target zone yourself. If the recalled part fails and someone else is hurt, you could be finding out about the "dangerous instrumentality doctrine" as it applies to "negligent maintenance" or "negligent entrustment" or some other legal nightmare.

This is in no way meant to be legal advice, but common sense suggests the best way to avoid all that is answering those recall notices when they come along. A little probing into the matter of your local court system's view of this might also be wise, to see how great the specific danger might be.

## Leaving Kids Or Pets In Car By Mistake

More often than you'd think, people forget they have sleeping children or pets in the back of their cars and it often leads to death. As a way to remind yourself to check in the back seat, store your purse, briefcase, house keys or some other essential item in the second row so you'll be forced to look there before you leave the car. Maybe a life-size stuffed animal can be kept in the child seat when it's not being used, so it would be moved to the front seat when you're child's in the seat and that would remind you. If these things don't work for you, think of something that does.

# Legal Rights for Passengers Change During Police Check In Traffic Stop

Good news if you're a passenger in a vehicle that's illegally stopped by the police and they find out you're doing something unlawful or are a wanted person.

The U.S. Supreme Court has ruled that passengers are "seized" within the meaning of the Fourth Amendment and can, like drivers, dispute the legality of a search.

This gift to society is the result of a trial involving a wanted man who was arrested when police stopped the vehicle he was riding in for a reason (suspected out-of-date license tags) that turned out to be invalid.

For all of you completely crime-free passengers in a vehicle stopped by police, this Supreme Court decision also means that as a "reasonable person" who has been "seized" that you are smart enough to know that you are not allowed to leave the scene when the vehicle's been stopped by the police and may be subject to the same treatment as the driver.

## Most Customers Happy With All New Cars

Overall customer satisfaction with cars and trucks reached 82 out of 100 on a national survey in 2007, the fourth straight year it had reached an all-time high.

Pretty much all brands did well, though it must be noted that consumer happiness went up for domestic brands (Chrysler, Ford, GM) and went down for the brands from Japan (including Honda, Nissan and Toyota) and South Korea.

For consumers, the best news was that the satisfaction gap between the top and lowest brands has shrunk from 18 points in 1994 to 12 points in 2007.

The study also found that consumer satisfaction with personal computers fell 3 percent to 75, and that Yahoo (79) passed Google (78) as preferred search engine.

# Make Sure Your Insurance Covers
# Uninsured Or Hit-And-Run Drivers

If it's not already part of your insurance coverage or if you're considering dropping it to save a little money, you might want to think again about "uninsured motorist" coverage.

This would be especially true when lots of people are looking to cut back on expenses to help them deal with tougher economic times, which would seem to be the case right now.

Without "uninsured motorist" coverage, you are pretty much on your own when it comes to paying the car repair and health care costs you incur in a crash.

And if the threat of having more drivers on the road without insurance weren't scary enough, the fact that one-eighth of all crashes are hit-and-runs should do the trick.

If the police can't locate the driver of the car that crashed into your car, you've got the same problem when it comes to repair and health care expenses.

## Thieves Target GPS Devices

The increased popularity of portable GPS-based navigation systems with smash-and-grab thieves is bad news for anyone who has one of those remarkably useful devices in their car.

But it also serves as a general warning to all car owners that it's not smart to leave anything that's easily transportable visible in your car when you're not there to protect it.

The GPS device is especially popular with thieves right now because it's popular with other people looking for a bargain on a navigation system.

Keeping it out of sight in the trunk or the cargo bay is the best bet, but it would also be a sensible step to register the GPS with its manufacturor so that it's harder for the thief to use. The satisfaction that might bring is up to you.

# Take Care When Passing
## Emergency Vehicles Or It Will Cost You

For safety reasons it's always been a good idea to approach emergency vehicles stopped at the side of the road with caution, which means slowing down and staying as far away from them as possible. But various jurisdictions across North America are starting to make it mandatory and are attaching hefty ($400 is not unusual) fines to the tickets.

It seems that clueless people are still crashing into police cars, ambulances and tow trucks with their lights flashing and their drivers are getting tired of it. This happens a lot.

The smartest and safest general approach to an emergency vehicle with its lights flashing is to slow down to about 40 mph (60 kmh) or less, depending upon the situation, and keep as far away as safety allows. If you're on a high-speed, multi-lane road, going that slow is not smart, but pulling into another lane so you leave the inside lane next to the emergency vehicle clear certainly is smart, and possibly mandatory.

## Parking Meters May Go High-Tech

The list of situations that computers and the internet are going to make change now includes parking meters.

Field trials are underway to test a computer-driven parking meter that does all kinds of interesting things, like taking a picture of your car when it's parked, letting you pay by credit card or with bills as well as coins, and phoning you when your time's about to run out.

On the down side for drivers, the parking meter also takes a digital image of your car's license plate so they can bill you if you do stay beyond your paid-for time.

This would mean more money for the local government and less enforcement cost.

## Company Tax-Free Commuter
## Benefits Can Save You Money

It might be worth your while to ask your employer about setting up a commuter benefits program, since it can save you and them money.

Under current U.S. tax law, employees who take part in the tax-free program can save more than a third of their commuting costs while the employer saves eight to 10 percent on payroll taxes for every employee that takes part.

Commuter programs take advantage of IRS Code Section 132(f), which allows people to set aside up to $110 per month pre-tax for transit benefits and $215 per month pre-tax for parking benefits.

The overall benefit to the driver can exceed $1,500 a year. Check it out with the HR or benefits people where you work.

## The Hot Gasoline Issue

Because gasoline expands in warm weather and shrinks in the cold, the people in balmier climates tend to get less gas for their money.

This fact of physics helps explain why gas retailers in the U.S. recently fought off an effort to make temperature-correcting devices mandatory on their pumps.

The gas companies claimed that such devices would be costly to them and the consumers and provide little benefit to people buying gas.

In Canada, where cold weather is more common and the customers would thereby get more fuel for their money, the very same gas companies have already installed temperature-correcting devices on their pumps.

Feel free to draw your own conclusions about this.

## Surprise -- Smoking In Cars
## Is Bad For You And Maybe The Car

More people are smoking in their vehicles now, it seems, probably because their car is the only place in the world where they're alone and not going to offend someone or break the law by lighting up.

But now there are efforts to ban even that, partly as a safety concern for people on the road with you or on the nearby sidewalks, and partly as a health concern for other people in the car, particularly children.

Before we get to those new issues, however, a reminder that there's also likely an economic component to smoking in a car. Many people won't buy a used vehicle that smells of smoke, which brings its value down. That hurts when you're selling your own car or turning in a leased vehicle, so there's no escaping that. And if you're one of those people who thinks keeping the window open while you smoke solves the problem, you are greatly mistaken.

On the safety front, the thinking is that the actions required to reach, light, smoke and dispose of a cigarette are at least as distracting as those necessary to handle a cell phone. And the dangers associated with dropping a lit cigarette are much worse than those related to dropping an active cell phone, even if both can result in serious driver distraction.

Since the political feeling to control cell phone use is getting stronger, it probably doesn't look like much of a reach to add smoking to the list of things you shouldn't be doing in your car while it's moving.

Banning smoking when kids are in the car is a newer concept, but the desire to protect children is a strong one in this society, so don't be surprised to see this one grow in favor.

If it's any consolation, the same kind of thinking is finding support in the UK, India and other countries as well.

# Device Created For People
# Who "Lose" Their Cars

Forgetting where you left your car is apparently such a common problem in the UK that Chevrolet has created a device that allows the vehicle to "shout" a personalized message to its forgetful owner.

One in five respondents to a British survey say they lose their car at least once every two weeks and spend over five hours a year searching for it. One in four drivers say they have actually thought of reporting their car stolen after spending more than an hour looking for it, the survey found, "only to realize that their memory had malfunctioned and their motor was in the car park all along."

A lot of this probably has more than a little to do with the fact that all levels of British society are a lot more fond of visiting pubs than people in North America are, but it is not mentioned by the survey takers since it's such a normal way to behave there.

On average, people in the northwest of England have the most trouble, the survey says, since they tend to misplace their car 14 times a year, with the Scots close behind at 13 times a year, and Londoners at 12 times a year.

To combat this, Chevrolet has produced the K.I.T.T.Y (Key Innovation That Talks to You), a compact remote-controlled talking alert. You press the button on this device and a car more than 200 yards away will hear it and respond.

Various officials at Chevrolet say the company's OnStar system would serve pretty much the same function, but there really wasn't that much of a demand for it to do that in the U.S. or Canada. Opening doors remotely for people is a big deal in North America, but not reuniting owners with cars.

If you ever misplace your vehicle, there are devices on the web or in auto-parts stores that will help you locate it.

# These Technologies Are Not
# Coming To A Car Near You

A woman in London, England, is responsible for our favorite ever suggestion for a special item in a car, followed closely by a gentleman in Texas who had a pair of requests.

After learning about the anti-theft aspect of GM's OnStar system, the man from Dallas asked if it would be possible to put a shotgun in the steering column that would shoot anyone who stole his Cadillac.

The answer there would be "no."

He then asked if it would be possible for the car to lock the thieves in, turn the heat up to max, blast the most irritating music (he suggested rap) through the sound system, and then come to a dead stop so the police could catch them?

All that is quite possible, but only the door locking and coming to a stop is used, usually by rental car fleets and the police in carefully selected situations.

The English lady actually had two things she believed would make life with her car more rewarding, and we're fairly certain only one of them has since been created.

That would be the fan that mounted on the bottom of the steering wheel and blew cool air up her skirt on hot days, which if nothing else speaks to the curious British reticence to put air-conditioning in their cars.

The other request is still in non-development, we fear, though it would probably have a wide attraction for many women.

The English lady wanted a mini-incinerator in the ashtray, one strong enough to vaporize small items. What she wanted to destroy without a trace were the wrapping papers from the "sweeties" she liked to indulge in when no one was looking, so she didn't have to revisit the guilt without the sugar fix to cover it when she emptied the ashtray.

# Putting All Your Eggs In One Basket's Bad But Putting Them In A Grocery Belt Isn't

If North Americans damage groceries in the drive home from the supermarket as much as the Brits apparently do, we could be wasting about $4 billion a year on things like wine, eggs, milk, flowers, breads, and cookies. That figure does not include the cost of cleaning up the mess, by the way.

The main problem in Britain is that most people (about two-thirds of the respondents to a large survey) put groceries on the back seat rather than in the trunk or cargo space of their cars, thereby increasing the possibility of damage by up to 20 percent.

Men are apparently more inclined to put the groceries in the back seat, the survey says, and more likely to drive in such a way as to put the groceries at risk. What a surprise.

On top of the cost of the lost groceries, there is also the danger created by having things loose in the car when a crash or rollover occurs.

GM's Chevrolet division in the UK is working on a seatbelt attachment that would carefully lash a few bags of groceries in place on the back seat.

According to the UK survey, the top ten shopping casualties on the journey from supermarket to shelf are:
-Smashed wine (29 per cent of all damaged shopping)
-Crushed flowers (20 per cent)
-Spilt milk (14 per cent)
-Cracked eggs (11 per cent)
-Broken cookies (8 per cent)
-Flattened bread (6 per cent)
-Squashed cakes (5 per cent)
-Shattered jars (4 per cent)
-Bruised fruit and vegetables (2 per cent)
-Leaking yogurt (1 per cent)

# Consumers Killed The EV -- Not One Auto Company Or Oil Company Conspiracy

Anyone who's seen the grossly-misleading "Who Killed The Electric Car" knows that the answer is supposed to be General Motors, with the other car companies as un-indicted co-conspirators. And surely there are general reasons to suspect the oil companies of being up to no good.

But the truth is that the buying public put EVs out of our misery by deciding in overwhelming numbers that they weren't interested, thank you very much, because they "didn't meet my driving needs."

Look at the numbers in surveys about electric vehicles and you see that most people wouldn't take an EV as a gift, let alone spend their own money on one. CNW Research of Portland found that the percentage of buyers who say they are "strongly" or "likely" going to purchase a pure EV has stayed below 2 percent for eight years. It started out at 1.16 percent in 2000 and went to 1.93 in 2007, for an eight-year average of 1.37.

The reasons a pure EV don't meet anyone's driving needs include its low speed and short range, the time it takes to recharge, the danger from batteries in a crash, the durability of batteries in general, the affect of cold on batteries, and an EV's high maintenance costs and general complications.

That doesn't even touch on the fact that it will likely cost a lot more than a traditional car.

Plug-in hybrids like the Chevrolet Volt and Saturn Vue that can run endlessly on electricity should be available in 2010 or so are another story, but the kind that you have to plug in every 40 miles or so are an open question. Nissan says it will have some here by 2010, but who knows. Even the raging media mania with Tesla and other pure EV startup companies is starting to fade as the realities set in.

# Problems With Run-Flat Tires
## Cause Customer Desire To Soften

For people concerned with their safety and security, the appeal of run-flat tires is obvious: even if they have a puncture they'll stay inflated enough to drive you out of trouble.

But there are various things in the picture now that make the purchase of run-flats on a vehicle difficult to endorse.

In the first place, ordinary tires will do the same thing in a limited and possibly expensive way. (See Page 15.)

Consider also the extra money you have to pay, the dubious nature of their durability, the difficulty in getting them serviced, and a growing feeling from existing owners that they're just not worth the trouble.

Owner dissatisfaction has already resulted in a class action suit by Honda Odyssey Touring owners against Honda Motor Corp. and Michelin North America, claiming that the two firms misrepresented the costs and convenience of repairing or replacing the run-flats on their 2005-2007 model year minivans.

Even if the suit eventually fails, the notion that so many people are cranky enough with a company that is widely believed to be a good place to buy anything automotive should give even the most faithful customer pause.

The biggest problem for run-flat owners seems to be that it's hard to get service for the tires, and costly when you do find it.

Car companies and their dealers are very cautious about providing expensive equipment and trained people to operate them, usually preferring that demand outrace supply. That means the poor consumer who bought the run-flats so she would have greater mobility will maybe have to wait days to have a tire fixed, and since there's no spare and probably no free replacement the vehicle is out of action.

# Carpooling Benefits Made Easier By Web For Anyone Who Wants Them

Send your average search engine off into cyberspace with the word "carpooling" and it's likely to come back with more than 2 million replies, which means you can likely find a stranger going your way anywhere in the world.

The more specific you get, however, the fewer the options you get back. But it must be said that the internet allows for a greater number of choices thanks to its role as the biggest bulletin board in history.

It also allows people interested in the concept of carpooling in general to investigate their choices without getting too close or too specific.

This means you have a better chance to look over possible car-mates before you agree to share a small space with them to wherever it is you're going.

Yeah, the idea of getting in a car with strangers is not at the top of every person's wish list, but carpooling does provide an opportunity to save yourself some time (the HOV lanes can be faster), money and aggravation (someone else drives while you read) while doing the environment a favor by keeping a few more cars off the road. These are good things.

If it sounds like something you might be interested in, at least the internet makes it easier to have a look at the possibilities of saving the planet through car-pooling.

## Toyota And Honda Are Boomer Favorites

Baby Boomers are by far the biggest buying group when it comes to big-selling cars. For Toyota Camry, boomers account for 68.9 percent of sales. Chevrolet Impala's next at 65.6, followed by Toyota Prius (65.2), Honda Accord (63.9) and Honda Civic (61.7).

# Parking Spaces Availability
# Opens Up To Web Users

Looking for a parking space in some big cities is no longer a shot-in-the-dark adventure, thanks to a growing number of Internet operations that keep track of where all the parking lots are and even how much they cost.

Sometimes they can even tell you where the empty spaces are.

There is sometimes even a feature whereby the parking operations in the intended area would make price bids to attract the consumer.

To top it off, the systems may even reserve a spot for you ahead of time.

The industry's just starting, so we can assume there will be some lumps in the early days but improvements to the service and the features will continue to expand. Check on the web to see what's available where you live or where you might be visiting.

## Two Key Rules For Jump-Starting Cars

When the time comes to jump-start a weak or dead car battery, there are only two really important things to remember:

1) The engine bay of a car has things that will hurt you, including the fan blade that can spin even if the engine's not running, so be very careful where you put your hands and wear gloves and protective glasses if you can.

2) Consult the owner's manual of the car with the bad battery AND the car that's running for the proper procedures for hooking up those magic jumper cables and everything else. Follow these rules very carefully, particularly the part about where you hook the negative (-) cable on the car with the flat battery. It almost certainly does NOT go on the negative post of the battery.

# Tire Ratings More A Marketing Ploy
# Than A Safety Or Performance Issue

Any new tire available in North America should be good enough for any vehicle sold here, even at speeds about 20 percent above legal highway speeds. The basic top speed on any new tire is 99 mph. So if you maintain your tires correctly (keep the pressure at its proper level, make sure they wear evenly by keeping them balanced and aligned), it's not necessary to spend a lot more for higher-rated tires.

If you're looking for new tires, most of the tire companies will give you an unbiased overview of what you need to know (www.Goodyeartires.com is pretty helpful). But bear in mind that the general intent of those places is to get you to buy more tire (i.e. one with a higher rating) and more tires (i.e. a set of summer tires and a set of winter tires, for example) than you may really need.

Speed is the usual reason for going up-scale with tires, but people with normal driving habits who never reach triple-digit speeds should look for tires that provide a softer ride or better fuel economy. That, too, is well explained on those websites.

As for those speed ratings, it's important to note that they do not concern themselves with a tire's handling or cornering abilities, just top speed.

Here's a list of the ratings' maximum speed limits:

Q-rated tires are good for 99 MPH (160 KPH), but there are six other grades: S-rated for 112 MPH (180 KPH), T-rated for 118 MPH (190 KPH), U-rated for 124 MPH (200 KPH), H-rated for 130 MPH (210 KPH), V-rated tires (there are two kinds) for 130 to 149 MPH (210 to 240 KPH), and Z-rated for 149 to 186 MPH (240 to 300KPH), depending upon their specific grades.

# Used Car Prices Should Go Down
# But Ownership Costs Going Up

With fewer people buying new vehicles, it's likely that more consumers will buy used cars instead.

That can have its financial benefits, since used cars always cost thousands less than new models. This appears to be particularly true in 2008, since there are endless waves of up-scale cars leased in 2005 coming onto the market.

The situation seems best suited for the folks looking to buy something German, since BMW and Mercedes have been crying the blues over the lease returns driving their prices down. They're not going to bargain-basement levels, but they should be a couple of grand less expensive than previously.

The problem for buyers of any used car from any brand is that these cars usually don't have any warranty left when they come on the market, so the buyer becomes responsible for greater costs as they relate to service, repair and parts replacement.

For various reasons, the prices of just about everything associated with cars (tires, batteries, engine oil and so on) have been going up, sometimes a great deal. This means that it will be a lot more expensive to operate a used car now than it was a couple of years ago.

On top of that, service centers associated with car sales facilities (new and/or used) will be feeling the pressure to replace the revenue the business has lost because of the drop of new car sales income, and that could mean greater labor rates.

As a result, a used car may not be as great a money-saving decision as was originally imagined, since the after-sales costs of new cars is a lot lower because of their warranties.

Maybe not a decision-changing consideration, but it's certainly worth thinking about.

**Alexander Law & Susan Winlaw**

# Tuning In To TV Is Now
# Available In Moving Cars

In terms of beyond-radio in-car entertainment, it took the auto industry about 40 years to go from the Chrysler Highway HiFi's turntable of the mid-50s to the Oldsmobile Silhouette Premiere's VCR in the late-90s. But the speed of technology since then has made TV reception in a moving car possible and improving all the time.

The technology's still far from cheap to install or easy to hide, the screens are small compared to what's in vogue today, tall buildings might block the signal, and quality's far below high-definition, but it is possible to offer your family many of their favorite channels while parked somewhere for the night, or (for more money) even while driving across town or across country

DirectTV and KVH Industries (www.kvh.com) are the big players in the in-car TV market and their choices are too complicated and/or evolving to explain here. Get ready to spend a couple of thousand dollars, however.

Chrysler actually sells an in-car TV system called Sirius Backseat TV in several of its vehicles now, but the programming is limited to a few children's channels.

If you do sign up for one of these services, don't forget that the driver is either legally or morally forbidden from watching TV while the vehicle is moving.


## What Kind of Auto-Related Services?

"All sorts of services will be provided to the customers in different denominations to meet the requirements, so that people ranging in all schedules will get satisfied." Sadly, these folks in Maryland are only describing their car transport business on the web.

# Traffic Reports From GPS
# Now Available In Cars

As remarkable as today's global positioning systems are with their ability to tell you precisely where you are on the planet, they may look like rotary telephones a few years from now.

That's because there are people who are finally going to start gathering the information from GPS devices to battle one of the greatest scourges of modern time -- traffic jams.

By using the data from a GPS device, it's possible to see how fast the vehicle is moving. If it's exactly here now and exactly there in 10 seconds and exactly down there 10 seconds later, then the car is moving at such and such a speed.

There are people who want to use all that data to keep track of real-world speeds around the country and report that, in detail, to the people who are contributing their own GPS information to the group picture. They also say they're not interested in giving your personal information to the government or anyone else, if that's worrying you.

This is actually happening now, through a device called the Dash Express, at MyDash.net. It works like many other hand-held GPS locaters in showing you where you are and how to get where you're going.

But it also sends that data back to a central computer that keeps track of your data and the data of other users and shows you all that real-time, real-world information on traffic flow.

This should at least give you a chance to take an alternate route, presuming one's available and presuming enough other people have signed up to make the incoming data worthwhile. This suggests that early adaptors will have to be very patient.

The device cost about $400 at launch and there's a small (about $10) monthly fee for the traffic-tracking information.

**Alexander Law & Susan Winlaw**   291

# Winter-Rated Tires May
# Not Do Much Good

If you live someplace where snow-covered roads are a common occurrence, you probably already know that it might be a good idea to get yourself some chains to strap to your tires in severe conditions, or maybe just winter tires.

You may know, then, that tires with a symbol of a snowflake in front of a steep mountain on their sidewall are said to be "winter-rated" by the rubber manufacturers of Canada and the U.S. That means they are supposed to help you and your car stay out of trouble in "severe winter conditions."

Well, the Canadian government's agency responsible for automotive safety, Transport Canada, recently tested a bunch of those snowflake-rated tires and found that the rating symbol did not guarantee similar stopping performance, or anything like it. In some cases, all-season tires did better.

The only suggestion for anxious buyers coming from Transport Canada was that snow tires seemed to do a better job the more expensive they were.


## WiFi Available In Your Car

If you're interested in having "a rich multi-media experience" in your car, companies like Autonet and others are ready to provide it. They're available, though not cheap, in many forms if you search "WiFi service car" on the net.

Those of you who might actually want to take advantage of something like this will probably already have it and those of you who are always on the lookout for signs of the apocalypse will be gratified to get one as exciting as this one.

There are also inexpensive little devices that look out for WiFi signals as you drive down the street, and all you have to do is hope its owners don't have the security restrictions up.

# Look To DMV.org For Guides
# To Car's "Administrivia" Side

Reviewing, selecting, insuring and servicing a car may be more or less continental concerns, but buying, registering and licensing them is a concern of the different states, and that is too huge and complicated a subject to review here.

But since the rules and regulations involving the administrative side of car ownership is too important to ignore completely, allow us to refer you to the best source we know of for such issues --- www.DMV.org.

The folks there have done a comprehensive job of outlining what you might call the nuts and bolts of car ownership in every one of the 50 states.

Along with explaining in details (rules, addresses, hours of operation) how each state's Department of Motor Vehicles work, www.DMV.org also includes information on traffic schools, driver's ed, local lawyers, tickets, rules for commercial drivers, and much, much more.

## New Cars Lose Ground As Status Symbol

Getting a new car was as good a way as any to impress your friends and neighbors in the early 1980s, which put it right up there on the status scale with a new house.

But a new car started losing its luster as a means of making people jealous in the early 1990s, with an extensive-expensive home renovation starting to register about as well. New cars went back up in 2000 but have since fallen to well below a reno that involves high-end appliances, furnishings and specialty roofing.

According to CNW Research's latest study, a new house is slightly ahead of a major home reno and several points above a new car. Buying a used car has always had some status attached to it, but it's still stuck in a distant fourth.

# A Paris Tour Men Will
# Enjoy Even More Than Women

If you and/or the men in your life haven't seen Rendez-vous, a 9-minute film by Claude Lelouche of a full-tilt drive through Paris at dawn, we can't recommend it enough.

On top of everything else, it's even romantic.

Before videos, Rendezvous was a cult classic raved about by the few people who stumbled upon it in theatres as a pre-amble to some forgettable feature.

It started to pick up steam with the public with VHS and DVD versions, but the internet has turned it into a sub-culture all its own. You can follow the drive on Google Earth's fabulous view of Paris, for example.

Do yourself a favor and search "Rendezvous Paris" on the web and begin your exploration with the film on YouTube.

As hypnotic as it is on a computer, the film is even more compelling on a big screen TV with a great sound system so you can hear the car as well as watch where it goes, so it could make an excellent present.

It may also engender more web searches as he and/or you investigate the many theories about what kind of car was used and so on.

YouTube will also provide you with an equally legendary video of a motorcycle going 180 mph on the Periphereque, which is French for "the circular traffic nightmare that runs around downtown Paris."

## Program Your Cell Phone For Safety

A common problem for rescue workers after a crash is that they don't know who to call in case of an emergency, so one of them came up with the ICE (think about it) listing on your list of pre-set phone numbers. Yes, In Case of Emergency.

| | | | | | | | |
|----|------|----|-------|----|-------|
| OR | 159 | CT | 2,190 | UT | 2,814 |
| NH | 250 | NM | 2,216 | NY | 2,826 |
| SC | 407 | MT | 2,222 | WA | 2,862 |
| AK | 538 | NJ | 2,252 | IN | 2,913 |
| DE | 1,011 | NC | 2,289 | MN | 2,964 |
| SD | 1,757 | MO | 2,313 | GA | 3,217 |
| VA | 1,760 | OH | 2,339 | CA | 3,282 |
| HI | 1,847 | DC | 2,357 | MA | 3,283 |
| MD | 1,882 | MS | 2,381 | TN | 3,316 |
| WI | 1,994 | RI | 2,439 | CO | 3,571 |
| KY | 2,004 | FL | 2,484 | WY | 3,659 |
| ND | 2,009 | AR | 2,604 | ME | 3,831 |
| ID | 2,037 | IL | 2,605 | KS | 3,851 |
| WV | 2,068 | OK | 2,615 | IA | 3,886 |
| PA | 2,124 | MI | 2,683 | NV | 4,036 |
| VT | 2,145 | TX | 2,691 | AZ | 4,232 |
| NE | 2,177 | LA | 2,715 | AL | 4,387 |

\* Based on regional average vehicle ownership costs for taxes and fees

# The Costs Of Fees And Taxes

The above figures make it hard to believe that these states are all part of the same country, working from many of the same basic national political premises.

There doesn't even seem to be a general geographic basis for the differences, as Oregon's figure is dwarfed by that of its Washington neighbor, New Hampshire's rate is way below that of Vermont and Maine, and Tennessee's rate is way above that of Arkansas.

Voters in Maine, Tennessee, and Washington must wonder.

## Alexander Law & Susan Winlaw   295

| | | | | | |
|----|-------|----|-------|----|--------|
| SD | 5,638 | OR | 7,885 | MT | 9,382 |
| WI | 5,956 | NC | 7,908 | PA | 9,438 |
| IA | 6,167 | TX | 7,997 | FL | 9,708 |
| GA | 6,355 | TN | 8,058 | AR | 9,793 |
| NH | 6,507 | MS | 8,156 | NY | 10,543 |
| MA | 6,640 | KY | 8,180 | NV | 10,616 |
| ND | 6,645 | MI | 8,186 | RI | 10,939 |
| UT | 6,694 | IL | 8,225 | NJ | 11,306 |
| ID | 6,788 | ME | 8,319 | MD | 11,445 |
| IN | 6,859 | MO | 8,449 | CA | 11,670 |
| NM | 6,940 | WY | 8,510 | DE | 11,780 |
| OH | 7,019 | AL | 8,590 | CT | 12,057 |
| KS | 7,020 | SC | 8,705 | DC | 12,293 |
| MN | 7,187 | VA | 8,708 | HI | 12,744 |
| VT | 7,539 | OK | 8,713 | LA | 12,874 |
| CO | 7,640 | AZ | 9,275 | WV | 13,031 |
| NE | 7,797 | WA | 9,284 | AK | 13,384 |

\* Based on regional average vehicle ownership costs for insurance

# A Record Insurance Premium?

If you think your insurance rate's too high, consider the family in Edmonton, Alberta, who saw their annual premium go from about $15,000 a year to $104,566.33 -- yes, that's $104,566.33 -- a year. The primary cause was the driving record of the 19-year-old son, who managed to get 10 speeding tickets between being in two fender-benders and a crash that totaled his car. Before that, there had been a pair of license suspensions. They went looking for another insurance firm and found one, which only wanted $50,000 a year.

# A Time-Saving Drive-Through System We'd Like To See

If you have to shuffle along in line for a few minutes while they prepare your drive-through food order, why can't you use the time to accomplish a couple of other drive-through chores as well?

We're thinking of:

-an ATM that only dispenses cash, like the ones in Vegas that don't want you putting money where they can't get at it, only this would be to save time, and

-a gas pump that provides maybe five gallons of gas at the most, which the racing world calls a "splash and dash".

There are probably some other quick transactions that could be accommodated (a lending library return box, for example), but the trick would be not to put in anything that would slow the line down.

It just has to have things that can be done in the time it would normally take to get through the regular line for food.

Sure it might require a little re-routing of the line, but that's why we train people to be engineers -- to work stuff like that out for the greater good, and in this case the greater good includes saving time and reducing emissions.


## A Movie About Love And Great Car Sex

One of the best coming-of-age films ever, Y Tu Mama Tambien, shows callow youths coming to terms with love, loss, loneliness, life itself and a hot older woman.


## A Movie About Love And Changing A Tire

The best movie scene ever involving people changing a tire (it's a short list but it's a great scene) comes early on in Return of the Secausus Seven, a fabulous boomer dramedy.

# Cost Of Ownership Ratings
# Not Much Help To Consumers

As helpful as cost of ownership studies seem, they're not much use to the individual consumer since they rely too much on conjecture, generalizations and even outright distortions.

Consider the cost of ownership study from Consumer Reports, at www.ConsumerReports.org.

As with all such charts, the Consumer Reports' effort does not relate to any one person, let alone the person looking for a little guidance. A person's age, sex, personal history, family, home address, driving record and style and everything else will affect how much it costs to operate a vehicle. A generalization for a non-existent person, then, is of little use.

On top of that, these studies rely heavily on variables that are simply impossible to forecast, such as depreciation, maintenance and repair costs. Consumer Reports uses vehicle histories from their survey respondents to predict the future, but things are evolving so much in the auto industry that you can't steer by looking in the rearview mirror.

For example, Honda and Toyota no longer deserve higher resale values because they no longer have a lead in quality and reliability. When enough consumers realize this, resale values will drop and invalidate the cost-of-ownership math.

And cars that used to be out of fashion (compact hatchbacks) could become more popular  and that would trash the future cost projections as well.

Insurance companies have a general idea what a specific model costs to insure, but that's because a certain type of person buys it. But if a different type of person buys it, the insurance price will change.

There are too many variables and conjectures required to guess the future (how well does that usually work out?) to make ownership cost charts useful.

| | | | | | | | |
|-----|--------|-----|--------|-----|--------|
| NH | 47,499 | MO | 51,926 | FL | 54,186 |
| SD | 49,483 | IN | 51,941 | AL | 54,435 |
| SC | 49,515 | NE | 51,959 | DE | 54,439 |
| OR | 50,268 | NC | 52,173 | NJ | 54,591 |
| WI | 50,418 | IA | 52,249 | WA | 54,909 |
| ND | 50,516 | VA | 52,353 | RI | 55,181 |
| MA | 50,968 | OK | 52,550 | MD | 55,939 |
| GA | 51,102 | TN | 52,681 | AZ | 56,081 |
| NM | 51,158 | TX | 52,724 | NY | 56,147 |
| OH | 51,233 | MT | 52,980 | DC | 56,737 |
| ID | 51,248 | IL | 53,125 | LA | 56,850 |
| MS | 51,419 | CO | 53,337 | CT | 57,303 |
| VT | 51,423 | WY | 53,541 | WV | 57,532 |
| UT | 51,803 | MI | 53,588 | NV | 57,763 |
| MN | 51,843 | ME | 53,770 | AK | 58,052 |
| KY | 51,852 | PA | 54,028 | CA | 59,348 |
| KS | 51,916 | AR | 54,053 | HI | 59,457 |

\* Based on regional average vehicle ownership costs, consisting of depreciation, financing, taxes, fees, insurance premiums, fuel costs, maintenance and repairs.

## Comparison Shows Big Cost Differences

While auto ownership cost ratings are never completely acurate (see story on facing page), they can shine a light on the differences of some hard costs between states.

For the most part, it's the costs for taxes, fuel, fees, insurance that create the difference, since the guesstimates for depreciation and repairs would be a constant number.

The major forces at work here are insurance, fees and taxes, with fuel costs playing a minor role.

Again, geogrpahic position seems to play no role.

**Alexander Law & Susan Winlaw   299**

# Drive A Rolling Billboard
# And Get A Free Car

If you're willing to drive a rolling billboard, there's a chance you might be able to get a free car, or a monthly payment for wrapping your own vehicle in some company's logo.

Companies such as FreeCar Media (www.freecarmedia.com) gather the names of people willing to drive a rolling billboard and show them to companies looking for a different method of promoting their product.

When you register your intent with FreeCar Media, there's an online application form that allows you to provide as much data about yourself as possible.

That allows a sponsoring company to search out the drivers whose personal situations will put their cars with the company's message in front of the kind of customers they're after.

If the sponsoring company thinks your car would be a good place to hang their message (which will be removed at the end of the agreement), they will offer to pay you about $400 a month for the privilege.

They may even provide you with a new vehicle to drive for a specified time -- say two years.

If you're really aggressive and creative, you might be able to find this kind of sponsorship arrangement on your own by approaching firms that might want to reach the people you see on a regular basis.

This sounds too good to be true, but apparently it works. FreeCar for one has lots of satisfied customers, and there are probably others around if you search.

You do need to be careful, however, since there are reports that some online companies that charge you a fee (one-time, monthly, whatever) to put you on a list that goes out to potential advertisers may not be entirely legit. Try approaching a rolling billboard for the contact information.

# Chrysler Car Built "By Special Appointment to Her Majesty...The American Woman"

The Dodge La Femme was a regular production model from the Chrysler Corporation in 1955-56, clearly meant to appeal to women who vacuumed in a voluminous wasp-waisted dress and pearls.

According to the official brochure, The La Femme (which is of course French for "The Woman") was made "By Special Appointment to Her Majesty… The American Woman."

La Femme was all about style, painted "heather rose" pink in 1955 and two-tone purple in 1956, with special tapestry materials with pink rosebuds on the inside.

Fashion accessories were also part of the deal, including things like an umbrella, a rain hat and coat and (for the first year) a bag that included a coin purse, a compact, a lipstick holder, a comb and (it was the 50s) a lighter and cigarette case. The bag fit into the back of the front passenger's seat while the umbrella and hat fit in the back of the driver's seat, addressing issues that women have with cars to this day.

The idea for a car to appeal to women's tastes in colors was born from a positive response to the La Comtesse showcar of 1954, so the La Femme became a $143 option on a regular Dodge model.

Hard sales numbers are impossible to determine, but it couldn't have been that successful or it would have been back for 1957.

Needless to say, if you have the purse and all its contents from the 1956 model you could sell it for more than the car itself was worth at the time.

For many years the La Femme was a fading part of automotive history, but like many other things once doomed to be forgotten, the internet has changed all that. Try www.dodgelafemme.com or Wikipedia if you want to know more.

## Driver Training Can Be Fun
## But It Has Limited Value

Across 20-foot discs of revolving pavement through fountains of water, up ski hills, around the face-off circles on a hockey rink, down twisty snow-covered passes in the Alps, along frozen lakes in the Arctic Circle, over endless acres of pylon-dissected asphalt, around endless racetracks on four continents, and through barrels and barrels of "camel snot" we have chased the value of "advanced" driver training.

But before we get to that, "camel snot" is the nickname given to a particularly disgusting concoction of chemicals whose sole purpose in life is to create a loss of traction between a vehicle's wheels and the road.

The general point is to give the driver the experience of losing control of a vehicle in a safe situation, so she or he can see what it feels like and perhaps pick up some skills that might help in a real world crisis.

This is more likely to be fun than helpful. After all, there's little use going on an expensive training program unless you use your own vehicle in the type of situation you might experience in your own life.

Vehicles react differently to a specific situation, thanks to a long list of variables that includes the condition of the tires, vehicle weight, where the drive wheels are, the road surface, the temperature and so on.

The best preparation for dealing with a situation that might require "advanced" driving begins with the choice of the vehicle. Most importantly, avoid any vehicle that does not have some form of stability control (see Page 23) and keep the tires prepared for trouble (see page 110).

Whatever vehicle you pick, take it for an emergency control test spin the first time there's snow, ice or lots of standing water. Wet pavement shouldn't give you a problem unless it's close to turning into ice, but standing water can send you skidding off the road in a heartbeat. Find a big, empty parking lot with nothing to crash into and drive around to test your vehicle's behavior in a curve or under braking.

This will give you some sense of what it feels like when your vehicle starts to slide and you can see how your vehicle behaves. It will be scary at first but in time you will see that there are things you can do to save yourself if you get past the shock and make some intelligent driving choices.

## Girl Scouts Promote "On The Road"

For a few years now the Girl Scouts have been actively trying to get young women interested in cars, and even working in the auto industry. The primary effort has been On The Road, a program "that encourage girls to be competent, smart and safe drivers." It aims to provide girls aged 14-17 with "innovative hands-on activities related to automotive safety and maintenance, smart driving and careers in the automotive industry."

There are events in which girls from the local council gather to discuss things automotive, a merit badge, online information and games, e-cards and a book.

Part of the funding comes from Firestone, which runs a chain of auto repair stores, and whose interest in putting its name in front of young women is pretty obvious.

What may be more surprising is the financial involvement of the US Department of Labor, which is trying to encourage young women to consider "career opportunities in the automotive industry." That may seem a little strange to some, but the American auto companies (particularly GM and Ford) at least are hugely interested in hiring women.

The web connection is www.girlscouts.org.

There's also a book called On The Road, for $5.95, which covers a lot of details about the program in general.

# Donating Cars To Charity
# Has Risks And Rewards

Donating a vehicle to charity appeals to good-hearted people as it looks like an easy way to dispose of an old problem while doing some good and picking up a tax deduction.

It's still a good idea, though it probably won't deliver as much money to the charity as you'd expect and the action can be fraught with peril if you don't exercise extreme care in picking a charity and doing all of the paperwork. There are horror stories on the web about the trouble the good-hearted got into when the recipients didn't hold up their end of the bargain with respect to completing the change of ownership process. If you are identified through the license plate or the VIN number as the last legal owner of a vehicle, you can be held responsible for parking tickets and other fines, even if you haven't driven the vehicle in years.

The good news is that your charitable donation of a vehicle is less likely to raise a red flag in the computers at the IRS. Abuses earlier in the decade caused the tax people to bring stricter regulations into affect.

To increase the amount the charity gets and to decrease your own future liability, consider selling your old vehicle through the normal means and giving all or part of the proceeds to the charity directly.

## The Car As An Escape Device

The time might come that you're stuck in your car behind a wooden or metal fence or some other type of impediment. If you really need to get to the other side of said impediment (say you're at risk), a careful application of the car's weight and engine power can make that happen. But pushing open a locked gate can have negative affects on the car, the gate and your legal status, so use this power only for good.

# Vintage Female Fashions Welcome
# At English Classic Car Event

If you like dressing up in vintage clothes (or shopping for them) and the man in your life loves vintage cars, you might want to take note of a unique annual event held near Chichester in southern England.

Every year around the end of August the Goodwood Revival attracts crowds of people who like to visit a particularly lovely patch of southern England wearing clothes from 1948 to 1966. Cooing over the veteran vehicles is an option, but so is drinking champagne, eating canapés on the terraces, and buying vintage clothes.

The men usually try to look like an RAF pilot, Cary Grant, James Dean or even Elvis, though some of them prefer the country vet look from All Creatures Great and Small.

Ladies tend to turn up in "kicky gear" from the 1960s that channels Twiggy, or "elegant" outfits that evoke Audrey Hepburn, Jackie Kennedy, Ava Gardner or Grace Kelly. There are also a few who try the voluptuous style of Marilyn Monroe.

There's a Ladies Day, during which a team of fashion gurus go looking for "the most immaculately-groomed ladies in the crowd" and giving them champagne and flowers, along with something delightful to talk about for the rest of their lives.

UK vintage clothes suppliers bring their wares to the Revival Market, a "unique shopping village dedicated solely and strictly to the design sensibilities of the pre-1966 period."

There are also a bunch of cars there from the same period, which are good to pose against. The event's run by the owner of Goodwood, Charles March, who is more commonly called Lord March because he's an earl. For more details, check out www.goodwood.co.uk.

It won't be cheap, of course, but it is an excellent event for lovers of olds cars, fashion and the English countryside.

# It's Easy To Increase Safety
# And Reduce Gas Use

If we're really, truly, madly worried about highway safety and air pollution, why don't we just order the car companies to create vehicles that will accelerate sedately to the legal speed limit and go no faster than that?

This would be easier and less expensive than you'd think, and could be done with virtually all the vehicles on the road today as well as vehicles yet to come.

Whether or not it's the right political, ethical, moral, economic, aesthetic, cultural or whatever decision is best left for another venue, but we should at least acknowledge the existence of a solution as simple as this.

Essentially, all that would be required would be new operating software for any vehicle on the road with computer chips controlling its engine management, which is virtually every vehicle on the road.

It would also be possible (though more complicated and more expensive) to provide vehicles with devices that would receive signals from transponders situated at points where the speed changes, so the vehicle would automatically reduce speed.

Sedate launches and moderate speeds would go a long way toward reducing fuel use and, it follows, air pollution, and the slower a car goes the less likely it is to run into something or someone (the driver has more time to stop and the car's less likely to be in a physical condition that ends in loss of control) and that would help with safety.

See how simple that is?

Auto companies would create computer code that wouldn't let a car go from 0 to 40 mph (a good maximum speed on urban streets) in less than six or seven seconds, and not allow them to get to 70 mph (a good highway speed) until they'd passed a transponder by the side of a high-speed, non-urban road that allowed them to go faster.

Since there are people who would undoubtedly rewrite that code so they could speed and continue to endanger other members of society, black boxes that keep a record of a how fast a car goes could also be added.

The police could easily download that information to allow for the timely issuance of tickets and points, and a new and harsher set of engine behavior codes could be installed in the offender's vehicle.

And if that didn't work, cars could be recoded to follow some other rules that worked better. It's just a software fix.

Technically, this stuff is not that big a leap for the auto industry. It shouldn't even add cost to the car, since it has to have a computer code that tells it how to behave in any case.

Even if the extra technology did cost more, think of the money to be saved from using less fuel and reduced medical care, with the police and doctors free to deal with more serious issues.

We know there would be serious resistance to these ideas and much of it would be valid, but it's worth making the point that we could actually take some serious but simple steps to deal with the problem of highway safety and air pollution if we really wanted to, but apparently we don't.

As a society, we are apparently not ready to let our elected officials get serious on these issues.

Just something to think about.

## A Car Movie Women Will Like

The Last Run is supposed to be about gangsters racing around southern Europe to escape a vengeful business partner, but it's really about love, loss, loneliness and life itself -- in a classic roadster from BMW with George C. Scott at the wheel.

# A Religious View Of Cars and Driving
# And How You Should Behave

It probably says something important about the world that when the Vatican issued its "Guidelines for the Pastoral Care of the Road" last year, the Ten Commandants for Motorists was primarily what the media chose to dwell on.

Media reports mostly ignored the fact that the document also talked about such "migrants and travelers" as prostitutes, homeless children and indigent adults, and included some extremely thought-provoking passages of interest to anyone even remotely interested in faith or religion. We can't recommend it too highly, so search the full document out at "Guidelines for the Pastoral Care of the Road" if you're interested in the total message.

To give these Ten Commandments their due, road carnage is a serious global issue, accounting for about 1.2 million deaths and 20 to 50 million injuries a year. But that will certainly rise sharply as developing countries add more vehicles to their roads, so any help is welcome.

For developed countries such as Canada and the U.S., the Vatican also has some thoughts about what we do with cars that many people, regardless of their religious feelings, will find worthy of note.

Here are some passages from the study that touch on North American concerns:

-"Mobility and wandering are therefore expressions of human nature and of our cultural development," the Vatican says, starting most famously with Mary and Joseph, but "our lives are conditioned by the car, as mobility has become an idol, which the car symbolizes." Roads should be "tools for facilitating life and the integral development of society. They should constitute a communication bridge between peoples, thereby creating new economic and human spaces."

-In addition to traffic congestion, "people are directly exposed to dangers deriving from other related problems, such as noise, air pollution and intensive use of raw materials. We must tackle these issues and not just passively put up with them, partly in order to limit the costs of modernization that are becoming unsustainable. In this context, it is a good idea to call for a commitment to avoid unnecessary car use."

-Cars may also "promote the exercise of Christian virtues -- prudence, patience, charity and helping one's fellow men and women -- in both a spiritual and corporal level. Finally, they may also provide an opportunity to come closer to God, as they facilitate discovery of the beauties of creation, the sign of his boundless love for us."

-Overall, the Bible affirms human mobility's "link with God's redeeming plan. Thus we may see traveling not only as physical movement from one place to another, but also in its spiritual dimension, due to the fact that it puts people in touch with each other, thereby contributing to the realization of God's plan of love."

-The Vatican paper says that "those who know Jesus Christ are careful on the roads. They don't only think about themselves, and are not always worried about getting to their destination in a great hurry. They see the people who 'accompany' them on the road, each of whom has their own life, their own desire to reach a destination and their own problems. They see everyone as brothers and sisters, sons and daughters of God. This is the attitude that characterizes a Christian driver."

-Even car racing can be okay in God's eye, the Vatican says. "When driving a car some people start up the engine to join a race, in order to escape from the troubling pace of everyday life. The pleasure of driving becomes a way of enjoying the freedom and independence that normally we do not have. This also leads to the practice of road sports, cycling, motorcycling and motor racing, in a healthy spirit of competition, even though risks are entailed."

-Road signs are often seen as "restrictions of freedom," the Vatican says in a section that might be heavily influenced by traffic conditions in the country that surrounds it. So some people, "especially when unobserved and unmonitored ... are tempted to infringe such limitations, which are in fact designed to protect them and other people." These people often find "certain prudent regulations that reduce traffic risks and dangers as humiliating," while others deem it intolerable -- almost a curtailment of their "rights" -- to be obliged to "follow patiently another vehicle that is traveling slowly, because, for example, road signs prohibit overtaking."

-Drivers' personalities are often different from those of pedestrians, the Vatican points out, and that can often "lead us to behave in an unsatisfactory and even barely human manner." Two of the principal psychological factors at work here are "the domination instinct" and a display of "vanity and personal glorification."

The domination instinct is the same as the feeling of arrogance, the Vatican says, and "that impels people to seek power in order to assert themselves ... By identifying themselves with their car, drivers enormously increase their own power," especially through the "thrill of speed," which allows them to "accelerate at will, setting out to conquer time and space, overtaking, and almost 'subjugating' other drivers," which are "sources of satisfaction that derive from domination."

As for vanity and personal glorification, "cars particularly lend themselves to being used by their owners to show off, and as a means for outshining other people and arousing a feeling of envy. People thus identify themselves with their cars and project assertion of their egos onto them. When we praise our cars we are, in fact, praising ourselves, because they belong to us and, above all, we drive them."

As a result of this, "unbalanced behavior varies according to individuals and circumstances, and may include impoliteness, rude gestures, cursing, blasphemy, loss of sense of responsibility, or deliberate infringement of the Highway Code. For some drivers, the unbalanced behavior is expressed in insignificant ways, whilst in others it may produce serious excesses that depend on character, level of education, an incapacity for self-control and the lack of a sense of responsibility."

The Vatican notes that, while "such unbalanced behavior may have serious consequences," it nevertheless falls within the "scope of psychological normality," which means you can be mostly normal but still do it anyway.

Whatever the reasons, the Vatican says, driving "brings inclinations to the surface from the unconscious that usually, when we are not on the roads, are 'controlled'. When driving, however, imbalances emerge and encourage regression to more primitive forms of behavior."

The Vatican suggests that "driving should be considered by the same standards as any other social activity, which presupposes a commitment to mediate between one's own requirements and the limits imposed by the rights of others."

Cars tend to bring out the "primitive" side of human beings, the Vatican notes, "thereby producing rather unpleasant results. We need to take these dynamics into account and react by appealing to the noble tendencies of the human spirit, to a sense of responsibility and self-control, in order to prevent manifestations of the psychological regression that is often connected to driving a means of transport."

Amen to that, say we, and suggest again that you view the other verses on the original document. Consider the "Moral responsibility of road users," for example, and how "Charity and serving one's neighbor" will make you feel better in heavy traffic.

# Ten Commandments For Drivers

(As shown on the Catholic Culture web site in the document Guidelines for the Pastoral Care of the Road, which is found in the Library section of the website.)

Thou shall not kill.

The road shall be for you a means of communion between people and not of mortal harm.

Courtesy, uprightness and prudence will help you deal with unforseen events.

Be charitable and help your neighbor in need, especially victims of accidents.

Cars shall not be for you an expression of power and domination, and an occasion of sin.

Charitably convince the young and not so young not to drive when they are not in a fitting condition to do so.

Support the families of accident victims.

Bring guilty motorists and their victims together, at the appropriate time, so that they can undergo the liberating experience of forgiveness.

On the road, protect the more vulnerable party.

Feel responsbile towards others.